MEDIEVAL LITERATURE, STYLE, AND CULTURE

MEDIEVAL LITERATURE, STYLE, AND CULTURE

Essays by Charles Muscatine

UNIVERSITY OF SOUTH CAROLINA PRESS

Published in Columbia, South Carolina, by the
University of South Carolina Press

Manufactured in the United States of America

03 02 01 00 99 5 4 3 2 1

Library of Congress Cataloging-in-Publication Data

Muscatine, Charles.
   Medieval literature, style, and culture : essays / by Charles Muscatine.
   p. cm.

   ISBN 1-57003-249-1
   1. Chaucer, Geoffrey, d. 1400—Criticism and interpretation.   2. Literature,
Medieval—History and criticism.   I. Title.
PR1924 .M87   1999
821'.1—dc21   97-45297

"The Canterbury Tales: Style of the Man and Style of the Work" was first published
   in D. S. Brewer, ed., *Chaucer and Chaucerians: Critical Studies in Middle
   English Literature* (Hampshire, U.K.: Routledge, n.d.), pp. 88–113.
"Chaucer's Religion and the Chaucer Religion" was first published in Ruth Morse
   and Barry Windeatt, eds., *Chaucer Traditions: Studies in Honour of Derek
   Brewer* (Cambridge: Cambridge University Press, 1990), pp. 249–62. Reprinted
   with the permission of Cambridge University Press.
"Chaucer in an Age of Criticism" was first published in *Modern Language Quarterly,*
   vol. 25, no. 4 (December 1964): 473–78.
"'What Amounteth Al This Wit?' Chaucer and Scholarship" was first published in
   Studies in the Age of Chaucer (1981): 3–11.
"Locus of Action in Medieval Narrative," copyright 1963 by The Regents of the Uni-
   versity of California, reprinted from *Romance Philology,* vol. 17, pp. 115–22.
Poetry and Crisis in the Age of Chaucer was first published by the University of
   Notre Dame Press in 1972.
"The Fabliaux," from *A New History of French Literature,* ed. by Dennis Hollier.
   Copyright 1989 by the President and Fellows of Harvard College. Reprinted by
   permission of Harvard University Press.
"The Wife of Bath and Gautier's *La Veuve*" was first published in *Romance Studies
   in Memory of Edward Billings Ham,* ed. by U. T. Holmes (Hayward, Calif., 1967).
"The Fabliaux, Courtly Culture, and the (Re)Invention of Vulgarity" was first pub-
   lished in Jan Ziolkowski, ed., *Obscenity: Social Control and Artistic Creation in
   the European Middle Ages* (Leiden, The Netherlands: Brill, 1998).
"The Emergence of Psychological Allegory in Old French Romance" was first pub-
   lished in *PMLA* (1953): 1160–82.
Erich Auerbach, *Mimesis,* reprint copyright 1956 by The Regents of the University of
   California, reprinted from *Romance Philology,* vol. 9, pp. 448–57.

To

NAOMI, SONIA *and* SAMUEL
WYNNE, COLE *and* MAX

CONTENTS

PREFACE

This book consists of those of my published writings on medieval literature—except for minor notes and book reviews—that have not found safer haven in volumes that are still in print or easily available.

The collection begins with four essays on Chaucer, my favorite author, and with an essay that defines the first of the two main foci of my work: literary style and its relation to meaning. The fifth essay expands the idea of style to include spatial form and applies it to the meaning of *Piers Plowman*. The next four essays, collectively entitled "Poetry and Crisis in the Age of Chaucer," were originally written together as Ward-Phillips Lectures delivered at the University of Notre Dame. They combine stylistic analysis with my other focus: literature as a source for evidence in cultural history. There follow three essays on the Old French fabliaux, where again my efforts, beginning with the study of style, have progressively moved over to the question of what literature tells us about culture. The last two essays, in genres by themselves, record in different ways two of my greatest debts as a scholar: to C. S. Lewis and to Erich Auerbach.

Except for technical corrections, the essays are presented here as first published. I am most grateful to the University of South Carolina Press for the luxury of being able to bring them together and hope that the press's generosity to me will provide some interest and benefit to readers as well.

C.M.

MEDIEVAL LITERATURE, STYLE, AND CULTURE

THE CANTERBURY TALES

Style of the Man and Style of the Work

If the whole of *The Canterbury Tales* can be said to have a single style, that style has within it an extraordinary variety, which derives from the great range of Chaucer's themes and the way in which his style supports or expresses them. The tales were long in the writing, but nothing suggests that their styles are in any way related to their chronology. Chaucer's mature style (like Shakespeare's) was a protean one. Medieval rhetorical theory described three styles, the high, the middle, and the low, corresponding to the social dignity of the subject matter. But the study of literature taught Chaucer much finer discriminations, and his mature works show a quite independent sense of style, transgressing decorum and even genre in the interest of meaning. *The Canterbury Tales* fulfil in a particularly satisfying way the familiar dictum that style and meaning in art are interdependent.

Though we shall be finally concerned with this aspect of Chaucer's style, with style as differing from tale to tale as it is deployed for literary effect, we should be aware that Chaucer's range is not limitless. In the very widest sense, his style is "late-medieval," inevitably rough-hewn by the traditions, issues, attitudes and forms of apprehension that belong to his epoch. On the other side, if the style of the work is shaped by Chaucer's immediate literary strategy, that strategy may be in turn influenced, limited, partly determined by his natural literary gifts, habits and propensities. The reader who attends patiently to the whole work will find beneath the local variations some constant traits, a peculiarly Chaucerian personality in style and language, an array of favourite stylistic devices. In the ensuing remarks I shall first attempt to describe some of the principal traits of this "style of the man," hoping thus to set the "style of the work" in relief and also to suggest how the nature of the one may be related to the formation of the other.

I

Perhaps the most common denominator of Chaucer's literary personality is a certain air of insouciance. His manner is indeed so relaxed that new readers have to be reminded that he was a highly sophisticated literary artist. But most critics are likely to err in the other direction. If we believe, with Kittredge, that Chaucer always knew what he was about, we must not forget that his sophistication includes a casualness and playfulness that we rarely associate with our greatest poets. Chaucer has none of the apartness and sense of the poet's special status that we feel in Milton or Wordsworth, little of the artistic self-consciousness of a Spenser or a Pope. Like all of these an artist to the bone, he seems nevertheless always to have prized his amateur status. He seems perpetually to be conducting a conversation with friends, and he cannot for long stand on ceremony with them. By inviting us at least once to "turne over the leef and chese another tale" he shows that he thinks of his poetry as something written down; yet it retains many of the qualities of the oral tradition, of poetry recited aloud, as no doubt it often was.[1] It is only occasionally a poetry of high compression or of jewel-like polish. Though one could cite scores of "great" single lines in *The Canterbury Tales,* Chaucer's characteristic triumphs are based more often on cumulation and sequence. We must always be prepared to tolerate, if not enjoy in him, a certain amiable inconsistency of tone, or of perspective, or of detail, as his narrative goes along. The fact is, Chaucer does not seem to have worried about consistency beyond a certain point.

No doubt the unfinished state of *The Canterbury Tales* exaggerates this quality. But by the same token, the rough edges and unmatched joints give us a sense of how he worked. Although we know that he revised some of *The Canterbury Tales,* one cannot imagine his being much concerned about merely factual matters. Chaucer is characteristically absorbed in the tactics of the passage he is writing, and careless of more remote correspondences. When the conception of the Nun's Priest was upon him, he gave no thought to fixing up the *General Prologue,* which barely mentions "prestes thre" (l. 164). His Cook is described in the brilliant *Manciple's Prologue* as if he had not already been heard from after *The Reeve's Tale.* The shy bumbler who tells *The Tale of Sir Thopas* is not quite the same as the gregarious character who narrates the *General Prologue.* The Knight's avowed dislike of tragedy in *The Nun's Priest's Prologue* seems at odds with the tone of *The Knight's Tale.* We are never explicitly told—or is this high artistic premonition?—the marital status of the Wife of Bath.

Many more of these mechanical flaws or inconsistencies could be cited, but none of them is very serious. What they tell us about

The Canterbury Tales

Chaucer's artistic stance is borne out by his occasional inconsistencies of perspective. The character Justinus, within *The Merchant's Tale,* cites as an authority on marriage the Wife of Bath, who is listening to the tale. The Summoner at one point is made comically aware of the literary structure of his own performance:

> My prologe wol I ende in this manere.

And once the narrator of *The Knight's Tale* transfers the sounds of trumpets and heralds from his tale to his audience as if there were no gap between them:

> The trompours, with the loude mynstralcie,
> The heraudes, that ful loude yelle and crie,
> Been in hire wele for joye of daun Arcite.
> But herkneth me, and stynteth noyse a lite,
> Which a myracle ther bifel anon.
>
> *(The Knight's Tale* 2671–5)

These minor and rather playful instances illustrate both Chaucer's awareness of perspective, and his disposition to be neither rigidly consistent nor too solemn about it.

Chaucer's basic quality of insouciance and naturalness is heavily contributed to by his language. Though he was no mean Latin scholar and a great importer of new words into English from French, though he was a courtier versed in international business and diplomacy, his language has an irreducible quality of familiarity—one might almost have said provincialism. I am not referring to his developed art of giving his realistic characters colloquial speech,[2] but rather to something deep in the grain of his own discourse, that at times seems to transgress literary decorum itself. It is in his rhythm and syntax and diction, but perhaps we sense it most clearly in the imagery of his figurative comparisons, where his choice of images is relatively unconstrained by the dictates of subject matter. Chaucer has a marked preference for similes over metaphors, as if the more discursive syntax of simile and its less pretentious reach of statement were more congenial to his rhythm and his personality. But in both metaphor and simile his imagery has a favourite range, which I can best illustrate by quoting at random and at some length from all parts of *The Canterbury Tales:* "his brydel . . . gynglen . . . as dooth the chapel belle"; "His eyen . . . stemed as a for-

3

Chaucer's language is thus something like that of a good politician. It can be either familiar or rhetorical and learned, but when rhetorical and learned it is never completely out of sight of the familiar.

Some Continental critics have found Chaucer irreducibly "middle class" on account of this language; but that is to be too pure as regards decorum. It is, rather, a great part of his delightful "Englishness," which must be acknowledged however much we may discover of his debt to the Continent in style, subject and genre. And it is even more than a source of easy geniality and of an appearance of artless spontaneity. At times, as we shall see below, it is transformed into a powerful medieval realism, and it enters into overtly comic and ironic combinations.

Another large trait which to modern eyes must contribute to Chaucer's artistic insouciance is his easy admission of rather "extra-literary" material, of *sentence* and doctrine into his poem. Thoroughly medieval, he does not seem to distinguish between belles-lettres and didactic literature:

> For seint Paul seith that al that writen is,
> To oure doctrine it is ywrite, ywis.
>
> *(The Nun's Priest's Tale* 3441–2)

So he includes in *The Canterbury Tales* his *Melibee*—which with a smile but without irony he variously calls "a lytel thyng in prose," "a moral tale vertuous," "this litel tretys" and "this murye tale"—and the long moral treatise which the Parson tells, calling it "a myrie tale in prose." As these tales extend the variety of the styles of the *Tales,* shorter passages of sentence and doctrine add to the variety of tone and temper we find in the verse. But it is not always easy to forgive Chaucer the stylistic effects of this medieval ingredient. Relevant learned commentary on the action of narrative, even if put in the mouth of a character, we can accept as medieval convention. We cannot easily accept such gratuitous *exempla* as fill the last thirty lines of Dorigen's complaint in *The Franklin's Tale,*[3] and there are many other passages in which sententiousness jostles art a little harder than we should like.[4] But we should rather be pleased that so much of the doctrine and learned diction in Chaucer are drawn into the folds of his style, sometimes supported by his theme, as in *The Knight's Tale,* sometimes concealed by his characterisation, as in *The Wife of Bath's Prologue,* or subsumed under his dramatics, as in the sermon of *The Pardoner's Tale.*

The frequent pile-up of *exempla* in *The Canterbury Tales* leads us to another of Chaucer's large stylistic traits: his predilection for making lists of things. In his use of the catalogue he follows antique literary tradition and also a number of typically medieval impulses. We have already mentioned sententiousness. There is also close beside it in Chaucer a kind of lay encyclopaedism, a symptom of the secularisation of learning in the Middle Ages, which produces vernacular bibliographies and recipes both for use and for sheer delight in the amassing of sonorous-sounding terms:

Wel knew he the olde Esculapius,
And Deyscorides, and eek Rufus,
Olde Ypocras, Haly, and Galyen,
Serapion, Razis, and Avycen,
Averrois, Damascien, and Constantyn,
Bernard, and Gatesden, and Gilbertyn.

General Prologue 429–34

Ther nas quyk-silver, lytarge, ne brymstoon,
Boras, ceruce, ne oille of tartre noon;
Ne oynement that wolde clense and byte,
That hym myghte helpen of his whelkes white.

General Prologue 629–31

I pray to God so save gentil cors,
And eek thyne urynals and thy jurdones,
Thyn ypocras, and eek thy galiones,
And every boyste ful of thy letuarie;
God blesse hem, and oure lady Seinte Marie!

(*Introduction, The Pardoner's Tale* 304–8)

Encyclopaedism here merges with the medieval rules of rhetoric, which are forever sanctioning the multiplication of instances. Particularly in the latter two quotations, though, we can sense Chaucer's curving of the figure toward functional literary use: suggesting the moral quality of the Summoner in the one, and a facet of the Host's character in the other. Similarly the great catalogues in *The Knight's Tale,* which merge with the description generally, help to create the rich chivalric background necessary to the tale's full meaning; and the catalogue of

7

alchemical equipment in *The Canon's Yeoman's Prologue* is made powerfully to suggest the futility and soullessness of pure technology.

In a certain sense the sequence of portraits in the *General Prologue* (and even the sequence of *The Canterbury Tales* as a whole) has the form of a catalogue; it is possible that Chaucer's liking for this form is related ultimately to the enumerative, processional, paratactic quality that pervades the structure of *The Canterbury Tales* in large and small. The individual portraits are themselves composed of catalogues of traits. But against the stasis and formality implied by the catalogue form, many of his portraits also create the complex characterisation and display the potential energy that on a large scale disarrange and make quasi-dramatic the sequence of tales as a whole.

Chaucer's portraits are among his most characteristic and successful literary devices, and are certainly his greatest technical innovation. They are based on the *effictio* of medieval rhetoric, a figure belonging mainly to the high style. In the French romances the formal portrait consists of a head-to-toe inventory of physical traits, often followed by a list of the character's moral qualities. The traits are mostly determined by convention. The figure lent itself particularly well to the description of allegorical personification, because in the conventional portrait the connections of the traits point in a single direction, thus creating the ideal figure contemplated by romancer and allegorist alike. Chaucer knew well the portraits in *Le Roman de la Rose,* and some of those in *The Canterbury Tales* are done in the same allegorical manner. The portrait of the Parson in the *General Prologue* eschews physical description for reasons of tone, but it has the allegorical simplicity of organisation. Equally conventional in structure are the highly concrete and decorative portraits of the kings Lygurge and Emetrius in *The Knight's Tale,* who virtually personify royal and martial magnificence. They well illustrate the fact that it is not simply concreteness of detail that is Chaucer's great innovation, but rather complexity of structure. Dante excepted (and his portraits are essentially different in kind from Chaucer's), no other medieval writer begins so well to introduce a second and third (or more) related systems of connotations into the portrait, creating the perspective—often with ironic tension—that we associate with characterisation in depth. Thus in the celebrated portrait of the Prioress we may roughly distinguish two groups of traits, compatible but not completely harmonious, one connoting religious sensibility and the other courtly delicacy. In this case the mere statement of the Prioress's occupation has such strong connotations that a large number of courtly traits can be played against it. Chaucer delights in finding traits that belong in both systems:

> And al was conscience and tendre herte.
>
> (l. 150)

The resultant ambiguity, as Professor Lowes long ago noted, is caught again perfectly in the final lines, describing the Prioress's rosary:

> Of smal coral aboute hire arm she bar
> A peire of bedes, gauded al with grene,
> And theron heng a brooch of gold ful sheene
> On which ther was first write a crowned A,
> And after *Amor vincit omnia.*
>
> (158–62)

In a similar manner one might be able to distinguish and disentwine the groups of traits that go to portray the Monk, the Pardoner, Alisoun in *The Miller's Tale,* Symkyn in *The Reeve's Tale* and the rest. But structural analysis will not account for the whole of Chaucer's success. For the portrait brought out other of his particular talents, too. Considering that the fourteenth-century associations of many of his details are beyond recall, and that others (as of his various kinds of horses) have become pale, it is remarkable that so much of his imagery is in itself so expressive as to have almost symbolic force. Thus he catches with economy and special point the preposterous family pride of Symkyn and his wife:

> And she cam after in a gyte of reed;
> And Symkyn hadde hosen of the same
>
> (*The Reeve's Tale* 3954–5)

female sovereignty in the Wife of Bath:

> A foot-mantel aboute hir hipes large,
> And on hir feet a paire of spores sharpe.
>
> (*General Prologue* 472–3)

and animalism in the Miller:

> Upon the cop right of his nose he hade

9

A werte, and thereon stood a toft of herys,
Reed as the brustles of a sowes erys.

(General Prologue 554–6)

The effect of Chaucer's portraits is also influenced by other devices, as of the placement or suppression of details. There is poetic force in the fact that the very *first* trait of the Prioress is that she "of hir smylyng was ful symple and coy." The portrait of Alisoun in *The Miller's Tale* depends on a submerged conventionalism, both in arrangement and in the categories of things described. Without it the rural imagery would lose some of its charm and meaning. But for the most part the portraits share that relaxed quality which we have seen elsewhere in Chaucer's style. He breaks up the formal arrangement of the conventional portrait, but does not seem to replace it with any other definable tactic. The resultant effect of spontaneity or informality is sometimes a splendid foil for such surprise effects as the final confidence concerning Absolon's squeamishness.[5] But such a sequence as the Friar's portrait seems almost too casual. Here Chaucer's Dickensian capacity to bounce us into acceptance of a character—by the brilliance of the details and the structure of their connotations—makes us forget the lack of surface arrangement.

Chaucer's style is all of a piece, and our discussion of catalogue and portrait has led us already to comments that apply to his descriptive technique generally. It is generally true of the descriptions in *The Canterbury Tales* that they transcend the purposes of mere ornament and dilatation that medieval rhetoric was content with. That Chaucer's portraits work deeply into the themes and plots of his narrative is well known. The same can be said of his settings and other extended uses of description. Those in *The Knight's Tale* are extraordinarily rich, in compliance with the subject's demand for high style, and under the beneficent influence of Boccaccio's example. This richness also answers and supports the tale's central exploration of the nature of the noble life:

The rede statue of Mars, with spere and targe,
So shyneth in his white baner large,
That alle the feeldes glyteren up and doun;
And by his baner born is his penoun
Of gold ful riche, in which ther was ybete
The Mynotaur, which that he slough in Crete.

(975–80)

10

The bisy larke, messager of day,
Salueth in hir song the morwe gray,
And firy Phebus riseth up so bright
That al the orient laugheth of the light,
And with his stremes dryeth in the greves
The silver dropes hangynge on the leves.

(1491–6)

Along with this bright imagery of chivalry and courtly Maying some description in the poem conveys a dark mood consonant with its awareness of death and disaster:

The northren lyght in at the dores shoon,
For wyndowe on the wal ne was ther noon,
Thurgh which men myghten any light discerne.
The dore was al of adamant eterne,
Yclenched overthwart and endelong
With iren tough; and for to make it strong,
Every pyler, the temple to sustene,
Was tonne-greet, of iren bright and shene.
Ther saugh I first the derke ymaginyng
Of Felonye, and al the compassyng;
The cruel Ire, reed as any gleede;
The pykepurs, and eek the pale Drede;
The smylere with the knyf under the cloke;
The shepne brennynge with the blake smoke . . .

(1987–2000)

Similarly the celebrated opening lines of the *General Prologue,* with their imagery of natural regeneration, transcend their origin in the conventional Spring description. April, sweet rains, and song birds, set beside pilgrimage and the holy blissful martyr, establish that double theme of nature and supernature, natural value and spiritual, which is at the heart of the whole work.[6] The critical reader should thus not pass by Chaucer's descriptions without pausing to savour their strategy as well as their decorativeness.

The reader will already have heard in the passages quoted above how well Chaucer manages sound and rhythm in support of his meaning. While the requirements of recited narrative, and also his temperament, prevent his writing a poetry of steadily high compression, he can rise to

11

the occasion at will, and many of his passages have a quality of heavily sensuous fitness worthy of the style of Keats or Spenser or Milton. Battle scenes brought out in Chaucer echoes of the Anglo-Saxon heroic measure, with its heavy beats enforced by alliteration:

Up springen speres twenty foot on highte;
Out goon the swerdes as the silver brighte;
The helmes they tohewen and toshrede;
Out brest the blood with stierne stremes rede;
With myghty maces the bones they tobreste.
He thurgh the thikkeste of the throng gan threste;
Ther stomblen stedes stronge, and doun gooth al.

(*The Knight's Tale* 2607–13)

He uses alliteration, the close coupling of stresses, and heavy pauses to convey the weight and solidity of the Miller's physique:

The Millere was a stout carl for the nones;
Ful byg he was of brawn, and eek of bones.
He was short-sholdred, brood, a thikke knarre;
There was no dore that he nolde heve of harre . . .

Conversely, the speed suggested in the next line is supported by the quick run of syllables:

Or breke it at a rennyng with his heed.

(*General Prologue* 545–51)

In *The Nun's Priest's Tale* Chaucer uses quick, lightly-stressed monosyllables to convey the effect of chickens' pecking, supported by the sharpness of an initial accented syllable:

Pekke hem up right as they growe and ete hem yn.

(l. 2967)

In his description of old January's singing, the emphasis of the "k" sound and the insistent flapping of the unaccented syllables beautifully underline the meaning:

. . . ful of jargon as a flekked pye.

12

The slakke skyn aboute his nekke shaketh,
Whil that he sang, so chaunteth he and craketh.

(*The Merchant's Tale* 1848–50)

The effect of Jankyn's fall at the end of *The Wife of Bath's Prologue* is expressed in the rhythm:

Al sodeynly thre leves have I plyght
Out of his book, right as he radde, and eke
I with my fest so took hym on the cheke
That in our fyr he fil bakward adoun.

(790–3)

Here the stressed syllable "doun" is given a memorable extra emphasis by the enjambement which speeds the passage toward it, and by the artful shifting of the preceding stress out of the normal iambic pattern, allowing a pause before the final, climactic thump.

While Chaucer thus shares this technical gift with all good poets, his peculiar talent, evident in the last quotation and remarked by many critics,[7] is his consistent ability to maintain the onward flow of his narrative verse in a lively and varied way. The Man of Law's disparagement of Chaucer's verse that

he kan but lewedly
On metres and on rymyng craftily,

is a joke that Chaucer can well afford to make. His narrative, while natural, is impeccably metrical, and his rhymes satisfyingly easy and accurate. To these ends he uses many resources: syntactic variations, the optional use of the final -*e,* a large vocabulary, and a great variety of parentheses, appositives, exclamations, pleonasms of all sorts. It is these "fillers" that give his narrative some of its leisureliness, and he has a marvellous trick of turning them to poetic account. As a first-person narrator (whether speaking in his own voice or through a Canterbury pilgrim) he can address to his audience phrases which both fill out his line or couplet and support his tone of easy colloquy:

And certeinly, to *tellen as it was,*
Of this vessel the Cook drank faste, *allas!*
What needed hym? he drank ynough biforn.

13

And whan he hadde pouped in this horn . . .

(The Manciple's Prologue 87–90)

Occasionally we can catch him squandering a handful of verses in warming up to his task,[8] and from tale to tale his inspiration seems to have had its ups and downs. Sometimes the movement is quite slow, with successive clauses having as much the effect of braking as of advancing the narrative:

The thridde day, this marchant up ariseth,
And on his nedes sadly hym avyseth,
And up into his countour-hous gooth he
To rekene with hymself, as wel may be,
Of thilke yeer how that it with hym stood,
And how that he despended hadde his good,
And if that he encressed were or noon.

(The Shipman's Tale 75–81)

At some notable moments it is extraordinarily spare and fast:

And with the staf she drow ay neer and neer,
And wende han hit this Aleyn at the fulle,
And smoot the millere on the pyled skulle,
That doun he gooth, and cride, "Harrow! I dye!"
Thise clerkes beete hym weel and lete hym lye;
And greythen hem, and took hir hors anon,
And eek hire mele, and on hir wey they gon.

(The Reeve's Tale 4304–10)

Generally, then, his narrative verse is flexible and versatile, flowing around the more static passages of description, lyricism, and sententiousness, and floating them, as it were, in a forward-moving current.

Chaucer's brilliant technique with dramatic verse has been so widely celebrated as to need no further exposition here. Where he has perhaps lacked due appreciation is in the other direction, in the sphere of undramatic lyricism and of formal rhetorical effects generally. Chaucer went to school to the rhetoricians; he knows well their "termes," "colours," and "figures," and it is a mistake to think that he uses formal rhetoric less in *The Canterbury Tales* than in the early works, or that he tends to use it only as it is sanctioned by dramatics.[9] Both of these ideas stem

14

from the feeling that because medieval rhetoric was based on bad theory and bad models, and practised by bad poets, its figures of speech are somehow inherently bad. To the obvious proposition that a certain concentration of figures of speech is normal to poetry, we must add the fact that *The Canterbury Tales* contains some very good poetry that is at the same time highly rhetorical. The question, of course, is not whether the rhetoricians' intricate patterns of words are used, but whether they work. Chaucer could make them work. To be sure, Chaucer in *The Canterbury Tales* seems very conscious of rhetoric. It is one of the subjects (like women and marriage) that he is forever making jokes about. The Host asks the Clerk not to use it; the Franklin says that he never learned it; the Squire claims to be a poor rhetorician who "kan not clymben over so heigh a style"; the Nun's Priest longs for the skill of a Geoffrey of Vinsauf (author of an *ars poetica*) to complain the abduction of Chauntecleer. Yet each of their tales uses rhetorical passages, and in many others Chaucer introduces them without self-consciousness.

Leaving out, for the moment, the consideration that many of Chaucer's characteristic devices (the long description, the portrait, the catalogue, the sententious amplification) have their origins in rhetorical tradition—taking into account, rather, only the local texture or feel of his verse—his poetry seems most formally wrought, most "rhetorical," when it approaches the lyric note, and especially within the formal apostrophe or invocation. Such passages as Arcite's death-speech and Constance's prayer on the beach are full of tropes and patternings of words from the rhetoric books: *exclamatio, interrogatio, pronominatio* (epithet), and the varieties of repetition *traductio, repetitio, adnominatio:*

> Allas, the wo! allas, the peynes stronge,
> That I for you have suffred, and so longe!
> Allas, the death! allas, myn Emelye!
> Allas, departynge of our compaignye!
> Allas, myn hertes queene! allas, my wyf!
> Myn hertes lady, endere of my lyf!

Chaucer uses his repetitions and antitheses so beautifully to build feeling that we hardly notice the rhetorical artifice that brings the passage to its climax:

> What is this world? what asketh men to have?

Now with his love, now in his colde grave
Allone, withouten any compaignye.

(The Knight's Tale 2771–9)

Similarly, the moving climax of Constance's invocation to the Virgin is the most intricate of four stanzas of "rhetoric":

Thow sawe thy child yslayn bifore thyne yen,
And yet now liveth my litel child, parfay!
Now, lady bright, to whom alle woful cryen,
Thow glorie of wommanhede, thow faire may,
Thow haven of refut, brighte sterre of day,
Rewe on my child, that of thy gentillesse,
Rewest on every reweful in distresse.

(The Man of Law's Tale 848–54)

The "style of the man," then, comprehends a great technical range, from this to the fully natural idiom and rhythms of the dramatic monologues.

I I

Turning now to the "style of the work," we may first repeat the observation that *The Canterbury Tales* in general show a close correspondence between kinds of style and areas of meaning. Chaucer continually makes choices among the technical means at his command, restricting and altering his style according to the attitudes he is expressing. The general lines of his strategy are those learned from literary tradition, particularly the French. French courtly literature presented to Chaucer a clearly defined style, which in its best exemplars, as *Le Roman de la Rose* of Guillaume de Lorris, was superbly designed to express courtly idealism. The courtly style in an impossibly pure form would be characterised by a slow tempo, unruffled rhythm, exotic setting, extensive description of a static, conventional, formal nature, formal portraiture, polite diction, rhetorical and lyrical discourse. Characterisation would be simple and allegorical. Essentially non-dramatic, the whole poetry would find its truest connection with human interest in its rendering of an ideal and longed-for world of the imagination. Side by side with this highly "conventional" (by which I mean "non-representational") poetry, the literature of the medieval "realistic" tradition presented Chaucer with the opposite style. The French fabliaux could teach him that along with comic disenchantment went rapid tempo, turbulent rhythm, spare and familiar settings, domestic imagery, colloquial and impolite discourse. The great dramatic monologues in Jean de Meun's continuation of *Le Roman de la Rose* showed him the beginnings of a complex, realistic characterisation; furthermore, they showed him that a realistic style could transcend farce, and begin to support other and more seriously "realistic" views of life.[10]

Secular literature, then, roughly oriented for Chaucer two styles and their related areas of meaning. Although for the sake of brevity I have greatly simplified the descriptions of both the styles and the traditions that produced them, the reader will no doubt still recognise that some of *The Canterbury Tales* belong to the tradition of courtly-conventional style and some to the "realistic." When he deals with extremes of attitude, Chaucer uses a relatively pure style, one or the other. *The Knight's Tale* with its slow pace, antique setting, elaborate, static descriptions, elevated speeches, and simple characterisation, is written in a conventional style which beautifully supports the idealism of its theme. *The Clerk's Tale,* not specifically a "courtly" poem, is nevertheless highly conventional; its style exhibits many of the traits which the courtly tradition shares with the idealism of pious legend. These poems, together with *The Squire's Tale, The Franklin's Tale,* and *The Man of Law's Tale,* admirably exemplify Chaucer's great range of tone and colour within what is essentially the same stylistic system. It corresponds to the whole range of feeling between Knight and Clerk, who yet have beneath their differences a common denominator of idealism.

At the other end of the scale we have the poems which are predominantly "realistic"— in the limited sense in which we are here using that term. They assert in various ways the primacy of matter and of animal nature in human concerns; accordingly their style is compounded of domestic imagery, natural discourse, local setting. They normally eschew formal rhetoric and extended description. Chaucer's tonal range within this style is narrower than that within conventional style, but his technical skill is, if anything, greater. Each of his realisms is different. The style that supports ordinary fabliau comedy in *The Shipman's Tale* is made specially acerb in *The Reeve's Tale*. The latter has a special sharpness in its descriptions, a special irony created by its use of dialect, which are acutely well suited to the Reeve's attitudes. The realistic setting of *The Miller's Tale* is similar to and yet unmistakably different from the worlds of domestic images built up in the course of *The*

Wife of Bath's Prologue and *The Summoner's Tale.* If the Miller's world is to him a congenial and manageable one, it is not as much owned and loved as is the Wife of Bath's; and neither's world is to be confused with the dark welter of the Canon's Yeoman's, which is neither loved nor manageable at all.

Both "realism" and "conventionalism" are tools to the mature Chaucer. The ultimate style of *The Canterbury Tales,* which I shall call the "mixed style," is the result of his management of the two traditional styles at once. This is evident in that many of the greatest tales are themselves of mixed style, and that in the context of the pilgrimage frame even the tales of relatively pure realism and conventionalism are set in meaningful juxtaposition to each other. The variety of style in *The Canterbury Tales* is thus great and yet artfully composed. It produces in large and small that distinctively Chaucerian effect of irony, perspective, relativity, humour; it supports the complex view of man's pilgrimage that is the subject of the whole work.

Let me here try to sidestep an obvious danger in this perhaps foolhardy attempt to deal with the "style" of so vast a poem. In implying that *The Canterbury Tales* is basically "ironic" in style, I do not wish to give the impression that the stylistic co-ordinates I have chosen—conventionalism and realism—are the only possible co-ordinates, or that certain themes and stylistic situations are not actually exempt from Chaucer's irony. One might profitably distinguish as quite separate Chaucer's learned or scholastic style, characterised by logical argument and Latin terminology. Assuredly one can isolate, somewhere between realism and convention, a Chaucerian "pathetic" style, composed with simple characterisation, plain diction, spare and humble setting, and reaching for great idealising power. It associates itself in Chaucer with the themes of parent and child and of wronged innocence, and its most successful exemplar is *The Prioress's Tale.* Here the pathos attaching to the little martyr is supported by a childlike tone, created in part through the use of simple, black-and-white contrasts, repetitions of words and phrases giving an effect of simplicity, a plentiful use of terms ("litel," "smal," "yong") denoting the diminutive, and a syntax that catches childhood's simplicity of expression:

> This litel child, his litel book lernynge,
> As he sat in the scole at his prymer,
> He *Alma redemptoris* herde synge,

As children lerned hir antiphoner;

"I kan namoore expounde in this mateere;
I lerne song, I kan but smal grammeere."

"And is this song maked in reverence
Of Cristes mooder?" seyde this innocent . . .

O deere child, I halse thee,
In vertu of the Hooly Trinitee,
Tel me what is thy cause for to synge,
Sith that thy throte is kut to my semynge?

(516–648)

We hear the pathetic note in the Hugelino episode of *The Monk's Tale,*
and at points in the tales of the Clerk, the Franklin, the Physician and
the Man of Law. In *The Clerk's Tale* it is attended by biblically simple
description and mostly by an admirable restraint of sentiment:

But ther as ye me profre swich dowaire
As I first broghte, it is wel in my mynde
It were my wrecched clothes, nothyng faire,
The which to me were hard now for to fynde.
O goode God ! how gentil and how kynde
Ye seemed by youre speche and youre visage
The day that maked was oure mariage!

(848–54)

But elsewhere in this otherwise superb poem, and more commonly in
the Man of Law's and Physician's tales, we can hear Chaucer squeezing
it a bit hard, and falling into sentimentality. Only in the description of
the "hoomly suffisaunce" of the poor widow at the opening of *The
Nun's Priest's Tale* are any passages associated with this pathetic style
directly exposed to Chaucer's searching comedy. The very sacredness
of the pathetic subject-matter exempts it from criticism or even from
ventilation; but by the same token it allows Chaucer to write some of
his least successful verses. In any event, while the pathetic contributes
to the variety of the *Tales,* it is not an important axis of his style.
Chaucer drew to an extent on the legends and lyrics in honour of the
Virgin Mary in his treatment of motherhood and children, but his sen-

timental pathos does not seem directed by a strong antecedent tradition of style, and he uses it only in *The Canterbury Tales*. There is none of it in the pathos of the earlier poems. It is late-Chaucerian as it is late-medieval. We may note that before this time little children do not figure prominently in medieval literature, and the literature is remarkably free from sentimentality.

On the other hand the "mixed style"—the interplay of conventional and realistic styles—has a clear basis in earlier medieval tradition and is a prominent feature of Chaucer's whole career as a poet. In him, indeed, the medieval comedy of a *Flamenca,* the irony of a Jean de Meun, the parodic elements in the *Renart* cycle and the fabliaux, found a particularly congenial development. The historical influence fell in, as it were, with a temperament and personality—not to speak of a technical range—that were admirably (almost explosively!) receptive to it. The brilliant variegation of *The House of Fame* and the ironic structure of the *Troilus* both show this.

We have already touched on some of the basic traits of Chaucer's literary personality that would be hospitable to the formation of a mixed style. His insouciance, his amateur stance, itself implies a requisite freedom from the strict bonds of decorum. Equally congenial is his tendency to play with perspective, for the mixed style is similarly based on the shift from one plane of reference to another. The first-person narrator's conventional and innocuous freedom to remind us of his own status as narrator—"This wydwe, *of which I telle you my tale*"—is always in Chaucer's hands on the verge of growing up into an instrument of perspective:

> Thise been the cokkes wordes, and nat myne;
> I kan noon harm of no womman divyne.
>
> (*The Nun's Priest's Tale* 2824; 3265–6)

The variety of narrative tones which he can assume—now knowing, now obtuse, now neutral—is of course not the same as the mixed style, but it bespeaks the temperament congenial to that style.

However, the richest source of the aptitude which Chaucer poured into the mixed style was in his language, particularly his natural propensity to speak in terms of familiar things, in terms of earth, rural nature, the human body. When energised, raised in intensity, given full context, it supports the most memorable recommendation of naturalness in English:

Lat hem be breed of pured whete-seed,
And lat us wyves hoten barly-breed.

Thise wormes, ne thise motthes, ne thise mytes,
Upon my peril, frete hem never a deel;
And wostow why? for they were used weel.

. . . me thoughte he hadde a paire
Of legges and of feet so clene and faire
That al myn herte I yaf unto his hoold.
He was, I trowe, a twenty wynter oold . . .

(*The Wife of Bath's Prologue* 143–4, 560–2, 597–600)

Conjoined with the French and the Latin terminology, with the sophisticated idiom of the courtier and man of letters, it creates on the level of language an ironic mixture analogous to Chaucer's mixing of larger units of style.

It is a miracle of Chaucer's style—of the same provenience as his unerring feel for expressive imagery—that his familiar language does not seem to collide with his high style except when he wants it to. One of the great pleasures in reading him is to attend to the nature of the language, to gauge when it is in ironic adjustment and when not. Chaucer can have it either way; it is a mistake to think that the current is always on. The knight's reference to the oxen in his plough does not create irony. Much of the time the familiar works harmoniously along with the learning and the formal artifice, leavening and lightening them as in this perfect *exemplum* from *The Manciple's Tale:*

Lat take a cat, and fostre hym wel with milk
And tendre flessh, and make his couche of silk,
And lat hym seen a mous go by the wal,
Anon he weyveth milk and flessh and al,
And every deyntee that is in that hous,
Swich appetit hath he to ete a mous.
Lo, heere hath lust his dominacioun,
And appetit fleemeth discrecioun.

(175–82)

While the connotations of "cat" and "mouse" and the rest have some bearing on the moral quality of Phebus's wife, who is ultimately being described here, their juxtaposition to such learned terms as "dominacioun," "appetit" and "discrecioun" is not meant to be comic, though we are forced to smile at the purely Chaucerian quality of the passage.

Even at his most relaxed moments, however, Chaucer is aware of the potency of the mixed idiom, and there is a sprinkling of its use for small local "ironic" effects throughout *The Canterbury Tales*. Chaucer can call at will for a satiric snap in the contrast between Latin polysyllables and plain speech:

> A somonour is a rennere up and doun
> With mandementz for fornicacioun,
> And is ybet at every townes ende.
>
> (*The Friar's Prologue* 1283–5)

> What spekestow of preambulacioun?
> What! amble, or trotte, or pees, or go sit down!
>
> (*The Wife of Bath's Prologue* 837–8)

Sometimes the natural enmity between barnyard imagery and educated judgment is stated while it is being used:

> Straw for thy Senek, and for thy proverbes!
> I counte not a panyer ful of herbes
> Of scole-termes.
>
> (*The Merchant's Tale* 1567–9)

> But, for ye speken of swich gentillesse
> As is descended out of old richesse,
> That therefore sholden ye be gentil men,
> Swich arrogance is not worth an hen.
>
> (*The Wife of Bath's Tale* 1109–12)

In *The Franklin's Tale* Chaucer sports with the pretentiousness of astronomical time-description:

> . . . the brighte sonne lost his hewe;
> For th'orisonte hath reft the sonne his lyght,—
> This is as much to say as it was nyght.—
>
> (1016–18)

22

Harry Bailly's unwontedly rhetorical invocation to Bacchus in *The Manciple's Prologue* is self-consciously brought to earth: "Of that matere ye gete namoore of me" (l. 102). A large measure of the humour of *The Tale of Sir Thopas* lies in its play with a mixture of romance convention and mundane imagery. Hardly one of the tales—the pious ones excepted—is without some mixture of this kind.

As I have already indicated, some of the best tales depend for their central meaning on the raising of the mixture of styles into a large structural principle. To speak in terms of genre, the Miller's and Merchant's tales radically combine stylistic traits of fabliau and romance; *The Nun's Priest's Tale*—to over-simplify grossly—combines animal fable and epic. In each the traits of the different styles are carefully exploited for the humour, the satire, the irony they produce when placed together. *The Miller's Tale* manages to remain fabliau, but there was never such a profound one. The tale needs its rich elaboration of courtly conventionalism to make such comic capital of its assertion of naturalness. We find the same mixture in *The Merchant's Tale,* but in very different adjustment. Here the cynically realistic undercutting of the pretence of romantic idealism produces a bitter humour. The mixture of *The Nun's Priest's Tale* produces yet another range of effects. It is *The Canterbury Tales* in little; its kaleidoscopic shifts of perspective, exposing a dozen important subjects to the humour of comparison, seems to exemplify Chaucer's basic method in the whole work. The tale illustrates, too, how much of Chaucer's technical range, how many of his favourite rhetorical procedures, can finally be enlisted in the service of the mixed style: courtly diction, and realistic, formal portraiture, rhetorical invocation, pathetic description; sententiousness becomes an instrument in his parody of learned discourse, and even the encyclopaedic catalogue appears, in an implied commentary on medical science:

A day or two ye shul have digestyves
Of wormes, er ye take your laxatyves
Of lawriol, centaure, and fumetere,
Or elles of ellebor, that groweth there,
Of katapuce, or of gaitrys beryis,
Of herbe yve, growing in oure yeerd, ther mery is;
Pekke hem up right as they growe and ete hem yn.

(2961–7)

In *The Pardoner's Tale* the mixed style is an instrument of the remarkable characterisation which finally dominates the poem. It is the very style of the Pardoner, who is the only pilgrim dramatically given literary powers comparable to those of Chaucer himself. The depth of the characterisation depends in part on the fact that in the Pardoner's mixed style, unlike in Chaucer's, the speaker is somehow made to fail in his irony. He turns out to be hardly humorous at all; his style rather deepens the curious blend of the grotesque and the pathetic already to be found in his portrait.

The stylistic components of the tale are easy to discern. The tale (with its prologue) is a dramatic monologue—that of Jean de Meun's character Faus-Semblant, but technically much more skilful. Within the dramatic monologue is a real medieval sermon, with its homiletic realism, its rhetoric and its *exempla*. On this level we are on familiar Chaucerian ground. The high-flown rhetoric of the sermon, in the context of the self-revelation of the monologue, produces a mock-effect which satirises the canned fireworks of the professional preachers. Chaucer underlines this effect by making the rhetorical outbursts glaringly ornamental, so that our attention is transferred from the meaning of the speech to the manipulations of the speaker. One can almost hear the Pardoner simulating the tears of St Paul:

> The apostel weping seith ful pitously,
> "Ther walken manye of which you toold have I—
> I seye it now wepyng, with pitous voys—
> That they been enemys of Cristes croys,
> Of which the ende is death, wombe is hir god!"
> O wombe! O bely! O stynkyng cod,
> Fulfilled of dong and of corrupcioun!
>
> (529–35)

John Speirs has well pointed out the conjunction in this sermon "of vigorous popular speech with scholastic phraseology," of "coarseness and . . . metaphysics." The realistic imagery here is inherited along with the learning from the ascetic-homiletic tradition, with its graphic descriptions of the fleshliness that must be condemned. But Chaucer makes it too vivid to remain simply satiric. It is presented with such a "thunderous overcharge . . . of feeling," Speirs points out, that it characterises the Pardoner as being unconsciously "both half-horrified and half-fascinated" by his subject.[11] This is going beyond the ordinary

Chaucerian irony; it makes the sermon both more ironic and less ironic than the Pardoner knows. His fascination raises his cyncism to a grotesque new power, while his horror reduces it to pathos. The sermon's great terminal *exemplum* of the three revellers who sought Death similarly breaks through the bounds of a simple satire on sermons. It is too convincing. The resulting stretch in the characterisation between redeeming sincerity and outright monstrosity is underlined stylistically in the sequence beginning at line 895. The whole gamut of Chaucer's styles can be found here in twenty lines, from the terrible rhetorical outcry, through the "broches, spoones, rynges" of domestic realism, to the touching special simplicity of "And lo, sires, thus I preche."

The juxtaposition of tales to each other and to the dramatic frame of the pilgrimage is the largest counter of Chaucer's style. It is the largest manifestation of what we can see in *The Canterbury Tales* from the mixed idiom up: Chaucer's endless interest in comparisons and relationships. "How shall the world be served?" is the question he asks. The great range of values and attitudes expressed in the tales represent his grand confrontation of it. The comedy and the tolerant irony, the relativism, the necessity to perceive: these are the answers implied by his mixed style.

CHAUCER'S RELIGION AND
THE CHAUCER RELIGION

One of the most useful truisms in the study of literary reception—of the ways in which texts are read in times and places other than their own—is that reception has two aspects: it reveals something about the text itself and something about its new readers or critics. The most secure and satisfying reception-study finds these two aspects mutually explanatory. The assumption, at any rate, is that different ages or cultures do not so much misread a great text as make from it special abstractions, acutely suited to their particular concerns. The text that survives from age to age, receiving variant and sometimes antithetical interpretations, is typically not so much a compendium of perdurable truths that are sometimes misunderstood and sometimes distorted, but a structure so richly and complexly organized that different cultures, different audiences, can re-orient it (rotate it three-dimensionally as one might rotate an image in a computer) and then interpret it in ways that, however special, do answer to the work. The interpretation may often represent a very limited reception, depending on the limits of the receiving apparatus; but it receives something that is, after all, there. It responds to, and reveals, both aspects of the situation at once.

This, at least, has for a long time been the finding of leading students of the Chaucer tradition. Caroline Spurgeon's great collection of Chaucer criticism and allusion (1925) and Derek Brewer's *Chaucer: The Critical Heritage* (1978) are immensely satisfying works in that they provide just such mutual illumination between Chaucer and six centuries of English-speaking culture. Thus Chaucer's rhetoric both answers to and illustrates the fifteenth century's passion for a new ornament and eloquence in English. Chaucer's creditable learning is praised as early Humanism in the sixteenth century, and the attribution to him of such works as the spurious *Plowman's Tale* explains his enlistment in this period as a Lollard by anti-papal reformers. The growing interest in "correctness" and polish, along with the progressive decay of the received text and the progressively antiquated appearance of Middle English explain, if they do not forgive, Chaucer's relative fall in popularity during the late seventeenth century and his frequently being modernized in the eighteenth. Brewer observes that during the eighteenth century, with the rise of the novel, Chaucer's poems "begin to be read as novels" and that Thomas Gray, in 1760, finds in Chaucer undeniable but rarely noticed traces of Gothic Horror.[1] Chaucer's tenderness and sympathy are richly evoked by nineteenth-century critics, who also begin that preoccupation with Chaucer's realism, fed by an age of realism in fiction, that is still going strong today.

Indeed, the twentieth-century reception of Chaucer is in most respects a remarkably sensitive and accurate reflection both of his text and of twentieth-century sensibility. The vogue of Chaucer the realist was overlaid at mid-century by a decisive interest in Chaucer's ambiguity and irony, qualities, as Brewer says, "that were not remarked on till the nineteenth century, and rarely then,"[2] but that must henceforth be counted among his most characteristic traits as artist and as personality. And who will claim, reading the emergent poststructuralist interpretation of Chaucer, that this perennially cheerful and confident poet never expressed a twinge of the anxiety of influence, never wrestled with the slipperiness and intractability of language, never wrote a poem whose real theme was the agony of writing a poem?

There is, however, one additional aspect of the twentieth-century Chaucer that is most surprising and puzzling: the religious, almost puritanical Chaucer who emerges powerfully and suddenly at midcentury and is with us still. This Chaucer is an essentially new element in the Chaucer tradition; but it is peculiarly difficult to connect to late twentieth-century sensibility.

The new religious Chaucer can easily be distinguished from the figure who emerges from prior discussion of Chaucer's religion; it is a matter of distinguishing between Chaucer's doctrinal position and the quality of his piety, that is, the nature, range, depth, and intensity of his religious feeling itself. It is the latter, his enveloping religiosity, that seems to me to be a late twentieth-century discovery or preoccupation. The issue of his doctrinal position—whether he was orthodox or a reformer, whether a Lollard or not—was at its height in the Renaissance, and lost much of its energy with the purging of the spurious works from Tyrwhitt's edition on. It is for now fairly settled, with general agreement that Chaucer was a safely orthodox Catholic in doctrine. But this issue touched only tangentially, at best, on the deeper question, "How *deeply* a Christian was Chaucer; or rather, how deeply does religion inform his work?" How deeply does his work express religious feeling? Where the doctrinal debate does touch on religiosity, it more often than not, and especially in the early twentieth century, lays Chaucer's religiosity open to serious question. Thus almost a century ago Thomas Lounsbury plausibly makes the case that Chaucer's temperament was not essentially religious at all. Chaucer's mind, Lounsbury thinks, was essentially sceptical. "There are those," says Lounsbury, "to whom faith is not so much a result of education or of conviction as it is a necessity of their being. It is natures of this kind that keep alive the religious flame in every age of doubt or unbelief . . . It is hardly necessary to say that to this class Chaucer does not belong."[3] To be sure, Chaucer has the capacity to feel "the beauty of the life of sacrifice and devotion which inspires the purer and loftier natures that enter into the service of the church" (vol. II, p. 518); but Lounsbury actually traces a progressive dwindling in Chaucer's religiosity: the apostrophe to the Trinity at the end of the *Troilus* marks the height of his early, relatively religious phase. Thereafter, sceptical passages in the *Legend of Good Women* and the *Knight's Tale* point toward the full scepticism of the *Canterbury Tales* (vol. II, pp. 509–30).

Opinion through the middle of this century by and large supported Lounsbury's judgement; Chaucer the sceptic, Chaucer the detached, is of course hardly surprising in an age of science and of secularism. But it hardly prepares us for the new religious Chaucer, which has by now become so heavily settled in as to need no demonstration here.

It would, however, be a mistake to identify this view simply with the school of scholarship and criticism that one would perhaps think of first: the exegetical school associated for the past forty years with medieval studies at Princeton. The movement is broader than that, and has been carried on by a more central group of Chaucerians, who by now may have in varying degrees been influenced by the somewhat embattled and controversial exegetes, but who have remained independent of them, and have by themselves decisively coloured our view of the entire canon. Since there is scarcely room here to embrace so vast a subject, and since they have been especially revisionist as regards the *Canterbury Tales,* the point of this essay will perhaps be adequately made by reference to their criticism of that work alone.

The ur-text is the remarkable Johns Hopkins dissertation, *The Unity of the Canterbury Tales,* published in 150 copies in 1955 by Ralph Baldwin. Baldwin is among the first to have attributed sovereign importance of the idea of religious pilgrimage to Chaucer's *plan,* and to have followed out the idea in its grandest and fullest implications. If

Kittredge had already dared say that the tales exist to illustrate the characters of the pilgrims,[4] Baldwin even more daringly finds that the pilgrims, along with their tales, exist for the pilgrimage. It, the pilgrimage, is the essential story that Chaucer tells:

> The drunken Miller, the rascally ecclesiastics, the Alisouns, the dutiful Parson and his brother—are all "framed" in that common piety, a pilgrimage. Despite frivolities and arguments, rancor and raciness, they have been conjured into existence as wayfarers and they activate a drama that does not cease for each of them with his tale. The via of Pilgrimage and the viae of the Pilgrims merge and measure off a story whose milestones are visible only in terms of Him "that hem hath holpen whan that they were seeke" [I(A) 18]. Some physical or spiritual sickness has put them *en route* to Canterbury, and one of the Enveloping Actions of the *CT* is the intercessory one of St Thomas à Becket, who is with them intentionally from the moment they convene at the Tabard. The "ways that lead to Christ" are as various as the Specific Actions of these convergent pilgrims. And our approach to the text seems to indicate that, using the Host's insistence on merriment as a foil, Chaucer has set his pilgrims on the road to glory.
>
> (pp. 78–9)

The secular tales are thus gathered and subsumed within the folds of a deeply religious conception: life as a pilgrimage to the New Jerusalem. It is a metaphor that Chaucer uses touchingly in his lyric *Truth,* and gives to the Parson to introduce his telling of the last of the tales:

> To shewe yow the wey, in this viage,
> Of thilke parfit glorious pilgrymage,
> That highte Jerusalem celestial.
>
> (x, 49–51)

Seen this way, the *Canterbury Tales* becomes an essentially religious work, the *Parson's Tale* becomes an unprecedently important part of it, and Chaucer, in his ripe maturity, becomes transcendently a religious poet.

The idea was apparently one whose time had come. By 1979, in a brief survey of the state of Chaucer studies, Florence Ridley could confidently say that "all the individual Canterbury Tales must be seen in the context of the last, *The Parson's Tale.* And in that light, even those tales which during the process of their telling do, indeed, 'sownen into synne,' become exemplars of the heedlessness and folly which each man must overcome if he is to reach the ultimate shrine of heaven."[5] In the same survey Ridley reviews Donald Howard's *The Idea of the Canterbury Tales*[6]—three times the length of Baldwin's book—devoted to the same general thesis, giving the same importance to the structural and metaphorical power of the pilgrimage, and thus the same crucial importance to the *Parson's Tale.* The idea is a commonplace in the pages of the present decade's Chaucer criticism, and comes to a peak of elaboration in V. A. Kolve's *Chaucer and the Imagery of Narrative,* an intensely close reading of the first five of the *Canterbury Tales.* Kolve not only seizes upon the idea of the religious Chaucer's religious pilgrimage as the overarching structural idea of the poem; he also finds a series of substructures of the same shape within the poem. Thus the pious and hitherto rather unprepossessing *Man of Law's Tale,* in his reading, becomes the climactic corrective, a "provisional palinode," to what Kolve takes as the first day's daring but unchristian excursions into pagan philosophizing and bawdiness.[7]

It is evident enough, then, that the religious Chaucer is a powerful new reading which should, like the other great readings of the past, lead us to deepened awareness of what is there in the text awaiting new appreciation. But the reading remains, in my opinion, both surprising and troubling. Before stating my misgivings, I should make clear what it is that I am not contesting. In the first place, there is little doubt that for all or most of his life Chaucer was a loyal Catholic, and—since his retraction seems both genuine and sincere—that at the very end he was in a mood of deep, Christian contrition. It is also clear that most of the mainstream critics, in contemplating the religious Chaucer, have not done so crudely. They have been aware of, and have confronted both aesthetically and historically, such apparent paradoxes as a fundamentally Christian poem's containing a majority of secular, bawdy fabliaux, or of its having to be retracted by its author at all.

In general they have offered highly sophisticated explanations. Thus Alfred David sees the whole of the *Canterbury Tales* as a sort of *agon* between the secular artist and the Christian moralist who is the final victor.[8] Donald Howard comes to see the poems as a single confrontation: there are "two books" within the *Canterbury Tales;* one book is the sequence of tales up to but not including the last, that represents the errant world, a world that is lost unless it be confronted, as it is, by the second, the Parson's tract on Sin and Penitence, which "puts a qualification on art itself."[9] Lee Patterson, rejecting the idea of pilgrimage or of anything else as the controlling pattern of the *Canterbury Tales,* sees the *Parson's Tale* (with the *Manciple's Tale* preceding) as the alternative offered to the meaninglessness and failure "of the whole poetic enterprise": "For his sober and prosaic treatise is a rejection of all personal speaking that does not confront, in the sacramental language of penance, the sinfulness of the human condition. It is not merely the qualifying complexities of language that are to be abandoned, but any language that does not deal with sin in the terms defined by the Parson."[10]

The very sophistication of this sort of criticism is a source of concern; the case being made here is too neat, and, in a way, too full of thought. Going back to the question of religious sensibility, and for touchstones thinking of half a dozen of the best religious poets—of Dante, Langland, the Pearl poet, Donne, Milton, Hopkins—what does Chaucer teach us to feel? What, on balance, is his legacy as a religious poet? Most of what is being said about the new religious Chaucer is telling us relatively little that is new about the religious *quality* of his poetry, however much about the ideas of pilgrimage, of penance, of sin and contrition, of pride and charity, of art versus morality, and about the difference between the sensibility of the Age of Faith and that of our own. For lack of a new and finer delineation of his *religiosity,* his religion remains a rather mixed and not altogether impressive thing.

There are, of course, great and religiously moving moments in Chaucer; perhaps the greatest is in the ending of the *Troilus* (v, 1835ff.):

O yonge, fresshe folkes, he or she,
In which that love up groweth with youre age,
Repeyreth hom fro worldly vanyte,
And of youre herte up casteth the visage
To thilke God that after his ymage
Yow made, and thynketh al nys but a faire
This world, that passeth soone as floures faire.

And loveth hym, the which that right for love
Upon a crois, oure soules for to beye,
First starf, and roos, and sit in hevene above;
For he nyl falsen no wight, dar I seye,

That wol his herte al holly on hym leye.
And syn he best to love is, and most meke,
What nedeth feynede loves for to seke?

The pity is that moments like this are just isolated moments, and they rarely appear in Chaucer's avowedly religious works at all. As has been observed before, his career as a religious writer seems to have had a number of phases. The first possibly includes the *ABC* and the *Second Nun's Tale*. A lyric on the Blessed Virgin and a saint's life, they are usually classified as standard medieval fare, and suggest a youthful and rather passive, conformist religiosity. But they have a kind of integrity about them. Both are translations, and both are unembellished, presented much as they were received; they seem to say that if Chaucer's feelings were passive and conformist, he at least was perfectly honest about it, and pretended no more.

Practised readers of Chaucer notice at once that these presumably early works have almost no trace of pathos in them; and that marks them off from what might be construed as a later stage of his religiosity, which is engaged much with the Blessed Virgin and with images of suffering women and children. This pathetic religiosity, one that conveys powerful feelings of tenderness and pity, is to my mind at the highest level that Chaucer's *sustained* achievement as a religious poet ever reaches. Its masterpiece is the *Prioress's Tale*. There are some unforgettable passages in the pious tale of the Man of Law; this one (II, 841 ff.) reminds us that Chaucer *could* write a great prayer:

"Mooder," quod she, "and mayde bright, Marie,
Sooth is that thurgh wommanes eggement
Mankynde was lorn, and damned ay to dye,
For which thy child was on a croys yrent.
Thy blisful eyen sawe al his torment;
Thanne is ther no comparison bitwene
Thy wo and any wo man may sustene.

"Thow sawe thy child yslayn bifore thyne yen,
And yet now lyveth my litel child, parfay!
Now, lady bright, to whom alle woful cryen,
Thow glorie of wommanhede, thow faire may,
Thow haven of refut, brighte sterre of day,

32

Rewe on my child, that of thy gentillesse,
Rewest on every reweful in distresse."

Moving as this note in Chaucer can be, it must be recognized as a very
special note, that explores, however beautifully, only a narrow sector of
religious feeling. It is not even an exclusively religious note, but can be
found in secular dress in a number of other poems: the Hugelino
episode of the *Monk's Tale,* the *Physician's Tale,* and the *Clerk's Tale,*
and is closely related in Chaucer's sensibility to an even wider range of
pathos (we might call it Ovidian pathos) to be found plentifully in the
Legend of Good Women and the Dido episode of the *House of Fame.*
Chaucer's pathetic religiosity, then, might more accurately be called his
pathos in a religious vein, which does not lessen its value, but underlines perhaps his limitations as a religious poet. We come up against
these limitations, almost embarrassingly, in the *Man of Law's Tale,* an
overtly religious legend in which Chaucer repeatedly challenges himself to rise to the expression of deep religious feeling, and, except for
the passages of pathos, fails. Chaucer—along with Langland and
Dante—was at times capable of generating religious sublimity with the
plain style, but here he reaches for it with high style, with rhetoric. The
Christian noblewoman Constance somehow escapes being slaughtered
with her fellow-Christians at a feast arranged by her pagan mother-in-
law in Syria. She then is set adrift by wicked pagans in a rudderless
boat, whence she drifts, in the course of years, to the coast of Northum-
berland. How, asks the poet, did she survive? His answer (II, 470–504)
is poetically one of the lowest points in his entire *oeuvre.* We need con-
template only a couple of stanzas:

Men myghten asken why she was nat slayn
Eek at the feeste? Who myghte hir body save?
And I answere to that demande agayn,
Who saved Danyel in the horrible cave
Ther every wight save he, maister and knave,
Was with the leon frete er he asterte?
No wight but God, that he bar in his herte.

God liste to shewe his wonderful myracle
In hire, for we sholde seen his mighty werkis;
Crist, which that is to every harm triacle,

By certeine meenes ofte, as knowen clerkis,
Dooth thyng for certein ende that ful derk is
To mannes wit, that for oure ignorance
Ne konne noght knowe his prudent purveiance.

(470–83)

Passages like this, with their fillers, awkward rhymes, uneasy management of rhythm, and slackness of diction, remind us of a fact of Chaucer's life suggested in the *Prologue* to the *Legend of Good Women,* but too seldom reflected upon, that the poet was from time to time bidden by important people to write things "and durste yt nat withseye" (F, 367). How else to account for work so ambitiously conceived and so cumbersomely executed?

Would that similar speculation could as readily account for the next problem that arises with Chaucer's new reputation as a religious author; and that is the unprecedented value it confers on the *Parson's Tale.* For there was never, perhaps, a less likely candidate for literary importance in the work of any great poet. The *Tale* is not poetry, of course, but a prose compilation from a sermon on penitence and a tract on the seven deadly sins, both originating in Latin. It is itself a tract, hardly intended that we should imagine it to have been recited aloud. (That would have taken about four hours and a quarter.) Until recently almost no one but specialists read it, and that under a species of compulsion. As literature, it rivals the work of Lydgate as a traditional object of derision. "Nothing much more wearisome can well be imagined," says Lounsbury, "than the worthy priest's disquisition on the various venial and deadly sins to which man's nature is exposed, and the various remedies against them. For the ordinary reader it is one long level of tediousness, save in two or three places where the preacher steps aside to denounce some particular manifestation of evil."[11]

The new view of the religious significance of the *Canterbury Tales* has made its way with astonishing blitheness through a thicket of uncertainties about the status of the *Parson's Tale.* The problem is complex, and its more intricate considerations have no place here; but to indicate a few of its major aspects will suffice to illustrate the force and confidence of the new view itself.

The very authenticity of the *Parson's Tale* has long been challenged. The challenge has just as long been beaten off, mostly by the sensible observation that we cannot banish works from the canon just because we don't like them. It is possible still to argue that Chaucer could have owned and studied it without having translated it. But I see no reason, given Chaucer's apparent taste for such a dull piece of edifying prose as the *Melibee,* not to imagine the *Parson's Tale* also as Chaucer's, as produced at the behest of someone who could not be refused, or in a mood of contrition, or, most likely, as a laborious act of penance. The real problem—it is no less than an embarrassment—arises not so much from the presumption of Chaucer's authorship, as from its inclusion in the *Canterbury Tales* and its newly crucial significance as the last of them. Here we run up against the entirely uncertain history of the putting-together of the *Canterbury Tales.* We don't know who put them together. There is almost full agreement that the earliest and best manuscripts were assembled by persons other than Chaucer in the second decade after his death. The evidence of the manuscripts suggests that he left his desk or his files in a mess; that some of the tales in the final collection were written before he had an idea of a collection, and that only some were securely attached by him to the collection. Some bear no particular relation to the teller assigned, and it appears that from time to time Chaucer or someone else may have switched tellers. We know that the editors or scribes of the fifteenth century had a field day inventing orders of the tales, writing links to make them fit, and making ascriptions of pilgrims to them. Chaucer, in fact, left on his desk no book of the *Canterbury Tales,* but rather ten groups or fragments. Except for fragment I(A), which opens the work; for a scattering of (often irreconcilable) references to places and times of the day; and for the *Parson's Prologue,* which sounds genuine and which will introduce the last of the tales, Chaucer had not worked out, or at least had not written down, a plan for the order of the fragments. The inclusion in the *Canterbury Tales* of any work that happened by chance to be lying among his papers is a distinct possibility, whether done posthumously by his executors or editors, or by his family, or even, at the last moment, by himself. The fact that there is appended to the *Parson's Tale* in all the best manuscripts the pious retraction by Chaucer of all his sinful works—a retraction listing the *Canterbury Tales* among other works but indicating no more specific connection to it—makes it more than possible that the *Parson's Tale* found its way into the *Canterbury Tales* under unusual circumstances, perhaps in anticipation of death, and unrelated to the literary and artistic making of the rest of the work. All arguments about the plan or structure or sequence or even the canon of the tales have to be made with the circumspection imposed by these conditions.

Let us turn to the context o the *Parson's Tale* in the action of the poem. The *Parson's Prologue* seems genuine, and there can be little doubt that Chaucer's sense of decorum led him to feel that the Parson should tell the last tale. Boccaccio had had a similar feeling about ending the *Decameron;* secular as the work might be, the accomplishment, the completion of so great a work was in itself a sobering event, an occasion for humble thanksgiving, as would also be the accomplishment of a pilgrimage. There is every reason to feel the rightness of the Parson's awareness of the grand analogy between a pilgrimage to Canterbury and "thilke parfit glorious pilgrymage / That highte Jerusalem celestial." It is an important moment. There is likely a special poetic resonance in Chaucer's locating of the action vaguely and yet precisely: "we were entryng at a thropes ende" (X, 12) he says, and it was four o'clock in the afternoon of the last day. The Host calls on the Parson "to knytte up well a greet mateere" (X, 28), but characteristically he calls for a "fable" (X, 29). The Parson will have nothing of fables, nothing even of verse. He will tell, he announces, "a myrie tale in prose / To knytte up al this feeste, and make an ende" (X, 46–7). There is no problem with the word "myrie"—we know enough about the terms for happiness and joy in religious contexts to accept "myrie" as a religious term. But in the brief discussion that ensues, the Parson's imminent contribution is once again called a "tale," once a piece dealing in "vertuous sentence" (X, 63), and twice a "meditacioun" (X, 55, 79). The Host, practical as ever, remarks that the sun is about to set—as it would be at four on an April afternoon in southern England—and asks the Parson to be economical—to recite "in litel space." Then comes, in the manuscripts, what we know as the *Parson's Tale.* The gross lack of dramatic verisimilitude here is one problem, though Chaucer did not always worry about verisimilitude if other and higher goals—as, for instance, philosophizing—were at hand. But it seems to me that the forecast of the *genre* of the *Parson's Tale* here must give us pause. A "tale"? A "meditacioun"? Well, a "tale" might be almost any recitation; but how well does the *Parson's Tale* answer to "a meditacioun"?

To my knowledge the question has not yet been given a satisfactory treatment; but for lack of a study of the meditation as genre in Middle English, we can at least consult the *Middle English Dictionary* under "Meditation." The overwhelming number—dozens—of examples of the word, dating from the early thirteenth century, illustrate its first meaning, which is "meditation; contemplation; devout preoccupation; devotions; prayer." A small second group of meanings simply show the first meaning in compound with certain verbs: to have or take or make or say one's meditation. Finally there is a third meaning, based on four examples which are reported to use "meditation" to mean "a moral discourse." However, since two of the four are from the very passage we are examining, we must suspend judgement on them. The only two remaining examples of the meaning listed, from 1400, are from a translation of the well-known thirteenth-century life of Christ of the pseudo-Bonaventura. One is a translation of an *incipit:* "Here byggynneth medytaciouns of the soper of oure lorde Ihesu And also of his passyun." The other reads: "Y wil the lere a medytacyun Compyled of crystys passyun and of hys modyr . . . what peynes they suffred thou mayst lere." What this text offers under the label of "meditation" is not any old moral discourse, but thoughts based on sacred biography, on religious narrative. And it is significant that among all the uses of meditation in the first and second senses, those that go beyond meditation or prayer in general or in the abstract, mostly refer to it in terms of joy, pleasure, the fervour of religious love; and for the single cited example that does suggest meditation on sin and hell, there are five that refer to meditations on the lives of Christ and of Mary, and their meaning. The repeated use of the term "meditation" in the *Parson's Prologue* suggests preliminarily, then, that the Parson may have been at one time intended to "knytte up" the "feeste" with a work quite different in character and in tone, more fitting to the occasion, and certainly closer to Chaucer's known talents and tastes in religious subjects, than the piece we have.[12]

The argument that the Tale is so hopeless as art as not to be admissible as Chaucer's work, while not itself a hopeless argument, we have already generously abandoned. Let us go on to a related but different issue: that is, that the *Parson's Tale* simply *sounds* wrong in subject and point-of-view for the last place in the Tales. Chaucer had done last places in texts in a religious vein before; the ending of the *Troilus* is one. One remembers too the ending of the fourth book of the translation of Boethius: "Goth now thanne, ye stronge men, ther as the heye wey of the greet ensaumple ledith yow. O nyce men! why nake ye your bakkes? . . . For the erthe overcomen yeveth the sterres." Chaucer knew great religious utterances when he heard them. From the ending of the *Troilus* and the very opening of the *Canterbury Tales* we are prepared for a generous, complex tension in Chaucer's view of the realms of secular and divine; we are prepared, even, for a ceremonially sober and conservative closure to the *Tales,* a beckoning to the contemplation of higher things. What, then, is he doing with this endless, narrow, small-minded, inveterately enumerative, circumstantially punitive list of sinful acts?

It would argue a sorry ignorance of Catholic doctrine or of medieval culture to suggest that such a document had no place in Chaucer's world. But the *Parson's Tale* doesn't sound as if it belongs to the end of the *Canterbury Tales;* it forces on the other tales a sharp and almost grotesquely narrow confrontation—a bald, unrelieved confrontation, without appreciation, or pity or regret—that Professor Howard senses and accepts, but which some readers still find profoundly unChaucerian. It seems, as E. Talbot Donaldson says, "wrong to read, as so many wish to do, the Parson's Tale as a reliable gloss on the rest of the *Canterbury Tales*."[13] If, as has been argued, the very baldness of the *Parson's Tale* signalizes Chaucer's explicit renunciation of art and even of literary language at this point, is it licit to yoke the piece retrospectively in any significant way with the literary art which it abandons? Would it not be more fitting rather to regard it as marking a trauma, a biographical or historical accident, something sudden, and rather pathetic?

I do not mean by expressing these speculations and doubts to assert facts that can't be proven. I mean only to suggest how speculative and doubtful it is to take so confidently the other position; and to raise a final question. Our experience of the Chaucer tradition, and its spirit, suggest that the new religious Chaucer should somehow be there, in the text; otherwise good critics and scholars, persons of talent and good will, would not have discovered him. Yet in this case the heavy weight of meaning that has been newly loaded upon the text suggests that a religious, almost puritanical Chaucer is less interesting as a discovery of twentieth-century critics than as their creation. I would almost call it a confection, that tells us perhaps more about the critics than it does about Chaucer. This reading of Chaucer involves the confident ignoring of so many of Chaucer's poetic and temperamental traits, the confident surmounting of so many factual or scholarly ifs and doubts, the ignoring of such palpable artistic embarrassments, that one is impelled to wonder—as one is even more easily impelled to wonder about the "exegetical" reading—what in the culture of the second half of the twentieth century explains or responds to the discovery of a newly religious Chaucer.

It is a subject for an anthropologist or sociologist. Unfortunately no one has done a survey of the religious tendencies of medievalists. It is difficult to imagine any relationship whatever between what we are studying and the recent recrudescence of popular religion in America.

tradition; the puritanical Chaucer may already be undergoing considerable deconstruction. Meanwhile, we may continue to wonder with Pandarus what sort of enemy it is

> That so kan leye oure jolite on presse,
> And bringe oure lusty folk to holynesse!

CHAUCER IN AN AGE
OF CRITICISM

"There is no good book on Chaucer's poetry," wrote Mrs. Q. D. Leavis in *Scrutiny* in 1943,

> because no first-class literary critic happens to have had sufficiently intense an interest in Chaucer to go to the immense trouble of acquiring the incidental specialisms and absorbing the masses of "factual matter" that would equip him to decide *as a literary critic* the critical problems Chaucer raises. And until such a critic does there will not be the book on Chaucer we all need, let what Bentley of mediaeval studies there ever may be edit the text, or if the authentic text were suddenly revealed from heaven.

But a sufficient mass of pertinent factual matter was quite easily available as Mrs. Leavis wrote; and there *were* good books on Chaucer. What Mrs. Leavis really awaited was a critic who would ask and answer a set of questions different from those of Kittredge, Root, Manly, and Lowes, and thus initiate a reading of Chaucer in tune with modern sensibility and modern literary theory. She had not far to look; for in the same issue of *Scrutiny* there appeared the last of a series of articles by John Speirs, which were later to be revised and expanded into his book *Chaucer the Maker* (1951). Raymond Preston's *Chaucer* appeared the following year. Between them—and despite numerous and very British infractions of the scholarly code that keep them still much underappreciated in America—these two critics ushered in the modern Chaucer.

Their lead, indeed, has been taken up so enthusiastically—borne on the high tide of an age of criticism—that there is no longer a real issue (if ever there was) between traditional factualism and modern criticism of Chaucer. The issue, as a group of recent books[1] on Chaucer can be seen to define it, is: what character, what emphasis, does modern Chaucer criticism seem to be taking, and what is its promise?

Wolfgang Clemen's *Der junge Chaucer,* which was first published in 1938, has now been revised extensively and translated into English as

Chaucer's Early Poetry. It makes a most successfully graceful reappearance, partly because Clemen's somewhat changed approach is in harmony with recent criticism, and partly because in 1938 the book was already in advance of its time. Without the slightest display of aggressive modernity, and with its basis still comfortably deep in a knowledge of the sources, *Der junge Chaucer* was incomparable in its time for its sensitiveness to the actual aesthetic and poetic character of the early poems. Like a typically "modern" critic, Clemen never strayed far from the text. He coupled this with a second virtue, which modern criticism has not yet exploited to the full: a continuous sense of the relationship of the poems, in theme and style, to the traits of late-medieval art and culture generally. He was (to my knowledge) the first Chaucerian to suggest that Chaucer's art clearly exemplified the rich *Spätstil* of the declining Middle Ages, that the mixed, alternating, experimental style of the *House of Fame* and the *Parliament of Fowls* must be related to the shifting uncertainty of fourteenth-century social, political, and ecclesiastical life. If the New Criticism has given way to a New Historicism— a historicism newly aware of art-style as a central datum in the history of culture—then Clemen will have been its prophet for Chaucer studies.

These qualities are fully preserved in Clemen's revised edition, along with his sensitive continuous account of Chaucer's alteration of sources. There is a welcome increase in emphasis on the role of poetic method in the generation of meaning, especially in the criticism of the *Parliament* (cf. p. 157). The treatment of the *Book of the Duchess* ends with new sections on "Style and Diction" and "Chaucer's Versification," and there are numerous new observations that arise from close reading, as in the analysis (pp. 151–53) of the introduction of the *Parliament* proper. Clemen is now more overtly and confidently concerned with rhetorical tradition—he uses Curtius' term "topoi"—and with such matters as "levels of style" and "technique of juxtaposition." But perhaps the most profound aspect of the revision, and a testimony to his continuous attempt to get an integrated view of Chaucer's achievement, is the appearance in his comment of a *leitmotiv,* of Chaucer's "new art of silence, of reserve, of cautious suggestion":

> By putting different elements together without comment, simply by the sequence of juxtaposition of his episodes or symbols, he can convey a definite way of interpretation, a train of possibilities, a line of choice. The reader is always left to draw his own conclusions. The "signifi-

cance" however lies in the realm of imaginative poetic logic, in the "logic of imagination" rather than on the plane of mere logical deduction.

Clemen has thus felt his way through the peculiar difficulties of the early poems to a solution that is distinctly modern. But while he fully recognizes its modernity, Clemen is not, one feels, imposing an anachronistically modern structure on Chaucer; rather, he is seeing aspects of the medieval poetry that the reading of modern poetry has surely helped him to see. This feeling is confirmed by observations of the same kind in the introduction to Derek Brewer's recent edition of the *Parliament* and in Robert O. Payne's book (p. 137) to be discussed below.

Chaucer's Early Poetry, then, maintains its preëminence as an introduction to the subject. Clear, judicious, responsible, it gives the impression that the modern Chaucer will have been built naturally and effortlessly on the basis of the traditional one, and it points to two main areas—close poetic analysis of the text and the relation of style to culture—as still fruitful ones for future investigation.

The two other recent books under consideration, however, belie any suggestion that the situation is either so clear or so peaceful, for they differ from Clemen's and from each other in fundamental ways. Robert Payne's *The Key of Remembrance* would suggest that Clemen does not go nearly far enough; Huppé and Robertson's *Fruyt and Chaf* suggests that both of the others go too far, in precisely the wrong direction.

Payne's book, subtitled "A Study of Chaucer's Poetics," is not limited to the early poems and pays important attention to the *Prologue to the Legend of Good Women* and to *Troilus and Criseyde.* It is a difficult book to read and a difficult one to describe, for the pressure toward new insights in it is so great as to have bent everything slightly out of conventional shape—and this goes for the style of the writing, which is by turns obscure, abstract, and diffuse, and for the sequence and structure of the argument, as well as for the interpretations of the poems. Nevertheless it is an interesting and challenging book, well worth the extra effort of reading.

Payne's main achievement is to have embraced in a comprehensive theory both medieval rhetorical tradition and Chaucer's "poetics." He is thus attacking anew the important set of problems raised (but hardly answered) by Manly in 1926 when he first called attention to the apparent naïveté of medieval rhetorical theory, to Chaucer's apparently close knowledge of the rhetoricians, and to the very sophisticated results Chaucer produces by conventional rhetorical means. The essential connection in Payne's theory comes in part from a rehabilitation of the rhetoricians themselves, a reinterpretation of their doctrine of amplification, which Payne sees not as a mindless love of ornament for its own sake, but as an implement of their neo-Augustinian orthodoxy. After Augustine, he argues, tradition—"a record of the way in which temporal events reflect eternal purposes"—replaced *inventio* in rhetoric, and stylistic elaboration, amplification, becomes the central process whereby the poet makes clear "the particular truth which he wishes to extract from his subject matter by elaborating and strengthening the portions upon which he wishes the emphasis to fall" (p. 47). Rhetorical elaboration reactivates traditional truth and connects accepted general laws with specific experience.

Chaucer's rhetoric, then, has a profound relationship to his view of tradition and of truth itself. His many references to the art of poetry are no longer of merely peripheral theoretical or biographical interest, but point to the center of a lifelong struggle to solve the problems posed by authority and experience, and, in other terms, of "the persuasive adjustment of language to truth" (p. 96). In this perspective such a text as the *Prologue to the Legend of Good Women,* with its extended discussion of the poet's mission, takes on an unprecedented importance in the ensemble of the poet's works. Although the author offers close rhetorical analyses at various points in his exposition, both "rhetoric" and "poetic" signify more often for him the very largest denominators of style and structure. The works are thus divided into three large rhetorical groups, representing successive major experiments in style, and the meanings of the particular structures of the separate works are in turn interpreted in the light of the central theory. I have no space to pause over the individual interpretations here—many of them are difficult and highly controversial—but I must commend the author's profound attachment to a grown-up theory of tradition and of poetry, highly refreshing in a field in which much sober and serious research is vitiated by the kindergarten theory accompanying it.

Payne's book actually contains quite a few fresh observations that are straightforwardly illuminating (as, e.g., on the diction of the *Prioress's Tale,* on the problem of characterization in *Troilus,* on Chaucer's audience as a created fiction), but the total impression of its modernity is that it is obscure, technical, and difficult. Its promise is large, but still cloudy. Payne shares with Clemen a sense, too, of the ultimate obscurity of Chaucer, particularly of the early poems, and of the difficulty of our ever penetrating Chaucer's defensive irony sufficiently to be certain of his attitudes. Not so, however, Bernard Huppé and D. W. Robertson! For them "Chaucer leaves no doubt of his own position." Here, right from the title's impliedly easy distinction between "fruyt" and "chaf," in the subtitle's easy assumption that the *Book of the Duchess* and the *Parliament* actually are "allegories"—here, one may feel, is perhaps too much certainty.

The fact that the authors' ideas have been so widely publicized in connection with their earlier works—Huppé's *Doctrine and Poetry,* Robertson's *Preface to Chaucer,* and their collaborative work on *Piers Plowman*—and the fact that the present volume, first written some ten years ago, represents no change in their general approach, will perhaps allow me to offer only the briefest (and admittedly incomplete) account. Let it suffice to say that the authors assume a homogeneous, untroubled, orthodox Christian medieval culture (well described and criticized by D. C. Fowler in these pages last March) and a universal Augustinian theory of literature for this culture. All of literature (including Chaucer) teaches charity and contemns vice, and where it does not appear to do so directly, it must be seen to be doing so covertly, in the form of an allegory or dark conceit. What might appear to the untutored as immoral or "secular" literature must be read, as the exegetes read the *Song of Songs,* as a congeries of symbols expressing the essential truths of Christianity. The meanings of the symbols, well known to such as Chaucer and his audience, may be recovered today from what still survives of the great array of Biblical commentaries, bestiaries, and other aids to exegesis produced for medieval theologians in the course of a thousand years. Read as such an allegory, then, the *Book of the Duchess* is a kind of sermon on the right curing of grief through Christ (the one "phisicien" of line 39), and the *Parliament of Fowls* a similarly covert homily against lust, against courtly love, and in implicit favor of Christian marriage.

In estimation of this argument, I would willingly align myself with those reviewers of Robertson's *Preface to Chaucer* who commended its learning while they deplored and rejected its main ideas. But *Fruyt and Chaf* has not that much learning to it, and it has not the capital importance of the authors' earlier works in making American medievalists memorably aware of the exegetical tradition and of Augustinian literary theory. That having already been done, it is hard to see why this thin and forced analysis needed to be revived and published. It is hardly likely to make converts, and to adepts it will be familiar stuff. Unless, of course, it is because the initial intellectual offering has now become a movement and a faith, and the spread of its doctrine a kind of piety. The footnotes to *Fruyt and Chaf* curiously enforce this impression, citing no contrary critical opinion, but giving notice of several forthcoming works of the authors' persuasion. It is, indeed, the suggestion that the book contains The Answer, that it eradicates doubt, that gives it even more of the air of a certain kind of modernity than does its rejection of the biographical-occasional approach or its concern with "symbolism." Neither psychoanalytic criticism nor mythic has taken quite the hold on medieval studies that they have on modern; perhaps exegetical criticism is their medieval equivalent. It has the same novelty, the same attractive capacity to marshal a great deal of data around a relatively few simple ideas, and the same promise of suddenly illuminating dark places and uncovering unapprehended mysteries. Like them, it is easily pushed beyond the legitimate bounds of its usefulness, especially by the young, the impatient, the seeker after certainty. "The problem, especially for the modern reader," say Huppé and Robertson, "is to find the one key" (p. 95). One may be permitted both to doubt and to regret. From this perspective, bands of loyal initiates preoccupied with sacred books and symbols promise not only the New Hermeneutics, but also the New Alexandrianism.

"WHAT AMOUNTETH
AL THIS WIT?"

Chaucer and Scholarship

"What amounteth al this wit?" The question, taken out of context and applied to Chaucerian scholarship and criticism, is not often asked among Chaucerian scholars and critics; it seems like one of those questions which, if you have to ask it, you probably would not understand the answer. We are, as a group, rightly assured of certain certainties—of the values of literature and history, and of the unchallengeable importance of Chaucer. In a particular sense, as medievalists, we know perhaps better than anyone else what the preservation of learning means. Our memory of the survival of scholarship and of its value for our culture goes back to barbarian times of a thousand years ago and more. In us, the preservation of learning is an unquestioned piety.

I bring this question—this rude question—into this company only because we seem currently to have entered times more barbarous than they were before, and because in the last decade we seem to be more and more surrounded by outsiders who in various ways are asking this question of us.

"What amounteth al this wit?" The question asked contemptuously by the hardened American anti-intellectual perhaps still does not merit a reply. But I must confess that I am moved to make an answer when the question is posed by persons who are young, and if not anti-intellectual then *un*intellectual, by persons who are not irremediably hostile, but who ask the question indirectly by refusing or ignoring what we have to teach. An answer is needed, too, for legislators and donors who have to weigh the claims of education and scholarship against those of other benefits to society.

The question takes on some added point when it is made in terms of social and cultural distinctions. Is it not true, we are being asked, that insofar as most of you work and teach in colleges and universities—is it not true that your whole discipline and approach to teaching was formed for the education of upper-class (mostly male) students? Until

48

recently your audiences have always come to you already conditioned with socially based assumptions about the value of literature and history. They have come with a knowledge of the Bible and of classical mythology, and perhaps some French learned in school or abroad. They have had the leisure, based on economic security, that afforded them the time to spend on your literature and your arcane philology. But now the last vestiges of nineteenth-century elitist education are being swept away (with the last vestiges of nineteenth-century culture). The demographic base in colleges has vastly widened to include persons (both washed and unwashed) of every sort of social and cultural origin. Many of them are completely oblivious of the Western tradition, if not hostile to it, and most of them are economically insecure. Why shouldn't the number of *your* students be dwindling, even though college enrollments in the last decades have doubled several times over? What have you medievalists got to offer to people from ghettos and barrios and immigrant ships and endless plastic suburbs—people getting ready to face life (if that is what it will be called) in the next millennium? What amounteth al this wit?

We are not hearing the question for the first time at this meeting, and our very presence here in fact constitutes an astonishingly emphatic and optimistic reply: "Chaucer scholarship is alive and well, you people, no matter what you may think of it." But we have been giving less optimistic replies, too, along with the majority of the humanities establishment, with the virtual dissolution of the liberal arts curriculum in many places in the 1960's, and with our slowness, so far, to re-think and re-locate the role of our studies in the life experience that faces our students. Some of us have already gone into psychological seclusion, as if the continued dwindling of our audience would leave us finally in a noble new monasticism.

As for me, I want that audience back; I want us to reach the new (and newly indifferent) student. Confidence in the value of what we have to offer calls for sympathetic advance, not retreat. But advance, I think, will be made more convincingly, our answer will be more credible, to the extent that it does not merely depend on the ancient a priori pieties about scholarship and learning. It must also relate our work as directly as possible to the central concerns of our culture.

Taking thus a position in favor of the re-validation of scholarship and criticism in these times, I am comforted by the idea that Chaucer would be in complete agreement. Of course, one does not get a sense from Chaucer that scholarship was in serious difficulties vis-à-vis the central

concerns of his own culture; and we know that from his day on the fortunes of scholarship—with minor ups and downs—were to be on the
rise for a long time. But Chaucer does give us a sense that scholarship
must tend to its filiations with the culture. Chaucer is, a bit ingenuously
for modern taste, an unabashed commender of relevance:

> For seint Paul seith that al that writen is,
> To oure doctrine it is ywrite, ywis;
> Taketh the fruyt, and lat the chaf be stille.
>
> (*NPT,* 3441–43)

The matter is a complicated one, and I am not prepared here to speculate on how much Chaucer's notions of scholarship and learning derive
primarily from the study of the Bible and thus perhaps make "relevance" an idea too vast to be useful. But we can see from Chaucer's
lifelong activity—if not as a professional scholar then as a part-time
gifted amateur and as an intermediary between professional scholars
and a less than intellectual but interested public—we can see in
Chaucer's notorious love of books coupled with his unfailing sense of
an audience a sympathetic model for our own activity:

> For out of olde feldes, as men seyth,
> Cometh al this newe corn from yer to yere,
> And out of olde bokes, in good feyth,
> Cometh al this newe science that men lere.
>
> (*PF,* 22–25)

The *bokes* in Chaucer are always old, but the knowledge provided by
their reading is made new. Elsewhere he says:

> . . . if that olde bokes weren aweye,
> Yloren were of remembrance the keye.
> Wel oughte us thanne on olde bokes leve,
> There as there is non other assay by preve.
>
> (*PLGW,* G25–28)

"There as there is non other assay by preve." The reservation is
utterly Chaucerian and, as with so much else in Chaucer, makes his attitudes all the more acceptable by showing that he does not come by
them uncritically. The world of books and authority is balanced off

against the world of experience in Chaucer's mind and life in just the way we would wish for ourselves.

No small sense of Chaucer's feeling for the nonscholarly audience for learning comes from his mostly comic recognition of anti-intellectualism or the cult of practical wisdom:

> Now is a nat that of God a ful fair grace
> That swich a lewed mannes wit shal pace
> The wisdom of an heep of lerned men?
>
> (*GP*, 573–75)

> "Straw for thy Senek, and for thy proverbes!
> I counte nat a panyer ful of herbes
> Of scole-termes."
>
> (*MerT*, 1567–69]

> "So ferde another clerk with astromye;
> He walked in the feeldes, for to prye
> Upon the sterres, what ther sholde bifalle,
> Til he was in a marle-pit yfalle;
> He saugh nat that."
>
> (*MilT*, 3457–61)

> "Myn hous is streit, but ye han lerned art;
> Ye konne by argumentes make a place
> A myle brood of twenty foot of space.
> Lat se now if this place may suffise,
> Or make it rowm with speche, as is youre gise."
>
> (*RvT*, 4122–26)

At points one is uncertain where Chaucer's amusement with redneck hostility to learning shades off into a shared satire of the excesses and limitations of scholarship itself. Chaucer is sensitive to the layman's response to the complexity of scholarly argument, sensitive and sympathetic too. Dorigen, contemplating the black rocks that threaten her husband's life, makes a moving appeal that has no use for argument:

> I woot wel clerkes wol seyn as hem leste,
> By argumentz, that al is for the beste,
> Though I ne kan the causes nat yknowe.

51

But thilke God that made wynd to blowe
As kepe my lord! this *my* conclusion.
To clerkes lete I al disputison.

(*FranT,* 885–90)

The *clerkes* do not necessarily come out on top in sympathy here. Else-where Chaucer can have fun with clerkly complexity, and make fun of it too. For this his favorite topic is free will and predestination:

Witnesse on hym that any parfit clerk is,
That in scole is greet altercacioun
In this mateere, and greet disputisoun,
And hath been of an hundred thousand men.
But I ne kan nat bulte it to the bren
As kan the hooly doctour Augustyn,
Or Boece, or the Bisshop Bradwardyn . . .

(*NPT,* 3236–42)

and the Nun's Priest concludes, after a brief but skillful summary of the issues:

I wol nat han to do of swich mateere;
My tale is of a cok, as ye may heere . . .

(*NPT,* 3251–52)

Perhaps the high point of this fun comes with the seventeen stanzas of speculation that Chaucer gives to Troilus, punctuated with the despair-ing cry:

"O, welaway! so sleighe arn clerkes olde,
That I not whos opynyoun I may holde."

(*TC* IV, 972–73)

Chaucer's good sense and balance concerning scholarship are validated, finally, by the evidence that he, too, has often enough become intoxi-cated with the thing itself. The amassing of notes, the piling up of instances, the gaudy display of erudition—Chaucer knew those sweet seductions. According to the *Prologue to The Legend of Good Women,* he has a collection of "sixty bokes olde and newe" about women. We can imagine a comparable collection (or at least a good set of notes) about dreams and about alchemy, and we know how much pedantic sport he had—sanctioned by the rhetoric of amplification—with these and other subjects. In his later years, though by no means cured of amplification, he came to see the potential pompousness in it; Chaunte-cleer shows us that—as Alice of Bath shows us the helpless desperation of an audience whom the next in a seemingly endless list of exempla might drive to violence; and Nicholas shows us the arrogance of intellectual pride itself.

As a user and transmitter of learning, then, Chaucer is on both sides of the transaction. In balance, he respects learning; but he does not accept it uncritically. He responds *most* sympathetically to learning when it promises a connection with practical virtue. His poor Parson, we remember, is "also a lerned man, a clerk," whose teaching is validated by practice: "first he wroghte, and afterward he taughte." It is similarly a practical or instrumental aspect of learning that is exemplified in his own best efforts as pedagogy. In the *Astrolabe* and the second Book of *The House of Fame,* in the clarity of the exposition, and in the tender regard for the wits of his audience, we get perhaps our best glimpse of the kind of scholar or teacher Chaucer would have been had he chosen that profession at all:

> "lo, so I can
> Lewedly to a lewed man
> Speke, and shewe hym swyche skiles
> That he may shake hem be the biles,
> So palpable they shulden be."

> (*HF,* 865–69)

Chaucer, lover of books but also practical man of affairs, vis-à-vis learning was a popularizer, and would have been proud to have been recognized as such. Indeed, some such idea may well have been on the mind of Eustache Deschamps when he called Chaucer a *grant translateur.*

After offering this brief reminder of some of Chaucer's opinions and practice, I am, however, not going to invoke him as a guide to what any one of us ought to be doing in Chaucer scholarship or criticism. Our subject is rich and difficult, and one could not define the degree of even the most arcane learning or of the most complex abstraction that might not still afford us profit, or at least scholarly pleasure. While it does look as if it would be highly un-Chaucerian to be too solemn or too pious about Chaucer scholarship, none of us is under the obligation, after all, to be Chaucerian. Chaucer would have been the first to insist, rather, on our being ourselves, and doing well what our talents and temperaments fit us for:

"What amounteth al this wit?
What shul we speke alday of hooly writ?
The devel made a reve for to preche,
Or of a soutere a shipman or a leche."

(Prologue of *RvT,* 3901–04)

Chaucer admires his Clerk perhaps as much for his being himself, pursuing his own bent, as for his clerkship. For another man "upon a book in cloystre alwey to poure" would drive him crazy. Chaucer has substantial sympathy for both; nor am I about to recommend the conversion of the reeves among us into preachers, much less the preachers into reeves.

Yet, the health of the profession in these and coming times will, I think, be better served by some moves in scholarship than in others. In this sense, if we cannot or should not try to remake ourselves or each other, we can at least be aware of what new talents the profession most needs, what recruits it might most welcome, what directions might be for us corporately most rewarding.

In this sense the Chaucerian advice might well be to look sympathetically toward our new audience—massively lewed as it may be—and to try to re-locate and re-define the connections between our activity and the culture in which we find ourselves.

The pedagogical aspect of moving in this direction is quite simply to make a generous outreach to students and to try to formulate—even at the expense of re-thinking them for ourselves—understandable answers to their questions about the value of humanistic scholarship.

On the professional side, the logic of the same argument would suggest that as researchers and critics, we would be best served if for a time we looked outward rather than inward—that we gave less emphasis to source studies and textual studies and narrow explication, and more emphasis to cultural history and the reading of medieval culture itself. We will, of course, always need and always profit from new textual discoveries, and explication will never go out of style. But we are in any case manifestly at the end of a phase in textual studies—conspicuously to be marked by the *Chaucer Library* and the *Variorum;* and we need some relief from the flood of explication that in its increasing inwardness and high focus seems to be telling us more and more about the lenses of the critics and less and less about Chaucer and his time.

By the time you hear this, our Program's first topic, *Contemporary Literary Theory and Chaucer,* will have been presented, and the matter may be already settled. I hope that we have already decided that for Chaucer studies it will be better that our messages be lucid and communicable rather than opaque and private; that the literary text be kept more important than the critic; that the text have a unique importance, but that part of its importance be its importance as cultural history. Looking outward—from Chaucer to his culture and to its place in cultural history—will take some of the emphasis away from ourselves and bring us into fresh contact with other fields, especially with sociology, historiography, and ethnography, themselves becoming more and more implicated in the procedures of literary discourse and analysis. The direction is an important and promising one suggested by modern critical theory itself. Viewing literature not so much as a separable part of culture but as one of its central traits; viewing literature not merely as illustrating history or as being illustrated by it, but as constituting the deepest history itself—this would be an exciting and productive direction to go. A new study of the place of Chaucer in cultural history might even turn up a new appreciation of the place of Chaucer studies in cultural history as well.

LOCUS OF ACTION IN
MEDIEVAL NARRATIVE

For investigation of locus in medieval narrative, we are given a provocative start by the art historians, who, working with spatial media, may be expected to have devoted more study to spatial notions than have the literary critics. Art historians find a number of successive spatial notions in the Middle Ages. Early medieval painting, they assert, is flat—planimetric. It lends itself easily to internal division representing scenes in different places, scenes so unambiguously framed off from one another that there is no suggestion of their existence in a single, continuous space. The spatial relations of the various scenes—being above or below, to the right or to the left—have a symbolic significance readily clear to the beholder. Like the relationships among the scenes or bands, the settings themselves in an early medieval painting, the indications of place, are emblematic rather than fully descriptive.

Of this handling of space and locus, strongly characteristic of medieval art, we can trace elements in the Italian Renaissance as late as Fra Angelico and Botticelli. Yet there exists a countertendency in medieval painting and sculpture—steadily increasing with time—to deepen, localize, and integrate space. This tendency finally emerges as the typically Renaissance concept, expressed in the invention of linear perspective, of a single, deep, three-dimensional space, containing a naturalistic setting which fills the space with objects of local and secular human interest.

One can isolate a period of extraordinary complexity in the interplay of these two concepts of space in medieval art. Because naturalism of detail came sooner than integration and depth of composition, in Gothic art the detailing and setting of a painting, the modelling of a sculpture, may have attained roundness and realism, while the framing and placing of the figure, its "spatial environment," was possibly still planimetric or schematic. In this case there prevails a typically "Gothic" tension between one system and the other.

These observations by the art historians help to orient our investigation of literary locus. Indeed, where the spirit of *Kulturgeschichte* has moved them sufficiently to look into literature, art historians have done some of our work for us. But my aim here is less to pursue the analogy with art than to try to sketch roughly some categories of literary space and to suggest a few avenues of approach.

Let me start with the assumption that while the establishment of a locus of action and its subsequent tending throughout a story may, in a way, be deemed decorative and separable from the story—"setting," one feels, is less important than action in narrative—, there is a degree to which locus is indispensable, inseparable from narrative. Within what Whorf has rather inelegantly but usefully called the "standard average European language-culture complex," at least, narrative requires an irreducible minimum of spatial sense. The very notion of events successive in time seems to generate a concomitant sense of locus. Indeed, to quote Whorf, "we can hardly refer to the simplest non-spatial situation without constant resort to physical metaphor." The sense of place, of the here, the elsewhere, the there, is so deeply embedded in our own patterning of experience that we cannot help imposing it on narrative.

For our present purposes let us suppress the notion of locus as mere decoration and with it the idea that locating action spatially serves only to endow the action with verisimilitude, to render probable the impossible by giving it some familiar aspects. Locus as ornament is less fundamental than locus as pattern. Rather than merely disguising the narrative with an air of probability, the orientation of the action in space (and thus in place) can be a mode of organizing the narrative and giving it more than probability; it can give it meaning.

In purely mimetic narrative, where locus and setting are crowded with suggestions of decoration and verisimilitude, this structural or patterning effect of locus is relatively difficult to perceive and to describe. For this reason I shall turn at once to allegorical narrative. In allegory we are free from ordinary verisimilitude and see space and locus in their deepest function. This perspective will fit our purpose well enough: mimetic and allegorical narrative are so intermingled in medieval literature that what we learn about one will illuminate the other.

Medieval allegory characteristically deals with moral rather than with physical space. Irrespective of whether the deeper action is supposedly taking place in the cosmos or in the human heart, the action of the surface allegory suggests relations of virtues and vices, relations that have almost nothing inherently spatial about them. Nevertheless, to

57

the extent that allegory is also a narrative rather than a tableau, it generates its own locus and setting.

Prudentius' *Psychomachia* shows us this locus in an early and simple form. As a setting for its successive armed conflicts between personified virtues and vices we have a field of battle materialized. It almost lacks local characteristics except for a pit dug by Deceit to trap unwary foes. (Unfortunately, during the battle Pride falls into it instead.) At the edge of the field one sees a palisaded camp into which the victorious virtues retire, only to be attacked from within by Discord or Heresy. After subduing Heresy the virtues erect a watch-tower against enemies and thereafter a sacred temple in which Wisdom sits enthroned.

Here all the elements of locus are used as direct and primary emblems of moral relationships, and operate in a space that has all the simplicity of the armed conflict it contains. This space, suspended somewhere outside the naturalistic world, is completely discontinuous with it. Though the poem renders the individual armed conflicts with a great deal of color and variety, the space in which they occur suggests values static, formal, ideologically fixed, suggests indeed that the victories of virtues over vices are permanent. The poem could be (and indeed many times was) represented pictorially. The one glimpse it affords of "Christ in the height rejoicing in his followers' victory and opening for his servants his Father's home in the deep of heaven"—the only other locus here mentioned—sounds like the description of a Romanesque tympanum beneath which, in a separate band, the victories of the virtues over the vices could be severally displayed. The use of locus in this fourth-century text is analogous to the use of space in early medieval pictorial art—some of which it actually influenced.

We can trace a set of changes in literary space, matching the set of those in pictorial space, down to the Renaissance. If Renaissance pictorial space is deep, natural, and rationally controlled by linear perspective, Renaissance literary space is natural and dramatic; the feeling behind it at its most extreme is expressed by the celebrated notion of unity of place. But we are still far from this point in the High Middle Ages, which show in allegory first a tendency simply to elaborate the kind of space and setting familiar from Prudentius.

This elaboration, traceable to Martianus Capella, reaches a kind of climax (or perhaps anticlimax) in Alain de Lille's *Anti-Claudian.* To the extent that Alain is dealing with cosmology he is using some concepts of locus and space already so deeply ingrained in medieval belief as to be almost equivalent to scientific report. (Who will say in what proportion the spheres, the fixed stars, and heaven above are for the High Middle Ages symbolic, and in what proportion real?) The patterned cosmos through which Prudence here ascends to the throne of God nevertheless superbly exemplifies the way in which the allegorist comes to use spatial references to organize and clarify such conceptual and spiritual relationships as are his proper subject. By the device of a journey through successively higher spheres with successive guides, Alain creates a kind of spatial epistemology: Reason and the car of the seven liberal arts raise the journeyer into astronomic realms transcending the senses: but past the celestial sphere Reason cannot guide. Theology carries on from there, and the guiding presence of Faith is necessary finally to reach "the supreme Palace of the eternal king." In describing the passage through the celestial spheres, Alain now and again uses the imagery of terrestrial journeying to express the hazards and difficulties of Prudence's flight. He mentions her circuitous path, the confused places (*loca dissona*), the unknown passes (*calles ignotos*), and so forth, but these images remain disconnected; their use is local and incidental. The overall character of the poem's cosmography (even granting the realism of Alain's astronomy), with its detailed descriptions of the various spheres and its heavenly garden and House of Fortune, is schematic. Spatial reference and spatial location have been elaborated to help organize conceptual relationships, but the space itself is not yet felt to be natural or even navigable, despite the continuous navigation. The quality of place and setting conforms beautifully to the Platonic idea that Alain himself expresses: God

> forms the outward appearance of things and the shadow of the sensible world from the pattern of the mental world, portraying the mental world outwardly in the image of earthly form. [v.288– 290]

The *Divine Comedy* displays Alain's scheme pushed to an extreme degree of elaboration; but superimposed on this scheme (or, rather, suffused throughout it) is a second spatial system or a second mode of rendering the sense of locus which bears out that well-established judgment that Dante's art stands in typically "Gothic" poise between two different systems of seeing, feeling, and being. Note, on the one hand, the rationalized pattern, with its numerical hierarchic orderings— reflecting by their locations immutable moral relationships; on the other, the continuously personal and humane response of the pilgrim who traverses this moral landscape, suffusing, I repeat, the abstract pattern with drama and immediacy.

Dante's devices for securing this second effect are many. The first-person viewpoint is accurate and consistent, so that the locus of action is described in personal perspective, from the beholder's vantage point. Dante, when he wills, can create a marvelous sense of height and depth, of falling and climbing. One discovers an impressively consistent tending of direction and location and time. Despite the omission of certain steps in the journey, there is continuity and connection between the places, from the almost terrestrial "dark wood" up to that single spaceless point "where every *ubi* and every *quando* converges." And there is a continuous play of minor touches that in their verisimilitude confirm the sense of human perspective: Dante's fear of a height or a ring of flame; his casting of a shadow; his need to be carried or led; the talk between him and Virgil, who chat and walk as men do; the fact, noticed by Statius, that a living person (unlike the souls of the dead) moves what he touches. Paradoxically, one of the most human responses to place or setting is that Dante has no sense of motion as he flies "faster than lightning" with Beatrice into the heavens. Beyond terrestrial space, earth-bound man cannot perceive motion. Only by watching Beatrice's beauty increase can he tell that he is ascending, and only by looking back can he tell how far he has come.

These two systems of creating a sense of locus are of course parts of two larger systems in the poem and in the culture; I need not belabor their meaning here. Let me only say that if the one inherited from Alain is the outward shadow of the perfect idea in the mind of God, the other, coming from the human breast, takes shape much as do the starving souls of the gluttonous in Purgatory. "How can one grow thin where there is no need of nourishment?" asks Dante. The answer: "The shadow takes shape according as the desires and the other emotions point it forth" [xxv.106]. The one system uses a patterned, a priori setting to express immutable moral relationships; the other, an irregular, humane, naturalized setting to represent psychological and emotional experience. Either setting is consistent, either is firmly wedded to the other; together they contribute greatly to the poem's structural strength and to its coherence of meaning. If (as Sypher and others maintain) there is Gothic tension here, there is also supreme poise and clarity.

The linear extension of Dante's narrative in space and time illustrates another quality of high and late Gothic art: its predilection for processional form. This form is omnipresent, from the Bayeux tapestry to the procession of the mystery plays. In twelfth-century literature we find it well-established in the episodic quests of Arthurian romance and in the moral allegory conceived as a journey or pilgrimage. The form was perpetuated well into the Renaissance. Moral allegory preserves it in the thirteenth century in Raoul de Houdenc's and Rutebeuf's dream-visions, then in Dante and Guillaume de Deguileville—a tradition extending all the way to *Pilgrim's Progress.*

The pilgrimage form was a great invention for allegoric narrative. It was much more sensitive a vehicle than the pitched battle, as C. S. Lewis says, for representing the movement of the inner life. Its aptness to express the stages of the Christian soul's progress toward salvation (or the reverse) received authority from Christian doctrine, on the one hand, and from the actualities of medieval pilgrimage, on the other. One could read it with effect on every level, from the literal to the anagogical. It was in fact a perfect meeting-place for those two spatial systems that converge in Gothic literature. The individual scenes or stopovers on the pilgrimage allow a certain realism, a certain local or personal or psychological interest. Meanwhile the succession of scenes, the linear sequence, the direction of the journey, can be made to suggest immutable moral relationships, immutable goals to be reached in immutable ways. For its meaning, Dante's ascent of the Mount of Purgatory—the pilgrim's progress in general—depends on the fixed sequence of events in time and space.

The pilgrimage shape powerfully illustrates the continuing importance, in the Middle Ages, of locus of action as structure or pattern. Even in non-allegorical medieval literature (which constantly seems to aspire to the condition of allegory) the line, or road, or series of settings functions to keep the separate scenes or events in order and scale. We can see this as clearly in the Canterbury Road, in the sequence of the *Canterbury Tales,* in the setting of the *Decameron* on a journey through successive pleasances and palaces, as in the *Divine Comedy.*

By the time of Langland's *Piers Plowman* (late fourteenth century), then, medieval narrative shows a strong geometry (or geography) of locus of action that is used structurally. I mention *Piers Plowman* because I should like to conclude my remarks by examining the locus of action in that poem. Though I shall confine my attention to the A-text (to avoid the authorship problem), my remarks will in fact apply equally well to Text B.

Langland's space seems surrealistic, unlike the space of any predecessor. For while he knows and in part uses flat, geometric, schematic,

Romanesque space; knows and uses in particular scenes naturalistic space; knows the intermittently uses the linear, pilgrimage form, none of these becomes a controlling locus of his narrative. The locus of the characters and actions and their spatial environments are continually shifting. This has a profound relevance to the peculiar character of the poem, and I am tempted to see in it a symptom, too, of Langland's period.

His opening suggests a single schematic locus, like that of Prudentius: a fair field full of folk, with a tower on a hill above and a dungeon in a dale below. In the description of the activity in the field we notice at once Langland's Gothic doubleness, his capacity to inject into his schematic plan figures, scenes, and tiny settings of realistic depth and vigor. The technique here is even swifter and more suggestive than Dante's. In the Prologue of the A-text no single scene is allowed extensive development; each gives way to the next with a curious inconsequence of spatial relations. There is a kind of artistic logic here in that no coherence but only a heaping and piling of tiny scenes is used to picture man's activities in this wilderness earth. But as this scheme dissolves, as one setting reels and melts into the next, as characters (sometimes whole troops of them) appear and disappear without notice and without trace, we become aware that something more than literary tactics is involved. Dante, at any turn of the road, can suddenly expose us to a shift of perspective, a change of scale, without this surrealistic feeling. In Canto iv of the Inferno, in the midst of darkness, we reach all of a sudden a seven-walled castle, and within it a green field in a place "open, luminous, and high," where the heroes of antiquity are visible. But then we turn back with the narrator and guide to "the part where there is nothing that shines"—that is, back to the spatial and locational frame that organizes the whole. In *Piers Plowman* there is no going back. The fair field, the vale, and the mountain are transformed without notice into a great encampment—with ten thousand tents for all the onlookers at the marriage of Meed. We suddenly witness the dickering over the marriage articles. Thence we go— by what road I know not—to Westminster, before the King.

In the next vision, the extraordinary shift of locus brought by the realistic tavern scene is righted by the continuity of the confessions of the deadly sins. But then in a completely unspecified locus, "a thousand men thronged together and prayed for grace to seek truth." They wander aimlessly as beasts over valleys and hills. After a long journey they meet a pilgrim who says he has never heard of St. Truth. At that instant:

"Peter!" says a plowman. "I know him"—and from nowhere Piers Plowman materializes into the poem. He describes to them the road, by way of meekness and conscience and the ten commandments, to where truth resides in the human heart. The next spatial reference finds them all on a rather different pilgrimage: helping Piers plow his half-acre. . . . And so the poem goes, existing in no one system of space and locations, invoking successive spatial concepts for limited and temporary effects, without tending to the relations between them. The peculiarity of space in *Piers Plowman* cannot alone account for the poem's character. But it works powerfully in concert with such other traits as the periodic establishment and collapse of the dream frame, the alternation of allegory and literalism, and violent changes of tone and temper, the peculiar equivalence of concrete and abstract terms, and the indistinctness of the genre. Along with these, the shifting locus of action produces an effect that, for lack of a better term, I have called "surrealistic."

Such a formal trait in poetry must have a profound consequence for meaning. It almost explains why this, among medieval English poems, is the greatest paradox. His sense of space almost betrays the poet. For while at every turn the discrete, isolable episodes—the overt statements—proclaim conservative Christian doctrine, the surrealistic spatial context creates a sense of instability. Thus it is, perhaps, that the preachers of 1381 could so easily use Langland's social orthodoxy as food for revolt, and later reformers make of him a violent Protestant. The poem's spatially isolated scenes invite being wrenched from so shifty a context. That sense of earnestness, of extraordinary urgency in the poem derives partly from the insecurity of its architecture. Unlike Dante's, Langland's fulminations seem not to be issued from under the arching security of a stable, permanent structure. The episodes, fragmentary in relation to one another, suggest shorings, passionately and hastily assembled—from heaven or earth—against some impending ruin.

In this, perhaps, the poem also reflects its time. Langland's knowledge of the great medieval formal schemes and his comparative failure with them—his failure to organize and to "see" by means of them—argues, in the context of his other traits, more than a lack of narrative skill. It means perhaps that for a man of his extreme sensitivity those schemes had begun to lose their clarity, hence their meaning and efficacy. The levels of goodness, "Do-Well, Do-Bet, and Do-Best the third," mentioned in the A-text as if they were clearly defined levels, might have been used to impose on the poem a Romanesque or Dantean clarity; but they were not. And the same is true of the consecutive, linear processional form. For Langland, the pilgrimage road to the New Jerusalem has too many detours to be called a road at all. His use of place and location—along with the other traits I have mentioned—suggests that for him, despite his doctrinal orthodoxy, the structure of the moral world—to which most of his predecessors could give coherent spatial expression—had become a thing newly problematic.

To pursue, finally, the analogy with space in pictorial art mentioned above, I know of no persuasive parallel to Langland's space—unless it be in certain Tuscan paintings of the 1360's and '70's, which, produced in an atmosphere of guilt and fear after the Black Death, have been described by the art historian Millard Meiss in much the same terms as we can use to describe *Piers Plowman:* with paradoxical space, a rejection of perspective, and a tension between the natural and the unnatural, the physical and the abstract. The systems which Dante had held in perfect poise and coördination have here lost their force, fallen into confusion. Whether or not the analogy with pictorial art holds good here, Langland's handling of the locus of action nevertheless provocatively suggests the late-Gothic style, or rather, the dissolution of Gothic style generally, but without the promise of reintegration to come.

POETRY AND CRISIS IN THE
AGE OF CHAUCER

To William K. Wimsatt, Jr.

FOREWORD

These four essays are in substance the Ward-Phillips lectures given under the title "Poetry and Cultural Crisis in the Age of Chaucer" in November, 1969, at the University of Notre Dame. I am grateful to the genial and learned company which sponsored the lectures, and particularly to Professor and Mrs. James E. Robinson, for their unforgettable hospitality.

The lectures are presented here with additional illustrations, with documentation (some of it more recent than that available in 1969), and with corrections and qualifications suggested by members of the original audience and by John Halverson and Larry Benson, who kindly read the lectures in manuscript. Much of the time for study and writing was provided by a grant from the National Endowment for the Humanities.

RELEVANCE, POETIC STYLE, AND CULTURAL CRISIS: AN INTRODUCTION

It is very much in the spirit of Professors Ward and Phillips, both of whom were devoted teachers of literature, that I address myself to the present topic. Proposing it, I am somewhat uneasily bringing into convergence a number of concerns that arise directly out of the problem of being a teacher of English literature in these particular times. It is perhaps a sign of the times that I can use the phrase *"problem* of being a teacher" for one of the most harmless and pleasurable occupations on earth. No teacher worth the name is without his moments of doubt and self-scrutiny. Yet recently—and particularly in the last five years—the teaching of humanities has become an authentic public "problem" recognized in international symposia and in massive studies. The central problem of the humanities is that of relevance. Are the humanities still relevant?[1] The question is always provoking, and is sometimes the occasion for either abject confessions of guilt and unworthiness; or for righteous, indignant, and closed assertion of the eternity of humanistic values. My own response falls somewhere in between. While I have not the slightest doubt of the value of what we are doing and teaching (in my case, medieval studies), I can imagine and forgive such doubts on the part of others. Students have a right (today a compulsive need) to ask what our relevance is; and in searching for clear answers, I feel, we may even find some new or at least fresh values in our enterprise for ourselves.

When confronted by the question of relevance, teachers of literature have at least three main areas to defend—the moral, the aesthetic, and the historical. The moral argument is perhaps the most ready at hand, but it is not satisfactory by itself. To argue that literature "embodies perennial truths" seems self-evidently true only in regard to a handful of texts. In defending the study of any texts apart from those currently considered direct repositories of practical wisdom or of insights into the "permanent" in human nature, if we do not invoke beauty, we are usually forced toward a relativist position, that is, toward the argument from history, and we make our appeal for appreciation or toleration of the "truth" as seen by someone else at some other time and place. This historical argument is actually more palatable than the moral argument to the many students who have reason to doubt the existence of any absolute truth at all.

The case for the absolute beauty of literature would seem to be stronger. It has been said that the new student hates beauty and history with an equal passion, but I do not believe it. Beauty, like health, is not hard to justify to the young; or at least there is not as much quarreling with a line of Spenser or Milton, or a speech of Marlowe or Shakespeare, that makes your knees weak and your eyes moist. Nor is there, on a more philosophical level, much difficulty in showing the permanent "relevance" of works of great formal achievement. For even if relevance seems timebound, and forever asking "what good are these things to me here and now, in confronting these issues?"—there is a readily available sense in which the beautiful, being timeless, is always relevant.

But to argue that the stuff we deal with is relevant because it is beautiful also has something incomplete if not wrong with it. In the first place, we know that a good deal of the appreciation of beauty in art depends directly on a historical sense, on knowing what the words really mean, what conventions are being invoked, and what audience is being addressed. Again, much of what we deal with is not that beautiful—interesting though it still may be. Furthermore, if the beautiful is timeless, why turn to the beauty of a medieval poem (with all the incidental pains the appreciation will cost you) in preference to that of a modern one? Finally, are we not, in choosing the aesthetic gambit, really dodging the question? The beautiful, virtually to be defined by its disinterestedness and its transcendence of issues, hardly answers a question born of passionate concern with issues.

Relevance is most persuasively to be shown, I think, in a mutually interdependent set of values—at once moral, aesthetic, and historical. For the historical sense sharpens our appreciation of the moral and aesthetic import of literature, while the value-laden characteristics of literature give it peculiar authority as historical data. But I should like to emphasize the historical argument even further. It is as some kind of history that much literature is interesting when it is not obviously beautiful; and it is as a peculiar kind of history that a beautiful poem is read just because it is a *medieval* poem. It is as history that we value medieval culture, seeing in it partly ourselves, partly what we no longer are, partly what we might be. As humanists we cannot escape being historians. Our "utopian end," as Roy Harvey Pearce has put it, "is as full and complicated a sense of the past and present as we can contain in our critical imaginations."[2]

If that is true, then part of the problem of being (and of training) teachers of literature these days is that for the most part we are poor historians. This is because for the last generation our own training has heavily emphasized the aesthetic rather than the historical, and because as historians we have been content with the notion of having our own thing: *literary* history.

Our problem is that the age of literary analysis—the New Criticism—seems to have reached a dead end. Conceived in reaction to a simplistic, "positivistic" kind of history, it turned our attention to the text in and for itself and taught us to read poetry with the minute intensity that is now part of our standard equipment. The New Criticism taught us that the archaeological parts of scholarship—editing texts, tracing sources—were ancillary to the great act of reading and elucidating the text in and for itself; that the text's meaning was somehow hedged against historical relativism; that the literary work enjoyed a special *is*ness, a special ontological status.[3] The new-critical position, despite all it has taught us, can no longer be defended as an end in itself; it has led us quite naturally into a concern with literary texts so narrow as to merit the label "aestheticism." Turning us away from a bad kind of history, it has tended to turn us away from history itself.[4] It has not turned us away, perhaps, from *literary* history, partly because literary history is necessary to full textual study and partly because our earlier Germanic and positivistic tradition of literary-historical research still survives. Both of these motives are strengthened by a certain territorial concern that was greatly promoted by the New Criticism. To purge literary studies of the irrelevant, the unliterary, was to fence them in against biography, psychology, sociology, philosophy. This territorialism fit beautifully into the American university departmental organization and into a certain aping of the hardness and specialism of more scientific disciplines on the campus. Now it is widely manifested even among secondary-school teachers as an anxiety—in the face of French, algebra, and biology—about having one's own subject matter.

We study and teach "literary history," then. The phrase itself suggests what a poor, incomplete thing we have if we have no greater end in view. It is as if we were concerned, when we are at all concerned with man in time, with the history of legs, arms, or livers. No need to belabor the point. Our obligation is to history itself; our problem is: How can we make literary research and literary understanding contribute to the full, rich, complicated whole that is the history of our culture?

We would be, in fact, in an excellent position to contribute to cultural history if we knew more history and if we were more expert in finding the terms and categories in which literature and history connect. For no one doubts these days that history consists as much (if not more) in currents of feeling, modes of seeing, transformations of values, revolutions of sensibility—as in political, military, and economic events. And there are no better data than poems for the history of sensibility. But how do they connect?

As the New Criticism has slowly changed from a doctrinal position to an incidental technique, researchers and critics have struck out toward new positions—new approaches, new emphases—but only a few of them hold out promise for a new leverage on history. The psychoanalytical, the structuralist, the mythical and the exegetical approaches, despite their intrinsic interest, seem to be alike in going away from history rather than toward it.[5] On the other hand the proponents of American Studies, as a group, seem closer to cultural history than most of us, perhaps because their material is presented to them in such a rich, mixed, and immediate form. Some of them—particularly Roy Harvey Pearce, R. W. B. Lewis, John William Ward, Henry Nash Smith, and Leo Marx—seem already to embody the thing we are looking for, a man expertly at home with literature who thinks and behaves like a cultural historian. But although Marx, Smith, Pearce and others have written provocatively about this subject, the Americanists have not developed a describable approach, and have not formed a school the rest of us could join.[6]

Unlike the Americanists, we medievalists suffer from a chronic lack of information. Ideally we should have to find ways of reading history from shards and fragments, from mutilated or isolated instances. For this purpose, one of the promising approaches is that of stylistics. By stylistics I do not mean the interesting commotion that has been going on recently in close proximity to the study of structural linguistics. We are justified in hoping that modern linguistics will sooner or later contribute powerfully to literary studies. If nothing else, a more accurate and refined grammar and syntax should enable us to be more precise than ever in the discrimination and description of verbal events in literature. But at the present writing the new grammatical tools do not seem quite ready, and a linguistics of action or of performance is only barely emergent. What I mean by stylistics is simply the study of literature that pays large attention to the contribution of style (and of structure, as in the New Criticism) to meaning.[7]

Style has, of course, long been recognized as one of the key terms in which both literature and history can be understood. It is a primary tool of archaeology and of art history. We can speak of the style of a work or of a writer, and the style of a period or culture. Terms such as "Renaissance" and "Gothic" have been felt to make sense describing a single poem or a whole culture.[8] There are general but no less powerful and interesting ways in which stylistic and structural aspects of poems like *Paradise Lost* and the *Divine Comedy* confirm, fill out, and even epitomize our notion of the culture in which they were produced.

This approach owes something to the European movement called *Geistesgeschichte,* deriving from Hegel and Dilthey and reaching its peak in the Germany of the 1920s and '30s. *Geistesgeschichte* sought to explain artistic phenomena, including style, according to the "spirit of the age," and in the work of such art historians as Heinrich Wölfflin, Wilhelm Worringer, and Max Dvořák it produced some of our most powerful notions of period style and of the historical alternations of style. It was not so successful in literary studies, and it has latterly, in general, been discredited for its impressionism and its unrealistic assumption that ages or cultures are homogeneous wholes wherein all the artistic symptoms can be expected to fall into the same configuration. *Geistesgeschichte* was rather easily dismissed, if considered at all, by the New Criticism.[9]

Modern literary stylistics, by contrast, incorporates the New Criticism; it can utilize all we know of literary analysis. If the New Criticism (or beyond the Atlantic the tradition of *explication des textes*) had been developed in the service of cultural history, this is surely one of the ways it would have had to be used. In paying attention to poetic style on a new-critical level of intensity, literary stylistics seems to offer an answer to the charge of vagueness that eventually discredited its predecessor. For stylistic analysis can describe a text, from its syntax and imagery through its narrative form and total structure (not to speak of many other possible stylistic categories), with a new precision and concreteness. Furthermore, the stylistics of an Auerbach or a Spitzer, starting from the text rather than from the culture, or at least paying profound initial attention to the claims of the text in itself, is not bound, as *Geistesgeschichte* tended to be, to find in the work of art merely confirmation of dominant tendencies in the culture. Stylistics is attuned as well to the variant and dissident as to the conventional note. Its emphasis on the nondiscursive elements of meaning, its attempt to penetrate through the area of what the words say to what the style says, indeed, sometimes leads us to intimations of meaning unbeknownst to or represented by the artists themselves. I am not sure that I accept fully Auerbach's reading of Dante's *Commedia,* but even the suggestions leading from his analysis of the meaning of the style of the Farinata-Cavalcante passage open exciting prospects for literature as cultural history:

In our passage two of the damned are introduced in the elevated style. Their earthly character is preserved in full force in their places in the beyond. Farinata is as great and proud as ever, and Cavalcante loves the light of the world and his son Guido not less, but in his despair still more passionately, than he did on earth. So God had willed; and so these things stand in the figural realism of Christian tradition. Yet never before has this realism been carried so far; never before—scarcely even in antiquity—has so much art and so much expressive power been employed to produce an almost painfully immediate impression of the earthly reality of human beings. It was precisely the Christian idea of the indestructibility of the entire human individual which made this possible for Dante. And it was precisely by producing this effect with such power and so much realism that he opened the way for that aspiration toward autonomy which possesses all earthly existence. In the very heart of the other world, he created a world of earthly beings and passions so powerful that it breaks bounds and proclaims its independence. . . . When we hear Cavalcante's outburst: *non fiere li occhi suoi il dolce lome*? or read the beautiful, gentle, and enchantingly feminine line which Pia de' Tolomei utters before she asks Dante to remember her on earth (*e riposato dei la lunga via, Purg.,* 5, 131), we experience an emotion which is concerned with human beings and not directly with the divine order in which they have found their fulfillment. Their eternal position in the divine order is something of which we are only conscious as a setting whose irrevocability can but serve to heighten the effect of their humanity, preserved for us in all its force. The result is a direct experience of life which overwhelms everything else, a comprehension of human realities which spreads as widely and variously as it goes profoundly to the very roots of our emotions, an illumination of man's impulses and passions which leads us to share in them without restraint and indeed to admire their variety and their greatness.

And by virtue of this immediate and admiring sympathy with man, the principle, rooted in the divine order, of the indestructibility of the whole historical and individual man turns *against* that order, makes it subservient to its own purposes, and obscures it. The image of man eclipses the image of God. Dante's work made man's Christian-figural being a reality, and destroyed it in the very process of realizing it. The tremendous pattern was broken by the overwhelming power of the images it had to contain. The coarse disorderliness which resulted during the later Middle Ages from the farcical realism of the mystery plays is fraught with far less danger to the figural-Christian view of things than the elevated style of such a poet, in whose work men learn to see and know themselves. [*Mimesis,* pp. 199–202]

This kind of approach is still only in its beginnings, and I think it is worth pursuing. Its development as a powerful mode of historical appreciation will depend upon the extent to which we can find plausible bridges between literary style and meanings that have resonance as history. The problem is not unlike that faced by the New Criticism (by R. P. Warren, Cleanth Brooks, and William K. Wimsatt, Jr., for instance) in its attempt to find terms in which close literary analysis could be made correlative with judgments of the aesthetic, and then the moral value, of literary texts. Thus the usefulness of terms of impurity—"ambiguity," "paradox," "tension"—in the New Criticism, and their gradual equation with "maturity," which becomes thereby an evaluative as well as a descriptive term.

The stylistic problem is difficult in that style is itself difficult to grasp: no one has succeeded, so far as I know, in creating a master list of stylistic categories. There seems to be no limit to the ways in which style can exist in literature, and the ways in which it can be taken hold of. From essay to essay, depending on the tactical situation, Spitzer will find primary stylistic meaning in the temporal adverbs of a novel; the variety of proper nouns in another; three separate linguistic features of a classical play; the rhythmical pattern of an essay.[10] Similarly Auerbach in *Mimesis* uses variously tempo, dialect, logic, narrative stance, dramatic devices, and dozens of other traits in stylistic analysis. It may be that apart from the most obvious characteristics—syntactic habits, imagery, lexicon, and the like—stylistic categories are as much dependent on meaning as meaning is on style, and that stylistic criticism is a kind of dialectical strategy, in which the critic attends just as much to felt meanings while he tries to locate their stylistic bases as he attends to stylistic traits and wonders what meanings they may be helping to convey.

In either case the question is the same, what is the style saying and what does it mean? The possible areas of meaning themselves are correspondingly various. Some aspects of style may be functional only in the single work and be unique to it. Others seem characteristic of the whole *oeuvre* of an artist; they contribute to the style of the man. Others yet again may be pointing also to meanings beyond the work and the peculiar situation of the individual artist and into the culture itself. Thus, in something of a critical *tour de force,* Auerbach in Chapter 3 of *Mimesis* can deduce from the "gestural" diction and showy syntax, the "powerful but distorted," "overrefined and exaggeratedly sensory" style of a passage of Ammianus Marcellinus, the quality of hopeless, unredeemed defensiveness of Roman civilization in the fourth century:

> Ammianus . . . belongs to the tradition of the antique historians in the elevated style, who look down from above and judge by moral standards, and who never make conscious and intentional use of the technique of realistic imitation because they scorn it as fit only for the low comic style. The particular form of this tradition, which seems to have been especially favored in late Roman times (it is already embodied in Sallust, but especially in Tacitus), is very strongly stoic in temper; it

delights in choosing exceptionally somber subjects, which reveal a high degree of moral corruption, and then sharply contrasting them with its ideal concept of original simplicity, purity, and virtue. This is the pattern which Ammianus obviously wants to follow, as appears from many passages of his work in which he cites deeds and sayings of earlier times in moralistic contrast. But from the very beginning we sense—and, in Ammianus, the impression becomes unmistakable—that in this tradition the material increasingly masters the stylistic intent, until it finally overwhelms it and forces the style, with its pretension to reserve and refinement, to adapt itself to the content, so that diction and syntax, torn between the somber realism of the content and the unrealistically refined tendency of the style, begin to change and become inharmonious, overburdened, and harsh. The diction grows mannered; the constructions begin, as it were, to writhe and twist. The equable elegance is disturbed; the refined reserve gives way to a somber pomp; and, against its will as it were, the style renders a greater sensoriness than would originally have been compatible with *gravitas,* yet *gravitas* itself is by no means lost, but on the contrary is heightened. The elevated style becomes hyperpathetic and gruesome, becomes pictorial and sensory. . . . Striking only in the sensory, resigned and as it were paralyzed despite its stubborn rhetorical passion, his manner of writing history nowhere displays anything redeeming, nowhere anything that points to a better future, nowhere a figure or an act about which stirs the refreshing atmosphere of a greater freedom, a greater humanity. It had begun, of course, in Tacitus, though by no means to the same extent. And the cause of it is doubtless the hopelessly defensive situation in which antique civilization found itself more and more deeply enmeshed. No longer able to generate new hope and new life from within, it had to restrict itself to measures which at best could only check decline and preserve the status quo; but these measures too grow more and more senile, their execution more and more arduous. . . . in Christianity itself—though Ammianus would not seem to be unfriendly in his attitude toward it—he sees nothing that might force a way through the prevailing futureless darkness. [pp. 56–57, 59–60]

This kind of connection between literary study and cultural history is my present subject; it is something of this sort that I shall be trying to explore in discussing in these essays three English poets—the *Pearl* poet, Langland, and Chaucer—in their setting in the late fourteenth century.

The age itself is apt for our inquiry, for two reasons. As ages go, it has pronounced character, for which we might expect to find clear stylistic symptoms; and it has pronounced resemblances to our own. It thus promises a special intensity of relevance. If not knowing history is to be condemned to relive it, then knowing this period may indeed save us some pains. I propose, then, to offer a brief characterization of the age—which I shall call an age of "crisis"—and then to investigate how each poet's style is related to it.

Of course, trying to characterize a whole age briefly is to deal in dangerous generalizations; as scholars and historians we do this unwillingly and at our peril. But every once in a while we must run the risk. Scholarly rigor and caution are admirable until they cut off contact between the researcher and his own culture. In any event, the general observations I shall offer herewith will be familiar ones. Though the study of specifically English culture in the late Middle Ages has for whatever reasons not yet produced a conspicuously broad, bold, and authoritative synthesis—an English cultural historian of Huizinga's breadth has yet to appear—there are numerous special studies, and some classical treatments of the enveloping continental culture of the period, on which to depend for guidance.

In calling Chaucer's age an age of "crisis" I may seem to be placing unwarranted confidence on a term that is more reliably used to describe people's reactions to certain conditions than to describe the objective conditions themselves. There were surely people in that age (as in our own) who lived through it without feeling that a crisis was going on. But for our purposes the label will do to indicate on the one hand conditions felt to be sufficient to generate a sense of crisis in the people who went through them, and on the other hand reliable testimony that a crisis was indeed felt.[11]

The age was one of contradiction as well as crisis, and it was by no means an age simply of decline. We would do well to recognize, for England in this period and for the Western European community it belongs to, some stabilizing events, and some signs of admirable accomplishment. The English parliament, particularly the House of Commons, is substantially the production of this period, as are some crucially important techniques of organizing trade and finance. Philosophy at Oxford and Paris, deriving in part from Ockhamite thought of the earlier part of the century, continues and enlarges the bases of modern scientific thought. The century sees important developments in military technique—with the introduction of the longbow and the cannon—and in technology generally. This is the century of the clock and the compass, of improved navigation and shipping. For England it is the emergent age of the great cloth industry. In northern Europe pictorial art, architecture, and sculpture make important gains in technique if not in spirituality. The English language comes into its own as a literary and administrative medium. The work of the very poets we are discussing is a capital achievement of the culture; apart from that of the fourteenth-century Tuscans, it is not to be rivaled in the Middle Ages at all. In religion the age sees the origin of movements that will issue in the Reformation.

Yet it persists in striking us more as an age of decline than of growth. It has a distinct character among periods of decline, in that decline does not come about gracefully. Rather, the elements of social and religious idealism are confronted with such great doses of intransigence, of nostalgia, of repression, or of bad luck as to create an atmosphere, not simply of decline, but of crisis. Thus the long economic depression that lasted from the end of the thirteenth till the middle of the fifteenth century was exacerbated by extraordinary attacks of famine in the first half of the fourteenth century and by the successive attacks of the Black Death, beginning in 1348–50, when perhaps a third of the population perished. The drastic speedup of the decline in population gave particular intensity to problems accompanying the slow but continuing decay of the feudal system. Agricultural workers in a period of labor shortage found their opportunities broadening, their expectations rising, their feudal obligations more irksome than ever. The response of the landlords and the government was repressive legislation. This is the century of the Jacquerie in France and of popular revolts all over Europe.[12]

In England in June of 1381 the peasants of Essex and Kent, goaded by antilabor laws, oppressive taxes, and other symptoms of corrupt and backward administration of the state, and led by radical reformers, revolted and marched on London. The government was taken completely by surprise. With the connivance of proletarian elements inside the city the mob came over the bridge and for two days were undisputed masters of a frightened city. Among the things they are reported to have demanded during the revolt were the handing over of all "traitors," the abolition of all lordships except the King's, the end of villeinage, the confiscation and distribution of Church property, and pardons for all. According to the chronicler Walsingham, the "mad" priest John Ball, one of the mob's leaders, preached before thousands at Blackheath a sermon from the text

Whan Adam dalf, and Eve span,
Wo was thanne a gentilman?

Ball thus converted an indigenous and hitherto rather harmless theme of Christian egalitarianism into a politically threatening call for social equality. "He tried," says Walsingham,

> to prove by the words of the proverb that he had taken for his text, that from the beginning all men were created equal by nature, and that servitude had been introduced by the unjust and evil oppression of men, against the will of God, who, if it had pleased Him to create serfs, surely in the beginning of the world would have appointed who should be a serf and who a lord. Let them consider, therefore, that He had now appointed the time wherein, laying aside the yoke of long servitude, they might, if they wished, enjoy their liberty so long desired. Wherefore they must be prudent, hastening to act after the manner of a good husbandman, tilling his field, and uprooting the tares that are accustomed to destroy the grain; first killing the great lords of the realm, then slaying the lawyers, justices and jurors, and finally rooting out everyone whom they knew to be harmful to the community in future. So at last they would obtain peace and security, if, when the great ones had been removed, they maintained among themselves equality of liberty and nobility, as well as of dignity and power.
>
> And when he had preached these and many other ravings, he was in such high favour with the common people that they cried out that he should be archbishop and Chancellor of the kingdom, and that he alone was worthy of the office, for the present archbishop was a traitor to the realm and the commons, and should be beheaded wherever he could be found.[13]

Whether or not under Ball's influence, the mob settled scores with the most prominent of their oppressors: they burned the palace of the Duke of Lancaster John of Gaunt, the greatest magnate of the realm and the patron of Chaucer, and beheaded, among many others, Chancellor Sudbury, Archbishop of Canterbury, as he took refuge in the tower with the royal family and council. Meanwhile the fourteen-year-old King Richard was negotiating with the rebel leaders. Aided by the rebels' touching confidence that the crown would put all to rights, Richard watched his men kill the principal rebel leader on the very next day. Proclaiming himself their chief, he granted all their demands, supplied them with charters, and sent them triumphantly home. The wave of revolt, killing, and burning that had spread to other parts of the country soon stopped. Then came the government's turn: the pardons were revoked, the judges set to work, and the movement's leaders were tried and executed. Walsingham reports that when a group from Essex asked whether the King intended to honor his charters, Richard answered; "Rustics you were and rustics you are still."[14]

"[The revolt] came as the last of three successive indictments of the government within a decade," writes May McKisack in her Oxford History volume, ". . . it created an atmosphere of general nervousness which long outlasted its suppression."[15] It thus serves to document the political as well as the economic crisis of the age. The century had seen Edward II deposed and murdered, and Edward III pursuing into his dotage an endless and ruinous war with the French. The latter part of Richard II's reign would see the French war relatively in abeyance, but the perennial struggle among nobles and crown continued in aggravated form in the appellants' successful revolt in 1387, in the merciless Parliament that followed, in Richard's subsequent recovery and revenge, and in the revolution which saw him finally deposed and executed.

In almost painful contrast to the corrupt and incompetent administration of government, and the prevalent cynicism and brutality of politics in the period, there is a surge of romantic and nostalgic cultivation of the outward forms of chivalry. This is the age of sumptuous tournaments, of the Order of the Garter, and the King's heralds, of the Court of Chivalry (before which Chaucer testified in a coat-of-arms dispute), and the sale of patents of nobility. Such pronounced concern with social status and its outward badges may well be a symptom of insecurity in a class massively beset by unrest from below. In any case the ethical norms of the cult of chivalry point up the disparity between the period's ideals and its actions. As Gervase Mathew charitably observes, "It was perhaps a central tension in late fourteenth-century English culture that its economics, its politics and its fiction were all too complex for so simple and individualistic a code."[16]

The condition of the fourteenth-century Church is too well known to need elaborate emphasis. The century begins with the captivity of the papacy at Avignon and ends with the Great Schism, in which Europe was treated to the spectacle of two popes excommunicating and making war on each other. The virtual destruction of the papacy as a spiritual force is only the symptom, however, of general decline in ecclesiastical prestige. There were of course great prelates and great priests in England. But their presence serves mostly to underline the Church's defects, from the secular and political pursuits of the episcopate to the widespread poverty of parish priests and the neglect of the parishes themselves.

The desperate case of the priests is exemplified in the Peasants' Revolt. It was a priest, John Wrawe, who led the mob which sacked the rich monastery of Bury St. Edmunds and beheaded its prior. John Ball, reports Walsingham, preached that "tithes ought not to be paid to an incumbent unless he who should give them were richer than the rector or vicar who received them; and that tithes and offerings ought to be withheld if the parishioner were known to be a man of better life than his priest. . . ."[17] Every reader of the literature of the period knows its satire on corrupt clerics: friars, pardoners, summoners, absentee priests. The period is full of complaint against pluralism, nonresidence, the sale of benefices, the baronial scale of monastic possessions, and ecclesiastical wealth. Anticlericalism there had always been, but in this period it is deepened by the growth of a theological and political rationale, and by the intransigence with which demands for reform were met and suppressed. In the eleventh century the highest officials of the Church had headed the reform movement; now the official position is everywhere one of reaction. Heterodoxy there had always been, but now because of the growing incapacity of the orthodox element to practice what it preaches, and because of the Church's failure to find a place or an outlet for reformist enthusiasm, it is being driven into heretical movements that finally issue into the Reformation.[18]

The Oxford professor John Wyclif is the great English reformist writer of the period. From 1374 on, he moves from an anticlericalism which earned him papal censure to denial of the doctrine of transubstantiation, and, just at the moment of the Peasants' Revolt, to the open heresy of his *Confessio.* He escaped trial as a heretic only through the influence of powerful friends like John of Gaunt, and, forbidden to preach or teach, spent his remaining three years of life in a tireless production of further documentary proofs of his fierce dissent. Himself no practical reformer nor leader of men, his obdurate teachings—that the Roman Church was capable of errors in articles of faith, that the Bible (which he caused first to be translated into English) was more authoritative than bishop, council or Pope—provided the nucleus for the heretical Lollard movement, which, despite its decline through assiduous persecution by Church and state, nevertheless survived into the English Reformation.[19]

The emergence of Lollardy in England was typical of many similar manifestations of the period in its basic ideas and values and its steady progression into open heresy. Not only institutional defects of the Church, but indeed the thought and spiritual temper of the time drove men to a crisis of faith. Heterodox ideas, some deriving from the Ockhamite, Joachite, and Spiritual-Franciscan thought of earlier periods, flourished and compounded themselves in an atmosphere of dependence on inner rather than on ecclesiastical authority. The cleavage between reason and faith, characteristic of post-Ockhamite thought, not only generated a certain unsettling scepticism, but also drove faith itself further and further into the realm of the irrational. Thus the age is one of the resurgence of a mysticism which, as Gordon Leff puts it, "was subjective, often to the point of being indistinguishable from histrionics."[20] The histrionic tone of late-medieval religiosity is fed in turn by a new resurgence of apocalypticism which the Black Death did much to validate.

In looking at the religious iconography and the art of the period, we shall have to stand back from late-fourteenth-century England, and take in materials from continental sources and from the surrounding periods. Because of the infrequent survival of substantial native works of art, and because in many ways the period is one of the free admission of continental artists and styles, it is difficult to characterize the native English painting and sculpture with any security. My general impression of the art of Richard II's reign is that it shows mainly the conservative side of the mood of the time; it does not much suggest a milieu of turbulence or crisis. Similarly English architecture, now in its great "early Perpendicular" period, suggests solidity and dignity rather than tension or decay.[21] Nevertheless the English, with French and Netherlandish, is part of a northern Gothic art which is entering its "late" phase, and it is in this loose but still meaningful sense that we can summarize the artistic manifestations of the culture of the age.

In the religious iconography of the time, as in religious thought, we find a shifting toward the emotional—Emile Mâle describes it in terms of an exaggerated Franciscanism—the emotional and finally the macabre. "The serene art of the thirteenth century," says Mâle, "is followed by the impassioned, unhappy art (*l'art passioné, douloureux*) of the fourteenth and fifteenth."[22] The progression of tone and style in medieval art in the fourteenth century is not a regular one and not easy to follow in its details, but the general direction is unmistakable. Comparing the religious art of the thirteenth century to that of the fifteenth, says Mâle, "one is almost tempted to ask whether it is the same religion that the artists are interpreting." The art of the thirteenth century rarely represents pain and death, and when it does, they are sublimated, dominated by a serene confidence. Even the Passion of Jesus itself fails to awaken painful feelings, he remarks. "In the fifteenth century," he continues,

> the majority of extant works are somber and tragic; art offers us no more than the image of pain and death. Jesus no longer teaches; he suffers: or rather, he seems to be setting before us his wounds and his blood as the supreme teaching. What we are going to come upon from now on is Jesus naked, bleeding, crowned with thorns, the instruments of his Passion, and his corpse laid out in his mother's lap. . . . The high middle ages represented almost nothing but Christ triumphant, the thirteenth century found its master work in the type of Christ teaching, the fifteenth century wished to see in its God only the man of suffering. From now on Christianity is presented in its pathetic aspect.[23]

Mâle cites further evidence in the late-fourteenth-century emergence of the Passion of the Virgin Mary or the *pietà,* first in painting, then in sculpture—a motif especially congenial to the mystics. The Pietà often displays along with suffering and death the new tenderness and familiarity, the new softness and sentimentality, that is clearly to be found in the representation of the Virgin and child, and of the saints.[24] At the same time pictorial art, pointing toward the superbly realistic painting of Jean Fouquet and Jan Van Eyck, is becoming an art of extremes, of the dissolution of high Gothic poise. The northern realism of the fifteenth century is a realism that finally denies the piety of its subject matter, or is rather the expression of a piety "so direct that no earthly figure is too sensual or too heavy to express it."[25] Sculpture too, freeing itself from architecture, is becoming increasingly realistic, but it is a realism with less and less spirituality. Gothic architecture on the Continent, finally, is dissolving into the tracery of the flamboyant style.

The literature of the age matches its art, particularly in the later stages. Chaucer's French contemporaries, Deschamps, Machaut, and Froissart—his first models—show some technical liveliness, but they are still largely dominated by the courtly forms and attitudes of a century before. They write a charming poetry (and Froissart a prose) that must be counted among the symptoms of the period's conservatism which we have already noticed. The same is true of John Gower, Chaucer's friend and the most important English poet after the ones that particularly concern us. Deschamps, who knew Chaucer's poems, does at the same time have a distinct bent for satire and complaint, but it too seems conventional, and does not link up with the age's deeper currents of social unrest. It provides a bridge, however, to the literature of the following age—the age of Villon, let us say—which shows clearly the inharmonious exaggerations of motifs that in the high Gothic period had been held in balance. As has often been observed, it is on the one hand a literature of complicated verse-forms, extravagant rhetoric, endless romances and decorative allegories of love. At the same time it is a literature of thickening realism, of crude satire, of deepening grossness, obscenity, scatology. Its humor is more trivial or more macabre, sometimes bordering on the pathological and sadistic. Its seriousness is one of melancholic disenchantment, of preoccupation with old age, decay, and death. It was about 1400, according to Huizinga, that pictorial art achieved a realism grisly enough to render realistically the details of human decomposition; at about the same time the motif spread from ecclesiastical to secular literature. The *danse macabre* was first so named in a French poem of 1376.[26] From all we can guess, all three of our poets, the greatest that medieval England produced, were living and writing at this moment.

If, as I have tried to show, the age has a pronounced character, so do the *Pearl* poet, Langland, and Chaucer. Our question is in what ways are they to be understood as poets of that time and that place? How do their works fit into a full and complex sense of their time? From the point of view of our methodological concern as students of literature: how has what we otherwise know of the culture left evidence of its condition in their art, and particularly in their style? And how does their art, reciprocally, modify and enrich our notion of their culture?

Our answers will be complicated, to say the least, by the difficulty, inherent in all studies of style-and-culture, of allowing for the particular character and situation of the individual artist. Although medieval decorum discouraged artistic idiosyncrasy, we can sense at once radical differences in the personalities of these three. There are also radical differences in the amount we actually know about them personally, and in the degree and kind of report of contemporary life found in their works. Each of them is in various ways still quite mysterious, for each in his own medieval way eschews journalism for an art more general and exemplary. All three are exasperatingly bare of direct allusions to specific contemporary people and events.

In the area of direct relationship to the history of the age we should expect most of Chaucer, who is incomparably the best known and most prolific of the three. We have a splendid new edition of the official records of his life.[27] While it is true that not a single one of these six hundred pages contains reference to his having been a poet, we have an excellent picture of his career as courtier and public servant. He came from a prominent commercial family with some connections at court. We first find him, in 1357, a page in the household of the countess of Ulster. He served in the army in France; was captured and ransomed; passed into the service of Edward III, making a series of trips to the Continent on diplomatic missions. For many years he was close to the family of John of Gaunt; his wife's sister, Katharine Swynford, was successively mistress and third wife of that important nobleman.

Chaucer's knowledge of court and international politics must have been equalled by his knowledge of commerce and of public works. In middle and late life he held a variety of responsible posts: Controller of Customs and Subsidy of Wools, Skins, and Hides in the port of London; Controller of the Petty Custom on Wines; Clerk of the King's Works; Deputy Forester of the royal forest of North Petherton. He was for four years a justice of the peace for Kent, and he sat in Parliament for Kent in the session of 1386. Shortly thereafter, he seems to have suffered financial reverses. But he survived extremely well the violent political vicissitudes of the reign of Richard II, including the deposing of Richard. In 1399, a year before Chaucer's death, the new king, Henry IV, renewed and increased his annuity from the crown.

Chaucer's earliest substantial poem, the vaguely allegorical *Book of the Duchess,* only thinly veils its occasion: it is an elegy on the death in 1369 of Blanche, Duchess of Lancaster, wife of John of Gaunt. It must have been composed within the year following. Similarly, "occasional" origin has been suggested for his unfinished *House of Fame,* which appears to be leading up to some momentous political or social announcement; and his *Parliament of Fowls* is a St. Valentine's Day poem, we do not know for what year. Actual prototypes have been suggested for some of his characters. But it is a good index of the paucity of contemporary reference in Chaucer that despite some of the most elegant scholarly research of our time, we cannot establish the precise

date of the composition of a single one of his substantial poems.[28] The
momentous crises and catastrophes of his time scarcely peep out of
these pages; his only undoubted reference to the Peasant's Revolt is in
a simile in the *Nun's Priest's Tale* describing the noise of the country
folk in pursuit of Reynard the Fox:

> Certes, he Jakke Strawe and his meynee
> Ne made nevere shoutes half so shrille
> Whan that they wolden any Flemyng kille,
> As thilke day was maad upon the fox.
>
> (3394–3397)

The reference is to the massacre of Flemish dockworkers by the London mob, a shameful little side-event in the occupation of the city. Here
it seems naked of political or social significance, as if Chaucer were
almost unaware of such.

Chaucer makes charming reference, occasionally, to his own life. He
can be glimpsed at work over his accounts in the customhouse; he char-
acterizes himself as a great reader; he makes fun of his fatness and his
unlikeliness as a lover. One of the most interesting accomplishments of
Chaucer critics in recent years is the uncovering and the delineation of
the "Chaucer" to be found in Chaucer's works. But it is becoming ever
more clear that this Chaucer is not the historical fourteenth-century
courtier and man of letters but an artifact. This artifact, this fictional
character or *persona,* is almost as much a creation of Chaucer the artist
as are Pandarus and the Wife of Bath. He is, in fact, a major implement
of Chaucer's narrative technique. There is no doubt that Chaucer, who
must have recited some of these poems to friends, continually employs
and manipulates traits of the historical Chaucer—i.e., of himself—in a
genial interplay between reciter and audience. But just as Chaucer the
Canterbury pilgrim is exposed as a hopelessly bad poet, so we cannot
be certain that any of the traits of the historical Chaucer are being given
to us "straight."

We can be more certain, indeed, that the artifact Chaucer differs fundamentally from his historical namesake. The shy, bumbling bookworm
of the early poems, the naive, transparently deferential, bourgeois good
fellow of the *Canterbury Tales* could never have survived in Chaucer's
actual milieu. As Kittredge memorably put it, "a naif Collector of Customs would be a paradoxical monster."[29] But I am not convinced that the

portrait that Professor Talbot Donaldson sensitively deduces from an awareness of the fiction itself is as realistic a reconstruction as we might make. The Chaucer his audience knew, says Donaldson, was

> a bourgeois, but one who was known as a practical and successful man of the court; possessed perhaps of a certain diffidence of manner, reserved, deferential to the socially imposing persons with whom he was associated; a bit absent-minded, but affable and, one supposes, very good company—a good fellow; sagacious and highly perceptive.[30]

This is probably true as far as it goes. But loving Chaucer as we truly do, we have not yet asked all the questions. If a naif customs official would be a paradoxical monster, one muses, a blameless one in this period would be—at the very least—surprising. Leafing through the *Life Records* one comes on the question of why Chaucer was not reelected to Parliament after the session of 1386. There were accusations made before that very Parliament of widespread corruption in the customs offices. Was it merely because of his identification with the King's party, or because of his conduct of office, that he shortly thereafter gave up his controllerships of customs? Why was Chaucer awarded in 1376 such a handsome reward as £71.4.6, the entire proceeds of the conviction of John Kent of London for exporting wool without paying customs duties? What elements in our portrait of Chaucer the man take into account his part (whatever it was) in the rape (or perhaps abduction) of Cecily Chaumpaigne?[31]

These are all small matters in the light of the kind of history we are pursuing, and I am not about to pursue them. In the absence of documentary evidence, biographical speculation is perhaps amusing, but not profitable. However, that no one has felt prepared to take an unbiased look at the personal trivia simply underlines the fact that we do not know the man in terms of many of his major, concrete activities. We do not know whether he was courageous or cowardly, and to what extent he practiced that Christian charity ultimately recommended in many of his works. We do not know how deeply he was implicated in the major social and religious issues of the time. We do not know what he thought of Wyclif, who was long protected for political reasons by John of Gaunt. (Chaucer was for a time a close associate of some Lollard knights; but on the other hand the Host in the *Canterbury Tales* makes fun of Lollardy.) One returns to the fact that we do not know where he was during the Peasants' Revolt, nor what he may have thought of or learnt from it. Is Chaucer in any other sense a poet of an age of crisis? How deeply is he relevant to his time?

That Chaucer *is* a man of his time has been proved repeatedly in the archaeological sense. Of course we praise the artist for his transcendence of journalism; for his capacity for symbolism—his capacity to invest the concrete image with broader meaning; his gift for giving what successive generations have felt to be insight into general human nature in his portraits of fourteenth-century characters. Yet at the same time we feel his picture of the times in general—its manners, morals, customs, speech—to be tellingly accurate. He is part of the time a master realist and comic satirist, and what we know from other sources corroborates his report: prioresses, monks, innkeepers, and even pardoners did indeed behave that way then.

This validation of the historical truth of Chaucer in his genre-painting is supported by another kind of validation to be deduced from the ideas and doctrines found scattered in his works. Chaucer was not a philosopher, but he was a great reader, a great considerer of ideas, and his ideas are safely and authentically medieval. Almost no one calls him a harbinger of the Renaissance any more. His fundamental position is Christian and a bit stoical. Trying to summarize his ideology, one might conclude that it was almost too safely a medieval, conservative one, perhaps more in tune with an earlier and securer phase of medieval culture. The only suggestion of its approaching the thinking of an age of crisis is its profound dependence on and affinity for the sixth-century *Consolation of Philosophy* of Boethius—itself supremely a product of cultural crisis, in which the last great thinker of the antique world, a Roman senator imprisoned by an Ostrogothic king, facing almost certain death on charges of treason, summons up all his philosophy in an effort to reconcile himself to God's ways. The book has been a comfort to men in every age since, yet the depth of Chaucer's sympathy with it, the pervasiveness of its influence on him, would, if we had no other evidence, argue in Chaucer some sense of the insecurity, the contradictoriness, and the brittleness of his own situation.

It is this sense which makes Chaucer seem most deeply sensitive to history, and we feel it in him at every turn. It is there pervasively and massively, not so much in his rather genial and tolerant realism, suggested only by inference and by turns in his Boethian conclusions and in the thematic material of some of his poems, but expressed in large and small in the texture of his poetry and in its gross structure by what I shall call here, summarizing, his ironic style. This style at its best embraces, inspects, and holds out for our delectation a world of alternate possibilities. It compares and tests the major value systems then in conflict—the Christian, the secular-idealist, and the secular-materialist—and does so with such comprehensiveness, clarity, and sympathy, that we must be satisfied that he, like the Wife of Bath, has had his world in his time. His poised, conservative, orthodox Boethian conclusions are validated by his confrontation of the major issues of value, and this confrontation is conveyed by Chaucer the artist in the style and structure, the typically ironic composition, of such masterpieces as the *Troilus* and the *Canterbury Tales.*

Chaucer the supreme ironist is of course not new to us. I have made my own argument for the dominant irony of his style elsewhere,[32] and will not repeat more of it here. What I shall offer instead, in a later chapter, are some reflections deriving from the fact that Chaucer was not always successful at irony, nor always an ironist. What alternatives did he try, I shall ask, and what further meanings may they suggest as to his relation to late medieval culture?

If the abundant documentary records of Chaucer, and his celebrated realism, yield so little direct evidence of his response to the age, we might well be discouraged at the case of our other two poets, for here there are, besides the manuscripts of the poems, no documents at all. We are not certain of the name of the author of *Piers Plowman,* if there was only one author, and if the work is one work rather than being two or three or four. At one time I felt, without regard to the so-called internal and external evidence, that no man in his right mind would twice *re*write a long, doctrinal poem—producing three versions in the course of twenty years, versions moreover which have defied all our efforts to find a consistent principle, either artistic or doctrinal or even political, governing the revision. Wordsworth produced less revision of the *Prelude* in fifty years, and that poem had not already been published to the world. Surely, among medieval texts the three versions of *Piers Plowman,* if written by one man, must be unique in this respect. Studying the poem a little more, however, one finds it to be unique in so many respects that one begins rather to feel that if anyone in the middle ages would have written and twice rewritten a long doctrinal poem it could only have been the author of *Piers Plowman.* Such evidence as there is, recently summarized by Professor Kane,[33] supports the idea of single authorship; I am content to call the shadowy historical figure who thus emerges by the name of William Langland, the more so because he seems so palpably in his poem to have placed before us directly his own personality and his own ideas.

We know Langland the man in ways that we do not know Chaucer. He is a moralist, a sermoner, a satirist, and a reformer, and there is little in his culture that we do not have his firsthand opinion about. Our investigation of Langland in terms of the literature of an age of crisis would seem to be almost redundant. On every leaf he deals with contemporary moral, political, and religious problems, which he envisions as parts of a single indictment of his age. We shall not need to dwell on this aspect of a poem that is mined for evidence by the social and cultural historians themselves. We shall, rather, turn from Langland the reformer to Langland the artist, and ask how they agree—to ask what (if anything) the poem as artifact has to add obliquely or stylistically to what the poem as moral tract directly says.

Speaking of poems as artifacts leads us naturally to our third poet, the author of *Pearl, Sir Gawain and the Green Knight,* and of a few lesser didactic poems: *Purity, Patience,* and perhaps *St. Erkenwald.* Of him we know precisely nothing, nor would we have any of his poems were it not for the unique manuscript of them that survived the great fire in the Cotton Collection in 1731. The poems, written in archaic or revivalist English verse-forms, and in a difficult provincial dialect, the dialect of the West Midlands, were not printed until the nineteenth century and have only recently—in the last twenty-five years—been properly appreciated as works of art.

Pearl and *Sir Gawain* are in a sense discoveries of the New Criticism; under close analysis they have been shown to have a depth and sophistication rivaling that of the best poems of Chaucer. Their author, like Langland, may conceivably have been a cleric. He is an orthodox Christian and knows both English and continental literary tradition. At the same time he has close affinities with feudal, aristocratic pursuits. He understands hunting and courtly love and country life. To judge by the contents of his poems, he may have been a priest attached to some back-country baronial court, far from the centers of power and the play of contemporary history. Entirely unlike Langland's, his poetry appears to say almost nothing of the late fourteenth century. It includes an Arthurian romance, a moral-allegorical vision-poem on personal salvation, and religious exempla based on Scripture and hagiology. The *Gawain* castle is thought architecturally to be a late-medieval one, but this and other touches of contemporary texture in the poetry are trivial.

Pearl and *Sir Gawain* present in perhaps the most acute form the problem of the relevance of poetry to cultural history; they seem so completely poetry, works of art, and so little history. Do they speak in any way to the actual condition of the age of Chaucer? This is the question to which we shall turn in the next chapter.

THE *PEARL* POET: STYLE AS DEFENSE

The moralist and the artist in the *Pearl* poet are so intimately related—the art of the poems and their meaning are so much entwined—that there is a certain violence in trying to part them. I shall do so only temporarily, considering briefly the moralist alone in order to show finally how much his true position depends on that of the artist.

The *Pearl* moralist, then, seems from his overt statements to be a surprisingly uncomplicated moralist, and a conservative one as well. Thinking of his having lived in the second half of the fourteenth century, we find him surprisingly untroubled for those troubled times, and surprisingly accepting and unquestioning of the orthodox forms of Christianity and of feudalism. These two major systems of thought, feeling, belief, and behavior were undergoing such trials and such patent damage in his time that his relatively slight reflection of actual conditions would seem to argue a kind of escapism or reaction.

It could not have been simple ignorance. A provincial court of sufficient culture to have evoked these poems is not likely to have been unaware of plague, corruption, war, revolt, schism. Indeed, if we look beyond the two masterpieces to the two lesser poems, we find ample reference to disaster and to moral decay. We may be hearing an indictment of the militarism of his own times in the poet's description in *Purity* of the brutality of Adam's descendants before the Flood:

He watz famed for fre þat feȝt loved best,
And ay þe bigest in bale þe best watz halden.

(275–276)[1]

[He who best loved fighting got a reputation for nobility; and ever the greatest doer of harm was considered the best man.]

Perhaps in his moving accounts of the dark anger of God—in his descriptions of the welter of the Flood, of the destruction of Sodom and Gomorrah and of the reigns of Zedekiah and Belshazzar, of the storm in *Patience* and the stink of the whale—we sense his own passionate concern with crimes and punishments of his contemporaries.[2]

But even when he is cataloguing specific vices to be avoided, in the manner of a preacher, his thrust is so general that we can make nothing distinctively local or contemporary out of it:

> For fele fautez may a freke forfete his blysse,
> Þat he þe Soverayn ne se—þen for slauþe one,
> As for bobaunce and bost, and bolnande pryde,
> Þroly into þe develez þrote man þryngez bylyve;
> For covetyse, and colwarde and croked dedez,
> For mon-sworne, and men-scla3t, and to much drynk,
> For þefte, and for þrepyng, unþonk may mon have;
> For roborrye, and riboudrye, and resounez untrwe,
> And dysheriete and depryve dowrie of wydoez,
> For marryng of maryagez, and mayntnaunce of schrewez,
> For traysoun and trichcherye, and tyrauntyre boþe,
> And for fals famacions and fayned lawez—
> Man may mysse þe myrþe pat much is to prayse
> For such unþewez as þise, and þole much payne,
> And in þe Creatores cort com never more,
> Ne never see hym with sy3t for such sour tornez.
>
> (*Purity,* 177–192)

[For many faults a man may forfeit Paradise so that he see not the Sovereign: one is sloth; for presumption and boasting, and swollen pride, man swiftly rushes direct into the devil's throat; a man may come to harm for covetousness, and villainy, and crooked deeds, for perjury, and manslaughter, and too much drink, for theft, and for quarreling; for robbery, and lechery, and falsehood, and despoiling and depriving widows of their doweries, for ruining marriages and supporting wicked people, for treason and treachery, and tyranny as well, and for false laws—for such vices as these men may miss the joy that is greatly to be valued, and suffer much pain, and nevermore come into the court of the Creator, nor, for such vile deeds, never set eyes on him.]

His poems are completely devoid of identifiable personal or political references. Ten verses near the opening of *Purity* (vv. 7–16) contain his only allusion to the vices of the clergy.[3]

On balance, furthermore, in his treatment of virtue and vice he addresses himself to the personal crisis more readily than to the social. Where in *Piers Plowman* we are continually reminded of the ordained function, behavior, and failure of groups, estates, professions—the *Pearl* poet's imagination polarizes around the moral condition of the individual: Jonah, the *Pearl*-Dreamer, Sir Gawain. He has a feeling for loneliness. Even in the most "social" of the poems, *Purity,* the argument periodically centers on single protagonists. Of course all of the individuals in this poetry are highly exemplary, but for the most part they exemplify crises of the private human will and judgment. While any of these *could* be generalized into social maladies, the poet does not in fact present himself as a satirist, a reformer, or even as a complainer of the badness of the times. In the two masterpieces that principally concern us, there is very little preaching on deadly sins and very little sense of retribution. Moralist he remains to the core, but somehow detached from current history.

His religious ideas, particularly on free grace, which were once thought to border on heresy—Carleton Brown called him an evangelist and anticipator of Protestantism—have now been found to be safely orthodox.[4] There is perhaps a flavor of protestantism in that his overt theology is not much a matter of the Church, the Fathers, and the Doctors, but rather depends much on Scripture. The moral fervor of *Pearl,* and the depth of its symbolism, would plausibly relate it to the flowering of devotional literature in the fourteenth century. But in it he never reaches that degree of mysticism or emotionalism, never really suggests that excess of feeling that we have come to associate with late-medieval religiosity.[5] He does not linger at all over Death's decay of the flesh; the Passion, briefly regarded along with the bleeding wound of the Lamb (vv. 805–814, 1135–1137), is not touched with horror or grotesqueness. Even the pathos that we should normally expect in an elegy, though unmistakably and movingly present, is restrained, muted in ways that we shall notice when we turn to the art of the poem.

I need not insist on the *Pearl* poet's allegiance to high-medieval feudalism. It is to be discovered just under the surface in *Pearl,* implicit in the diction and in the relationship of the characters. God and the elect are themselves conceived as a feudal hierarchy, which has taken to itself, spiritualized, and perfected that ideal of Courtesy[6] which it now shares with high medieval aristocracy. The same fusion of religious with feudal idealism is even more apparent in *Sir Gawain.* We might be tempted to see in the poet of this highly heraldic poem, with its emblematic band worn crosswise, its color green, its pentangular symbol, some of the gaudy ceremoniality of the period; but if so, the moralist has raised the ceremony to something finer than the typically late-medieval assertion of rank and class-consciousness.

The *Pearl* poet as moralist is a remarkably pure and uncompromising moralist. He seems in fact to have a passion for purity. It is, in a way, all he ever writes about: in *Patience* it is the purity of Jonah's obedience to the Lord; in *Cleanness* (or *Purity*), the impurity and the corrective cleansing of God's vassals; in *Pearl,* the salvation of the pure, and in *Sir Gawain,* the slight impurity of Gawain's *trawþe.* In the latter two poems—which turn on delicate distinctions, degrees of purity—we find much of the obverse and concomitant motif, of spottedness and imperfection. Whatever critics decide to be the precise sin of Gawain—be it pride, cowardice, carnal frailty, or what not—he wears the green girdle "In tokenyng he watz tane in tech of a faute" (v. 2488). The innocents in *Pearl* are "Wythouten note oþer mascle of sulpande synne" (v. 727). The pearl in its various manifestations is *wythouten spot, maskeles, wemles, unblemyst;* it has no *teche* or stain. This imagery of spotlessness is dominant enough to constitute the refrain linking the stanzas in three sections of the poem, including the very first, and it is a strong factor in the contrast of the two main groups of images; in Wendell Stacy Johnson's terms:

> on the one hand, images out of the world of growing things, images of the garden and the vineyard which are associated with the dust of the earth; on the other, images of light and of brilliant, light-reflecting gems, free of any spot (dust) and associated with whiteness and with emblems of royalty.[7]

There is no question, in any of his poems, of his fundamental purism. In morals, tolerant of human imperfection as he may be, he is always aware of the ideal: the pure, the perfect.

It is not surprising that these terms can be applied to him wholly as artist as well. His awareness of integrity in morals seems to be of a piece, in his total personality, with his sense of form. He is almost unique among medieval poets in having a passion for unity, for utter discipline of form. I say "almost unique" thinking of Dante, of Dante's moral purism, of the formal regularity of the *Commedia,* which is emblematic of the rightness of the universe, and of the stunning interplay of formal correspondences within this regularity which amplify and celebrate unity, order, the regular correspondences of all things.

Even in verse-form the two poets have comparable impulses. Dante's extraordinary feat in never repeating a rime (the endless fecundity of God's sounds!) and the endless linkage of the *terza rima* have something of the same effect as the extraordinary linkedness of lines and stanzas in *Pearl*.

Both *Pearl* and *Gawain* end on a note reminiscent of their beginnings. They come full circle like Gawain's pentangle, an endless knot, and remind us of the roundness and integrity of themselves. Within this integrity, the poet has furthermore, in each case, set himself difficult formal tasks, the performance of which is a kind of celebration, as in Dante, of the ultimate unity of the work—whether it be God's or the poet's. In *Pearl* much of this performance is in the verse-form itself. Each twelve-line stanza has only three rimes, one of them used no less than six times per stanza. The stanzas are grouped by fives, the last line of each stanza in the group being connected to the first line of the next by a repeated syllable, word, or phrase, and all the stanzas in the group ending with a repeated phrase, something like a refrain. Since the last riming syllables in the stanzas are always part of this repeated phrase, all the stanzas in a group are further linked by having the same rime in lines 10 and 12. There are twenty of these groups, which are themselves linked at beginning and end by similarly repeated phrases. This meterical form is "probably the most complex in English."[8] The metrical task in *Sir Gawain* involves stanzas of unrimed alliterative long-lines followed by a brief rimed "bob and wheel," scarcely less complicated than in *Pearl*. In *Sir Gawain* the echoing alliteration, the linking of words by sound, has much of the same repetitive, unifying effect as have the rimes and refrains in *Pearl*.

The sense of order, correspondence, and linkage in both poems is powerfully supported by a certain amount of numerical symbolism. It would not be surprising to find such symbolism in the work of a poet who could give us the description of the pentangle, Sir Gawain's device, along with the exegesis (vv. 619–665) explaining that it stands for five interlocking sets of five interlocking virtues. But the poet's interest in repeated pattern goes well beyond mystical numbers to produce those repetitions of words, images, scenes, and actions that every reader recognizes and that seem to constitute a dominant artistic habit. In *Pearl* there is the astonishing ubiquity of the pearl symbol itself, and the pattern of successive gardens which are the locus of the action. In *Sir Gawain* patterns of time, place, and action are everywhere: "Things are arranged in pairs— there are two New Year's days, two beheading scenes, two courts, two confessions; or in threes—three temptations, three hunts, three kisses, three strokes of the ax."[9] There is a major sequence of repeated actions in the arming of Gawain and description of his shield, his journey to the castle, his three temptations, and his confession to the priest—taken up again in his second arming and the description of the girdle, his journey to the Green Chapel, the three strokes of the ax, and his confession to the Green Knight. There is continued patterning in the exchange of gifts in the castle, the exchange of visits between Gawain and the challenger, and so on and on.

To pursue this theme longer would be to defer unduly the observation that, despite this extraordinary insistence on unity, pattern, order, regularity, the poetry in its full effect has nothing of the monotony, the stiffness, the rigidity or intransigence or dogmatism that we might expect such a formal structure to support. Trying to account for this will bring us closer to the center of the poet's art and meaning.

The poet's use of some important elementary contrasts may contribute to his avoidance of a monochromatic effect; surely it contributes to his avoidance of simplicity and monotony. We have already mentioned the elementary contrast of nature and super-nature, heaven and earth, in the imagery of *Pearl*. *Sir Gawain* is similarly planned across contrasts between civilization and wildness, warmth and cold, company and solitude. But these and other contrasts have so powerful an effect that they may at the same time be taken as reinforcing rather than blurring the sense of pattern in the poem. Earth and heaven, spottedness and purity, the old hag and the beautiful hostess, winter storm and Christmas fireside juxtaposed in this poetry, as often intensify as modify each other. This leads me to feel that it is not only the elementary contrasts in the patterns of the poetry, but also the almost incredible richness of oblique *variation* on these patterns that accounts for the poetry's final effect: not of a simplistic black and white purism, but of a purism that comprehends the whole shimmering range of possibilities in the variants from pattern or perfection. Thinking now of the total effect of these poems and how unobtrusive the patterning often is, we might guess that it exists as much to provide a basis for the variation as vice versa. My thesis here, at any rate, is that the interplay between formal unity and variation is at the core of both the style and the meaning of the poetry,[10] and I shall point to some characteristics in *Pearl* and *Sir Gawain* in turn to illustrate.

"'O spotless pearl in flawless pearls, that wears,' said I, 'the precious pearl'"—

> "O maskeleʒ perle in perleʒ pure,
> Þat bereʒ," quod I, "þe perle of prys."
>
> (745–746)

The poet who could write those lines and get away with it—nay, set them vibrating with meanings as subtly related to each other as are their sound-effects—is a poet for whom variation is a passion, and whose feeling for language is marked by the same play of repetition, synonymy, and symbolic variation that we find in the grosser pattern of the poetry. The extraordinary rhymes and refrains (and, as here, the occasional alliteration) of the *Pearl* verse-form play directly into the hands of a man drunk with words.

Semantic variation in *Pearl* is so rich as to defy exhaustive analysis. My impression is that almost any group of stanzas would yield up the same kind of variations as do the first two stanzas, where the idea of the uniqueness of the pearl is rendered in two ways:

> Ne proued I neuer her precios pere
>
> (4)

and

> I sette hyr sengeley in synglere;
>
> (8)

the related idea of her extreme beauty, in five ways:

> To clanly clos in golde so clere,
>
> (2)

> So rounde, so reken in vche araye,
>
> (5)

> So smal, so smoþe her sydeʒ were,
>
> (6)

... þat pryuy perle wythouten spot,

(12)

My priuy perle wythouten spotte.

(24)

Her special value to the speaker is rendered in seven or eight ways at the same time by "my privy perle," and picked up again with great variety in the speaker's exclamation, "Allas! I leste hyr" (v. 9), his pining away, his love-longing, the heaviness of his heart, the swollen feeling in his breast, and the contrary feelings of pleasure, of hope, of reminiscence of former joy, of the silence, sweeter than song, when he thinks of her.

In the first two stanzas his losing of her is expressed in three variations:

Allas! I leste hyr in on erbere,

(9)

Þurgh gresse to ground hit fro me yot,

(10)

... in þat spote hit fro me sprange;

(13)

the variant motif of her being in the ground is itself varied, in the second and third stanzas, in yet four more ways:

To þenke hir color so clad in clot,

(22)

O moul, þou marreʒ a myry iuele,

(23)

Þer such rycheʒ to rot is runne,

(26)

Þer hit doun drof in moldeʒ dunne;

(30)

and a comparable set of variations grows up in the bouquet of herbs—spices, blooms, flowers, fruit, grass, wheat—that must follow the planting of *so semly a sede*. The image of the *sede* (v. 34) is itself the fourth (or perhaps the seventh) way that the poet has found to refer to her. When we go on to the fourth stanza we find along with new motifs some further resonations of those already introduced.

At the same time the refrain in the final lines linking the stanzas is making its turn of the phrase "perle wythouten spot"—and the word *spot,* according to the system already described, is picked up again in the first line of each stanza. Critics (particularly Wendell Stacy Johnson) have already shown how the poet revels in the ambiguity delivered into his hands by this sort of repetition, and how the play with language, here the variant meanings of *spot,* contributes to the sense of paradox, important to his meaning at this point: that the spotless pearl should be spotted, in the earth, and yet be perhaps without spot, without wordly location.[11]

We must pass reluctantly by the gorgeous verbal display of the second group of stanzas describing the dream-garden, in which the variation of the language seems particularly apt for rendering the glint and gleam of its "reflected brilliance" (in Johnson's phrase). But I cannot resist quoting one stanza:

> The dubbemente of þo derworth depe
> Wern bonkeʒ bene of beryl bryʒt.
> Swangeande swete þe water con swepe,
> Wyth a rownande rourde raykande aryʒt.
> In þe founce þer stonden stoneʒ stepe,
> As glente þurʒ glas pat glowed and glyʒt,
> As stremande sterneʒ, quen stroþe-men slepe,
> Staren in welkyn in wynter nyʒt;
> For vche a pobbel in pole þer pyʒt
> Watʒ emerad, saffer, oþer gemme gente,
> Þat alle þe loʒe lemed of lyʒt,
> So dere watʒ hit adubbement.

(109–120)

[The adornments of those splendid depths were fair banks of bright beryl. Swirling sweetly the water did sweep, flowing right on with a whispering sound. On the bottom lay shining stones, that glowed and

shimmered like light through glass, and as streaming stars, when earth-
men sleep, shine in the heavens on a winter night. For every pebble set
there in the pool was an emerald, sapphire, or precious gem, so that all
the pool gleamed with light, so precious was its splendor.]

The shimmering quality of this passage, if not to be found in every section of the poem, is somehow typical of it and of its meaning. The central meaning of the *Pearl* symbolism is developed through variation and
reflection about a boldly repeated image which gradually increases in
richness as the poem progresses.[12] The poem, in fact, is one of the most
beautiful examples we have of the synthetic, accretive power of symbolism, its capacity to bring together related significances into unitive
simultaneous apprehension. The poet who wrote

"O maskele3 perle in perle3 pure,
Þat bere3," quod I, "þe perle of prys"

was not challenging us to figure out what the meaning of the pearl is,
but rather to appreciate the multiplicity of meanings that the symbol
could be made to interrelate: a girl, perhaps named Margery, a jeweler's
precious stone fit for a prince; a kind of beauty such as might be found
in an earthly Paradise; an emblem of moral purity; a sign of salvation;
a badge of the company of the elect; a similitude of the kingdom of
Heaven; the gates of the New Jerusalem. Finally, the *precious perle3
vnto his pay* of the poem's last line, where "he" is God, measures the
range of meanings that have been traversed and linked up by the echo
of the first line, with its simple-appearing *Perle, plesaunte to prynces
pay.* It is no wonder, then, that in the course of the poet's rich unfolding
of variant meanings for his central symbol, critics have felt impelled to
reach for deeper and fuller significances in the dramatic action of the
poem as a whole: to feel that the treatment of the speaker's personal
loss, of the salvation of his little girl, and then of his own salvation,
must also imply the problem of all mankind's loss of innocence and salvation, and the pearl's including in its significance the very soul of
mankind.

Variation in the central symbol as the poem progresses is accompa-
nied by a certain dramatics in the dialogue between the dreamer and the
pearl-maiden, and here again we find a quality akin to that in the
poem's poetics and symbolism. The relationship between the two

speakers is curiously varied. Or rather, one had better say, the dreamer's felt relationship to the maiden is varied. For her attitude toward him is stable: a mixture of firm pedagogy and respectful sympathy, expressed even in the confident tone and rhythm of her speech. Here again we have sameness played against variation, and it functions (among other ways) to keep the elegiac pathos firmly in hand. One can begin to pick out the variations in the dreamer's view of the maiden simply by collecting some of the epithets he uses to refer to her. On first sight she is a *faunt,* a child (v. 161), and then a *mayden of menske, ful debonere* (162), then successively *þat gracios gay* (189), *þat frech as flor-de-lys* (195), *þat gyrle* (205), *þat precios pyece* (229), *that juel* (253), *þat damyselle* (361), *blysful* (421), *þat gaye* (433), *maskelleȝ bryd* (769), *þat specyal spyce* (938), *þat lufly flor* (962), *my lyttel quene* (1147), *my frely* [beauty] (1155), and finally, after the vision of her disappears, *my perle* (1173) again.

The dreamer's partial adoption of the stance of a courtly lover is unmistakable here; it is supported by such conventions as the garden setting, the elaborate description of the lady, with her "vysayge whyt as playn yuore [ivory]" (178) and her exquisite manners, who takes insufficient notice of *luf-daungere* (11) [the power of love] and of his burning grief (387–388). This stance is part of the poem's deep identification of Christian and courtly virtues, common also to *Sir Gawain* and perhaps even more central to that work. But we should not let the religious overtones of the idea make us insensitive to the erotic, and to the psychological penetration with which this variation of the relationship is admitted into the poem. It is, of course, one of several variations on the relationship between father and daughter, man and pure maiden, the living and the dead, that are by turns exposed to us in their dialogue.

The psychological delicacy with which the meeting is handled is prefigured in the dreamer's slight hesitance in pursuing his way through the garden and in his precarious mixture of fear and hope when he first sees her. At his speechless wonder she respectfully bows, like a daughter and also a lady, doffs her crown, and greets him with *a lote lyȝte,* a glad sound (238). But a moment later in response to his too ready complaint of his loss, she replaces her crown and soberly corrects him. He excuses himself for the error, but the rush of his affection and relief carry him into a second error, his desire to live forever after with his pearl in the bright groves. This error elicits a certain impatience and shortness in her response:

"Jueler," sayde þat gemme clene,
"Wy borde ȝe men? So madde ȝe be!"

(289–290)

["Jeweler," said that clear gem, "Why do you men jest so? You are so
mad!"]

The tone, surely, is that of a daughter who enjoys the privileges of a
lady as well.

And so the conversation goes, the dreamer learning little by little to
accept his loss as he accepts little by little the paradox of salvation, and
making some more backward steps, some more errors, in progress. As
soon as he has some intimation of his daughter's high estate he grows
more humble, as might a countryman whose daughter had married a
foreign prince. "Let's not argue now," says he, "we see each other so
seldom":

"We meten so selden by stok oþer ston.
Paȝ cortaysly ȝe carp con,
I am bot mol and manereȝ mysse."

(380–382)

["We see each other so seldom by tree or stone. Though you know how
to speak courteously, I am just dust, and lack manners."]

But his humility leads him to another error; he does not quite understand how his little girl should have become a queen. A countess perhaps, yes:

"Of countes, damysel, par ma fay,
Wer fayr in heuen to halde asstate,
Oþer elleȝ a lady of lasse aray;
Bot a quene! Hit is to dere a date."

(489–492)

["By my faith, young lady, it would be fine to have the position of
countess in heaven, or else be a lady of lower rank. But a queen!—that
is too high to reach."]

It is too high a mark for one so young. I emphasize the domestic and

99

social overtones here at the expense of the theological point that is about to be expounded, but they are presented together, and if the former functions in the service of the latter, it never becomes purely metaphorical. Her reply—the parable of the vineyard—ends on a note of injury:

"Bot now þou moteȝ, me for to mate,
Þat I my peny haf wrang tan here;
Þou sayȝ þat I þat come to late
Am not worþy so gret fere."

(613–616)

["But now to contradict me you argue that I have taken my penny wrongly. You say that I that come too late am not worthy of such great fortune."]

Her tone of asperity sustains the emphasis given to the long passage of noble stanzas that follow, with their refrain:

For þe grace of God is gret innoȝe.

At the end of the maiden's discourse, by far her longest in the poem, the dreamer is moved to the point of veneration of the queen before him and makes invocation to her. It is perhaps no accident that the pearl symbolism reaches its highest point of intensity here, in verses that we have already noticed:

"O maskeleȝ perle in perleȝ pure,
Þat bereȝ," quod I, "þe perle of prys. . . ."

(745–746)

The ensuing conversation serves to fill out the maiden's account of the state of the elect and the dreamer's glimpse of the New Jerusalem; their disagreement is forgotten. But the ambiguity of their relationship persists to the end. Mortal man's unfitness to conceive of the splendor of the New Jerusalem is mirrored in the dreamer's renewed sense of social humility, his reluctant presumption to ask yet another question:

"I schulde not tempte þy wyt so wlonc,
To Krysteȝ chambre þat art ichose.

100

I am bot mokke and mul among,
And þou so ryche a reken rose. . . ."

(903–906)

["I should not test your noble judgment—you who are chosen for
Christ's bridal-chamber. I am just muck mixed together with dust, and
you are so fair a fresh rose. . . ."]

But as the perspective lengthens in his vision of the procession of all
the elect toward the throne of God, and he sees the maiden once again
as one among many maidens, the old fatherly and loverly emotions are
renewed:

I loked among his meyny schene
How þay wyth lyf wern laste and lade;
Þen saȝ I þer my lyttel quene
Þat I wende had standen by me in sclade.
Lorde, much of mirþe watȝ þat ho made
Among her fereȝ þat watȝ so quyt!
Þat syȝt me gart to þenk to wade
For luf-longyng in gret delyt.

(1145–1152)

[I looked among his shining troop, how they were loaded and laden with
life. Then there I saw my little queen that I thought had stood near me
in the valley. Lord, she was rejoicing greatly, looking so white among
her companions! That sight made me decide to wade across, for love-
longing, in great delight.]

My lyttel quene . . . For luf-longyng in gret delyt: almost the whole
range of their relationship is compressed in those words. They give the
last touch of psychological rightness to the dreamer's final error: his
mad urge to cross the stream then and there, and his consequent awakening out of his vision.

This awakening, the imperfection of the dreamer's understanding
and of his self-control, are essential to the meaning of the poem, which
comprehends here something of the pathetic inadequacy of ordinary
mortal thought and feeling to grasp the full nature of God's love, God's
grace, God's kingdom. The poem at its end, as throughout in the
maiden's discourse, and as in the unity of its structure, never lets us

doubt the fullness and perfection of that kingdom; but through its diction, style, and dramatics at the same time it always makes us feel the variousness, the imperfection, and the manifold partial intimations of it that we perceive in this life.

Fullness, perfection, on the one hand, variousness, imperfection, on the other—these motifs are just as deeply involved in the style and meaning of *Sir Gawain and the Green Knight*. But the two are not the same poem, and some of the same stylistic and structural traits in the serio-comic romance will be found to be supporting rather complex variants of the meanings we detect in the moral elegy.

The same rich synonymy and the same analytic, variational syntax supports in *Sir Gawain* much of the same subtly various and shimmering quality we find in *Pearl*. The daring white-on-white coloration of *Pearl* finds a suggestive parallel in the green-on-green of *Sir Gawain*. But as the various greens in *Sir Gawain* are often also mixed with some reds and golds, so the variety and fullness of detail which the style produces seems to support a greater sense of fecundity and, finally, of energy than in *Pearl*. The picture seems more crowded with detail, and if it indirectly hymns the manifold and various works of God, it also reflects a joy in the open-handedness and handiwork of men. The richness of the formal descriptions has often been noted. The armor of Sir Gawain, for example, is crowded with fringes and gold nailheads and gems, turtle-doves and true-love knots "so thickly embroidered as if many ladies had worked on it at home for seven years" (vv. 612–613). This sense of fullness of detail is picked up in the birds and butterflies and green stones and knots and bells that adorn the Green Knight and his horse, in the enticing costume of the lady of the castle, and even in the elaborate get-up of Morgan le Fay, "Toret and treieted [latticed] with tryflez aboute" (960). It is the same motive, I feel, and not wholly a faithfulness to late-fourteenth century architecture, that describes Bertilak's castle as having so many painted pinnacles scattered and clustered about it that it seemed pared out of paper (802). Very generally it is of a piece with the superlative feasts in the poem, full of music, double the usual number of dishes, with great variety of soups, fishes, and seasonings (189–197), and generously provided with leisure time and entertainment. Arthur's Christmas party lasts "ful fifteen dayes,"

With alle þe mete and þe mirþe þat men couþe avyse.

(45)

It is a world superlatively rich in content, even when the content is unpredictable or unfavorable to men, as in the splendidly concrete winter scenes, with their suggestion of a great multiplicity of hardships and adventures.[13]

As it expresses this sense of richness, fullness, and variety, the poem also generates a sense of superabundant energy. The description is itself one source of this feeling, for it either directly bespeaks the energy of fabulous handicraft, or that of nature. It is hard not to see in the Green Knight an overt symbolism of natural energy.[14] The vegetative associations of his appearance (the holly in his hand, his beard like a bush) would be enough to suggest it; but so do his size, his muscularity, and his manner both at Arthur's court and at the Green Chapel. When he is transformed into a country baron, the three hunting scenes superlatively perpetuate this symbolic role. But special energy is not reserved to the Green Knight; it is generated at every corner of the poem: obviously in the youth of Arthur and his guests, and in the martial reputation of Gawain. Less obviously but more profoundly in a widespread kinesthetic imagery, an imagery of muscular force, of tension and release, of the springing of steeds, the swinging of weapons, the exertion of grasping and leaping and catching, even of laughing, embracing and kissing. For even in the poem's quieter moments, the verbs seem to work overtime, possibly because of the continuous stretch that this poet applies to their meanings. So that between the hunting scenes, at bedtime in the castle,

Vche burne to his bedde busked bylyue.

(1411)

each man hurried to bed; the cock had *crowen* and *cakled* only three times when the lord *watz lopen* from his bed, and the company *dressed* to the wood before any daylight *sprenged,* to *chace.* While her husband is on his third hunt, the beautiful lady cannot sleep. She *ros hir vp radly* (1735), *comez* within the chamber door and *closes* it after her, *wayuez* open a window and *callez* on Gawain to wake up. The verbal energy persists even into the description of their general good cheer:

With smoþe smylyng and smolt þay *smeten* into merþe,
Þat al watʒ blis and bonchef þat *breke* hem bitwene
. . .

103

With luf-laȝyng a lyt he *layd* hym bysyde
Alle the specheȝ of specialté that *sprange* of her mouthe.
(1764–1765, 1777–1778)

[With pleasant and gentle smiles they fell into mirth, so that all was joy and happiness that broke out between them. . . . With a little affectionate laughter he parried all the provocative speeches that sprang from her mouth.]

This combined sense of superabundant fullness and energy—a sense not only of variety but of endless potentiality—always works in *Sir Gawain* in counterpoint with the extraordinary formalism to produce the total effect of the poem, which, like that of *Pearl,* is one of a surely-felt sense of order that nevertheless comprehends a great variety of experience. The contribution of the verse-form to this counterpoint is evident in the great freedom and variability of the alliterated main body of the stanza and the rather prim, delicate formality of the terminating rhymed bob-and-wheel that control and set it off.[15]

The Religion in *Sir Gawain* is by no means decorative or mechanical, but it is subordinated to the Courtesy, and although they remain versions of each other, it is the secular emphasis rather than the religious that is chiefly felt in the poem. So the order invoked by the poem is not chiefly that made by God, but rather the order made by men. It therefore requires no frame in a dream-vision of a better and higher world, but is rather framed by human history. The poem fittingly opens, then, with reference to the siege and the assault of Troy, that archetype of disaster, and continues with an account that is divided between the recitation of the subsequent successive foundings of Rome, Tuscany, Lombardy, and Britain—that is, successive restorations of order—and the reminder that Britain's building did not prevent the alternation of *werre and wrake and wonder,* and *blysse and blunder,* of the generation of bold men who loved strife and brought about *tene,* trouble, mischief. Many marvels have occurred here, continues the poet, and he will tell us concerning Arthur, the noblest king of all, something that he variously calls an *aunter in erde, a selly,* and *an outtrage awenture* (27–29).

The poet's variational structure, his synonymy here, three times brings into such close collocation historical events, marvel, and adventures as to suggest that the marvelous adventure to be narrated is not only historical (a forgivable poetic stance), but will constitute a comment on history and on the alternation between those two faces of history, *blysse and blunder,* that is, between order and confusion.[16] In a general sense the variational style in *Sir Gawain* supports and expresses a sense of variation—vicissitude—in human history.

The historical alternation between *blysse* and *blunder* is carried into the poem's pattern in many forms: *Sir Gawain* is much more a poem of contrasts and alternations than *Pearl.* But the thing to be primarily noted is that its alternations and contrasts, its moments of danger as well as of happiness, are all penetrated by a sense of ritual, caught up in a sense of pattern. It has been said that the three essentials of the festival spirit are that it involve excess, revelry; that it be affirmative, that it "say yes to life"; and that it display contrast, that it be the exceptional.[17] Correspondingly, the richness and energy which characterize the life of this festival poem are not merely decorative or celebratory, but rather pose the contrasting challenge of containment, of self-control, of rule, without which neither festivity nor civilization is possible.

Thus the vigorous action of the poem is intricately laced and bounded with dozens of variations of ritual, bargains, covenants, expressed or unspoken, which men make among themselves as an order in the world. The action is not only governed by social convention and formal agreements—that would be true of any society poem—it is preoccupied with them. We see, furthermore, that a great deal of the aesthetic patterning of the poem, of the unity of balanced and numerical repetitions, is a matter of social pattern, of ritual, custom, or mutual agreement. Even the poet's mode of viewing the action, his way of describing scenes, is penetrated, as Marie Borroff has shown, by a sense of the reciprocal.[18]

In this context we can take with maximum seriousness the recent suggestions in modern criticism that the element of *game* in *Sir Gawain* is highly meaningful.[19] For game is nothing other than a variation of the systems of covenants or agreements, the adopted sets of rules, by which humans submit their energies and passions to limits and defend themselves from unruliness and chaos.

The challenge of the Green Knight is at once an adventure, a game, and a bargain; its full answer by the hero Gawain is a test of his capacity to play the game according to the bargain or the rules. The element of death that obtrudes loomingly in the midst of this Christmas frolic and provides the romance with its greatest dose of seriousness does nothing to diminish the game going on. With the final laughter of Arthur's court at the end and the revelation that, after all, sorcery and shape-shifting have been at work, the action never loses completely its quality of play. We are never sure, in fact, when the game leaves off and earnest begins, for the game by itself has a serious import.

So many details of the poem fall into place in this pattern that I can only indicate a few of them here. That King Arthur has *ʒonge blod* and *brayn wylde* (v. 89) is of course an element of the poem's energy, its vitalism, which is carried out in the youthfulness of his court and in the crowded and superlative quality of the feasting scene surrounding it. Energy is curbed and civilized at the same time by the nice sense of holiday ritual—it is a recognized occasion for revelry—and by the sense of courtesy and precedence that are observed throughout. The fact that Arthur's awaiting some *auenturus þyng, sum mayn meruayle,* some challenge *in iusting* (93–97) is itself a *custom* expresses precisely the dialectic we are tracing; and the fact that the Green Knight's challenge comes heralded by this custom has some effect on the way in which the poem's action accepts and contains that challenge. The mention of the challenge to jousting as among the possible adventures that Arthur awaits introduces some imagery that does more than prefigure the Green Knight's challenge; it perpetuates the notion of *reciprocity* that infuses the whole poem's sense of life and of play:

> To joyne wyth hym in iustyng, in jopardé to lay,
> Lede lif for lyf, leue vchon oþer,
> As fortune wolde fulsun hom, þe fayrer to haue.
>
> (97–99)

> [To join with him in jousting, a man to stake life for life, each one to let the other have the fairer lot, as fortune might help him.]

The rules of the game could hardly have been better put. They have already been taken up in a lighter vein in the gift-giving game (with its payments in kisses, no doubt),[20] and I need not belabor this element in the bargain struck by Gawain with the rude stranger; it is this bargain, this game, with the system of reciprocal duties it entails, that forms the central action of the poem. It is perhaps worth noting, however, the words used by the Green Knight to describe it: *þe gomen* [game] (273), *a Crystemas gomen* (283), *oure forwardes* [agreement] (378), *þe couenaunt* (393), and the solemnity with which Gawain is sworn to reciprocate. "Game" and "solemn agreement" are synonymous.

The splendid description of the passage of the seasons—with its play on change, variety, growth, and decay, all encircled by natural law (vv. 500–533)—is entirely in harmony with the structure we are following. The ritualism of the arming of Gawain and the description of his shield invoke the norms of chivalric and Christian behavior which are part of the rules of the game; and of the same significance, and even more prominent, are the rules of the game of love and courtesy which come to the fore at Bertilak's castle. The richness of the poem's morality is that all of these are great games, great systems, and that Gawain must play all of them, consummately, at the same time.

The motif of the exchange of gifts intensifies the complexity and the difficulty of the test that Gawain undergoes. Most obviously, it obliges him to reveal his favors from the lady and thus makes concealment of the girdle an overt fault, an act of *vntrawþe,* perfidy. It also reinforces on an apparently sportive, inconsequential level the motif of reciprocity and of covenant which is at the heart of the deeper, life-and-death action:

"Ʒet fuie," quoþ þe freke, "a forwarde we make:
Quat-so-euer I wynne in þe wod hit worþez to yourez,
And quat chek so ʒe acheue chaunge me þerforne.
Swete, swap we so, sware with trawþe,
Queþer, leude, so lymp, lere oþer better."
"Bi God," quoþ Gawayn þe gode, "I grant þertylle,
And þat yow lyst for to layke, lef hit me þynkes."
"Who bryngez vus þis beuerage, þis bargayn is maked". . . .

And efte in her bourdyng þay bayþen in þe morn
To fylle þe same forwardez þat þay byfore maden:
Wat chaunce so bytydez hor cheuysaunce to chaunge,
What nwez so þay nome, at naʒt quen þay metten.
Þay acorded of þe couenauntez byfore þe court alle.
                                        (1105–1112, 1404–1408)

["Furthermore," said the man, "let us make an agreement: whatever I win in the woods will be yours, and for that, exchange with me whatever advantage you get. Fine sir, let's make the swap and give our words, whether we lose or come out better." "By God," said good Gawain, "I agree to it; it delights me that you want to play." "The bargain will be made as soon as someone brings us a drink". . . . And again in their jesting they agreed in the morning to fulfill the same bargain that they made before: no matter what might befall, to exchange their winnings, whatever new things they got, when they met at night. They agreed to the covenant before the whole court.]

For the poet to have balanced the love scenes and love tokens with the scenes and the prizes of the hunt seems tonally and thematically perfect. The hunting scenes are neither decorative nor excrescent nor even overdeveloped. For the hunt (pursuit of game) is a game of a most ancient and vital form, and by describing these lively chases the poet in the first place powerfully perpetuates the poem's sense of wild energy, barely to be controlled by the rules and custom of the hunt. It is surely the function of describing the careful dismemberment of the deer and boar to reestablish the sense of ritual order after the vital rush of the hunt itself. The envelopment of each love scene between the halves of a hunting scene put beyond doubt an artistic intention. Professor Savage long ago suggested some analogies between the character of the lady's quarry and that of Bertilak's, with the capping observation that on the third day Gawain acts the fox in the bedroom as the hunters hunt the fox in the field.[21] Surely a prior poetic relevance is in the fact of the hunts themselves. It will perhaps trivialize my point—but clarify it nevertheless—to quote a bit of Chaucer here:

She was so propre and sweete and likerous
I dar wel seyn, if she hadde been a mous,
And he a cat, he wolde hire hente anon.

(Miller's Tale, 3345–3347)

The poet knew, as we know, that the game of dalliance and love-talk is the containing and civilizing of animal sexuality. Our sense of Gawain's being tested is intensified, then, not only by the seductive charm of the lady, but by the imagery of the chase, of natural energy, deeply masculine, deeply sensory, with which the hunts surround his temptation and almost promise to validate his taking the lady. The life-and-death struggles of the hunted animals, finally, are played against Gawain's risk of his own life. If the lord's brutal courage in the face of the boar underlines the touch of prudence in Gawain, the deaths of the animals and the counterpointed vitality of the lord do in fact help to extenuate (if not validate) the love for life which motivates Gawain's one act of *untrawþe*. We can see in this perspective, indeed, how the felt vitality, the festive "saying of yes to life" in the whole poem's imagery and style, finally enters deeply into the poem's moral significance.

To turn back again to the theme of covenant and reciprocity, we may observe that the crucial dialogue between Gawain and the lady is embedded in a web of preliminary *exchanges*. There is the context of the exchange of general courtesies in the castle; the exchange of wit and compliment which constitutes their love dialogues; and such small but suggestive variations of the theme of chivalric rules as her suggestion of a military truce as she captures him on the first morning, and his refusal to countenance on the second morning a kiss taken by force, *geuen not with goud wylle* (1500).

The ending of the third dialogue is literally *about* exchange and reciprocity. The lady requests a gift, a token, in remembrance (1799). And Gawain's replies are politely ambiguous. He is unhappily not provided with baggage full of precious gifts; but he makes clear that while the lady deserves the most precious token of her hospitality—something he can and should reciprocate—it would not be right, it would not be to her honor, to give her a token for *drurye,* for love (1805). That, it is clear, would be a false token of reciprocity. The lady reverses the terms and offers him the gift of a ring. He refuses it and then refuses the green girdle on the same grounds:

"I haf none yow to norne [offer], ne noȝt wyl I take."

(1823)

His final acceptance and keeping of the girdle stands out from the poem's tight weaving of mutual exchange and agreements, not only as the only violation of his pledge with Bertilak, but as the only reward accepted without fair exchange given.

The rhetoric and imagery of ungrudging reciprocity, answering, unflinching truth to one's covenants, is very strong in the final episode, and I have of course passed over a great many other incidental examples of it in this discussion. The churlish behavior of Gawain's guide functions both to set off the ignorance of those (churls) who do not understand the world of covenants and to underline the terror of a state in which no such civilized restraints exist. The churl's picture of the Knight of the Green Chapel is of a monster unreasonable and uncontrollable, whose only occupation is slaughter—even of innocuous priests. In the face of the churl's terror, Gawain's reply is to invoke the ultimate covenant, that between man and God, and ride on alone.

Gawain's most obvious moral test is the test of chastity in the castle, which is presented less in and for itself than as a test, rather, of *trawþe* to the rules of hospitality.

> He cared for his cortaysye, lest craþayn he were,
> And more for his meschef, ȝif he schulde make synne,
> And be traytor to þat tolke þat þat telde aȝt.
>
> (1773–1775)

[He was concerned about his courtesy, lest he should be boorish, and even more about the trouble he would be in if he committed a sin, and betrayed the man who owned that house.]

But this test is only preliminary to the confrontation at the Green Chapel, which, precisely because it has no doctrinal content but consists in naked adherence to the covenant itself—because it is, in fact, the final inning or period in a Christmas game—is the deepest test of all. The poem seems to exemplify precisely what Huizinga means in *Homo Ludens* when he says: "The play concept as such is of a higher order than seriousness. For seriousness seeks to exclude play, whereas play can very well include seriousness."[22]

Much as in *Pearl, Sir Gawain* contains a strong sense of the ideal, delights in the variations from it, and ends with a tolerant sense of the difficulties of perfection. Even Eneas, *þe trewest on erthe*—the poet has reminded us—was once tried for treachery.[23] As in the *Pearl,* the style and structure of the poem are based on a deep interplay between formal unity and variation. *Sir Gawain* is the larger and more complex poem, its setting is more social than private, and it gives greater emphasis to the notions of disorder and of the imperfectness of human arrangements than does *Pearl,* so we might naturally expect to find in it a more suggestive connection with the sensibility of its own time. And in a sense we do. *Sir Gawain,* which is about *trawþe* and faithfulness in men, may be implying more about treachery and churlishness in its own culture than *Pearl* suggests about religious scepticism and the capitulation to grief. But the poems seem to me nevertheless more alike than different. The man who wrote these poems cannot have been ignorant, unobservant, or insensitive, and the times cried aloud for a reassertion of faith in God and in the integrity of men. The variational style in *Pearl* images precisely the imperfection of man's vision of the divine perfection. In *Gawain* the style supports the poem's sense of fecundity,

110

but also its sense of vicissitude, of disruptive energy, of the inconsistency and surprise that attend human affairs. But in both poems the extraordinary integrity of form, the sense that the variations are variations from an ideal order, continually asserts the primacy of that order. We come in each poem to a vision acutely aware of man's imperfection but unshakably confident in his religious and chivalric ideals.

If the *Pearl* poet is responding to the troubles of his times, his response, especially in the two masterpieces, is mostly oblique. Crisis touches him, no doubt profoundly, but in these poems it is completely absorbed in his art. Indeed, the richness of the poems combined with their artistic purity, the self-containment of their meaning, the sublime control and assurance with which they are composed, the total poetic energy they absorb, suggest a man for whom the perfection of his art has become a kind of defense against crisis. Each of the two poems is composed of exactly one hundred and one stanzas, and I take that extra stanza in each case to be a sign of humility. But it is the humility of an inveterate artificer. The *Pearl* poet has been compared as a writer to George Herbert, to Gerard Manley Hopkins, and to James Joyce, and there are good reasons for each comparison. But I like even better the observation made by one of my students not long ago, that for his time he is very much like the late Wallace Stevens: a "cubist" artist, with a fractionating, variational vision; and as artist, totally an artist—immersed in an age of crisis, but somehow beyond it, refining out through his art almost all of its accidental qualities, rendering finally, through form, only its shimmer, its beauty, and its moral essence.

PIERS PLOWMAN: THE POETRY OF CRISIS

In the last two decades Piers Plowman has been the object of concentrated attention by an impressive array of scholar-critics. Impressive not so much in their gross number, for there are many more investigators of Chaucer, for instance; but relative to its bulk and complexity, the poem has attracted extraordinary resources of talent to its elucidation. Unlike the works of the *Pearl* poet, it is not at all a modern discovery. It survives in over fifty manuscripts, making it one of the best sellers of the English Middle Ages, and it has been well known and a focus of theological, social, and scholarly controversy ever since. But as with *Pearl* and *Sir Gawain,* modern criticism (along with modern textual scholarship) has added a full new dimension to the study of the poem, and that consists of nothing other than regarding it *as* a poem. Recent investigators have been notable for a complexity of equipment that answers the complexity of the task: an acute awareness of the textual problems, a deepening understanding of the theology of the time, a broad knowledge of medieval literature, and an appreciation of artistic form and poetic language. A respect and love for the artist himself is axiomatic; in addition, some have been able to bring to their studies a personal religious commitment which makes it possible for them to accept the meaning of the poetry with total sympathy, simultaneously as art and as faith.[1]

In terms of equipment and of sympathy, then, much of what we have to bring to bear on the study of the poem has in fact been brought to bear in recent years. Of course this is not all we shall ever have. Our knowledge of fourteenth-century culture is still notoriously sketchy; and we can look forward to the completion of the reediting of the text, which is now in progress, and to advances all along the line. But I advert, perhaps ponderously, to the impressiveness of what has been done, to the learning, ingenuity, insight, and sympathy that have been lavished upon the work, to suggest the validity of the results of modern criticism—namely, its extraordinary inconclusiveness—and the validity of the meaning of those results: that *Piers Plowman* must in important ways *be* inconclusive; that its form and style are symptomatic of some sort of breakdown.

The problem with which *Piers Plowman* confronts us has been variously expressed by its most sympathetic critics. "Surely the starting point," George Kane writes, "is this paradox of total greatness and local failures"; and his essay goes a long way toward explaining the paradox without removing it. A. C. Spearing speaks of an "effect of potent vagueness" as being typical of the poem. Morton Bloomfield speaks of "a basic uncertainty" in Langland's mind. John Lawlor finds "penetrating clarity and largeness of vision . . . side by side with the very taste of purposelessness." Elizabeth Salter and Derek Pearsall attempt mightily to account for "the apparent inconclusiveness and deviousness of the poem's movement"; they describe the reading of the poem as "an experience . . . both richer and, at times, more confusing than any analysis or abstract can suggest."[2]

The puzzling quality of the poem is thus widely felt, and variously located, and one is forced to observe that despite our real advances in knowledge, modern criticism does not dispel one's sense of puzzlement, but rather tends to substitute new and more complex puzzles for

112

the old. Thus in sharing the modern concern with the problem of the poem's art, we must nevertheless recognize that older questions—the question of authorship, for instance, and the question of the "thought" of the poem—have now been subsumed in the problems of the poem's form, structure, and coherence, which virtually all modern critics recognize.

Medieval literary theory does not lean heavily on the ideas of form, structure, and coherence, preferring rather to dwell on the methods of amplification and ornamentation, which in too many cases obliterate form and structure. But general aesthetic theory is full of the awareness of proportion, order, and composition in art.[3] In any case the medieval poet, no matter how unsophisticated his aesthetic, had numerous other occasions for controlling his form or structure. In religious poetry there was always the clarity of form imposed by theology, by belief itself. A highly rationalized and numerical theology and a belief in the significance of formal or typological correspondences will help to produce an ordered and rationally divided work: if on God, then on his three aspects; if on the afterlife, then divided into Hell, Purgatory, and Paradise; if on penitence, then dealing successively with the four stages: repentance, confession, satisfaction, absolution.

Gothic art derives formal characteristics from related but more general habits of thought. The emergence in the twelfth century of dialectic as the chief method in philosophical exposition does not originate but only caps and gives final validation to a deep-seated formal tendency in the Gothic mind, a tendency which shapes whole classes of poems: *conflictus, tenson,* debate, the body and soul, the knight and the clerk, the Owl and the Nightingale, Winner and Waster.

Another Gestalt that is most congenial to Gothic art is that of the procession, the linear progression through stages or stations, as in a journey. It can be used in describing the succession of bays, leading to the altar, in the nave of the Gothic cathedral. In the other arts is can be found everywhere from the Bayeux tapestry to the procession of the mystery plays. It is a formal or structural factor in the *Divine Comedy* and the *Decameron.* As the pilgrimage it underlies the *Canterbury Tales* and many a moral allegory; as the quest it is the formal basis of much in romance.

Finally, the traditions and conventions of genre provide formal directions for the conduct of the poem: the dream-vision, the allegory, the romance, the fabliau, the sermon; each has accepted characteristics which contribute to form and structure.

The first thing to be observed about Langland is that although his work bears traces of almost all the large formal resources I have mentioned, it is finally controlled and explained by none of them.

There have been impressive attempts to discover a theological architecture of the poem. These attempts were for a long time focussed on what seems to be a perfectly clear and typically medieval division of its concerns into four parts. The full, completed poem consists of a "Vision of William Concerning Piers the Plowman," being about a third of the whole, and then a series of visions concerning "Do-Well, Do-Better, and Do-Best." What could be clearer? The initial vision should be an introduction describing the problem, the present ills of society, and the successive sections Do-Well, Do-Better, and Do-Best should treat of successively higher levels of right conduct. But beyond this all remains cloudy. The poet is not consistent in his use of the terms "Dowel, Dobet, and Dobest the third." He uses them often enough— one critic has called them "a kind of maddening refrain,"[4]—but we do not know what they mean. We could linger for the rest of our discussion with the theories on this one point: that Dowell, Dobet, and Dobest are the active life, the contemplative life, and the episcopal life; that they refer to the purgative, illuminative, and unitive stages of mystical contemplation; that they deal with the gifts to Man of, respectively, God, Christ, and the Holy Spirit;[5] and so on.

One sympathetic and remedial suggestion is that the multiplicity of possible meanings of the three ways of life is intentional, and that any and all may be present.[6] A related view is that each of the successive meanings of the three lives somehow augments the others.[7] More pessimistic is the observation that apart from one passage in Passus XIX, and in the manuscript rubrics, references to the triad all come in the Dowell section "and nowhere else, and that there the three Do's are defined in six or seven different ways."[8] Other critics have turned from the schema completely, suggesting that the poem does not operate on a conceptual structure at all, and may even be explicitly rejecting "the method of precise intellectual distinction."[9] Taken together, the best criticism of the poem suggests that what might have been a great tripartite medieval structure does not rise here, or at least that it is neither clearly outlined nor solidly based.

Turning now to other major possible sources of coherence, we find similar difficulties. *Piers Plowman* is really too long to be a debate as such, but the several dialogues between the Dreamer and interlocutors, as well as doses of dualistic and antithetic structure, give us some suggestion that its essential organization might be dialectical. This suggestion is very strong at the beginning, where the narrator, clothed as a hermit, is wandering on the Malvern Hills, falls asleep by a brook, and dreams that he is in a wilderness. High in the east, toward the sun, he sees a beautiful tower on a hilltop, and beneath it, in a deep dale, a dungeon. In between is a fair field full of folk, busy about all the activities of the world (Prologue, vv. 1–19). That this tower and dungeon, the high hill and dark dale, represent opposite alternatives, Jerusalem and Babylon, Heaven and Hell, would be a normal inference for allegorical poems. This inference is confirmed when, after an extended description of the fair field full of folk, in Passus I a beautiful lady named Holy Church instructs the Dreamer, telling him that the tower is the tower of Truth (or God) and the dungeon is the dwelling of Wrong (or the Devil). The conversation between Holy Church and the Dreamer is reminiscent of that of a host of other pairs of figures in medieval dialogue. Sometimes such figures engage in equal debate (which has been called "horizontal" debate), as in the *Owl and the Nightingale*. At other times they take the "vertical" roles of master and pupil, as in Boethius' *Consolation* or in *Pearl*. The forms can be combined, as in the second part of the *Roman de la Rose,* which is a horizontal debate among the various exponents of love, but has a vertical character in that each one successively takes the part of a master instructing the Dreamer (or Bel Acueil). Here in *Piers Plowman* the debate or dialogue is vertical. After Holy Church instructs the Dreamer concerning Truth and charity, in Passus II she points out to him another beautiful lady, clad in scarlet and jewels, named in the poem Meed; she is the daughter of False, as Holy Church is the daughter of God, and when Holy Church departs we expect the Whore of Babylon to have *her* turn in the dialogue that seems to be developing.

But Langland, in then going on with an extensive treatment of some of the evils of the world, wanders *out* of the dialectical genre framework thus established. Instead of sermon or polemic by Meed, he writes a semidramatic allegory on the relations between Meed and Falsehood, and Meed and Conscience, in a setting explicitly named the English court at Westminster (Passus III and IV). The following section of the poem shows Reason or Conscience preaching to the people, bringing on Repentance and the confessions of the Seven Deadly Sins (Passus V). Thus, in turn, the three or four-part pattern of the stages of Penitence temporarily becomes the organizing principle of the poem, and this in turn soon merges with the pilgrimage form. Confession over, the poet has a moving vision of the throng of repentant sinners inspired to seek Truth, but not knowing the way. Here for the first time enters Piers or Peter, a simple plowman, who gives the simple prescription of a life of honest work and doing good—doing the work that God has cut out for one—as the way to Truth. Piers is conceived here as a guide on a pilgrimage; but the plowman's pilgrimage is to plow his half-acre. After dealing with the problems of man's laziness and malingering, the poet shows Truth sending to Piers and his followers a pardon and a promise of eternal life (Passus VII).

Thus ends the first part—possibly to be called the Introduction—of the poem. The vision which follows shows us the narrator in lonely quest of Dowel. If the dialectical structure seems to have dropped out of sight, we might rediscover it in the series of debates in which the Dreamer now engages with such figures as Thought, Wit, Studie, Ymagynatyf, and Conscience. There are enough of these debates to establish that Langland set great store by the form. But in the final analysis the poem does not *proceed* by means of them. On the one hand, the Dreamer never finds, as a pupil in his "vertical" debates, any master with whose teaching he seems finally consoled. The multiplicity of subsequent masters, as Bloomfield has noted,[10] casts some shadow even on the role of Holy Church. She never reappears in the poem, although, paradoxically, it is surely her teaching which comes closest finally to providing what resolution the poem contains. Nor is Piers the Plowman, the most authoritative figure in the poem, ever brought into true dialogue with the Dreamer. Meanwhile, as Rosemary Woolf has said, "There is no poetic resolution to the opposing arguments" in the debates; "they are merely accumulated and put on one side."[11]

The quest pattern as the formal basis of the poem has an impressive number of supporters; but there is a serious issue whether the quest is effective artistically, that is, as a formal device in the poem, or biographically, that is, as a way of looking at the life of the poet, of which the poem itself is a record or symptom. The quest pattern reappears now and again in the poem, with the Dreamer ever seeking instruction on the means of salvation or perfection, but it is so distorted by digressions and alterations that its literary status is open to doubt. It is a quest that has many beginnings, no middle, and an ambiguous end; the quest leads back to where it started, in a pathetically hopeful vision of the human Conscience vowing to become a pilgrim to "walk wide as the world lasts to seek Piers the Plowman," destroyer of Pride. We cannot demand a compulsive neatness from medieval poets, nor impeccable theology or logic. But we expect to recognize some form, some control; if the poem is a quest, a spiritual autobiography, it is like none other of its time.

Sympathetic criticism of the poem as quest has tended toward accepting its incoherencies, somehow, as part of its art. Langland saw the Dreamer's quest, say Elizabeth Salter and Derek Pearsall, "as a search for truth which was complex, often contradictory, and cumulative." In successive bouts with the same problem these critics point out at least six searches in the poem, which exist neither in simple sequence nor in isolation, but which, they assert, "can be gradually or dramatically revealed as similar, even identical in direction and end-point." We must agree that all the searches in the poem are for Truth, early designated by Holy Church as the best of treasures, and the object of Piers Plowman's pilgrims. But in describing the literary relations of the successive journeys *in the poem,* the critics fall back on comparisons that suggest abandonment of a literary conception of form for something like real life. The searches, they say, "unfold out of the first search in a way which is more like a process of organic growth than deliberate literary design."[12] George Kane grasps the thorns more boldly:

> Indeed the figure of a search affords an excellent analogy for the progress of the poem; the false starts and changes of direction, frequent pauses, anxieties, hesitations and impatience which characterize it are thus excellently illustrated.[13]

This comes close to invoking the fallacy of imitative form; and many a reader has felt that the poem more than merely *represents* "the false starts and changes of direction, frequent pauses, anxieties, hesitations, and impatience" of the search for Truth. It not only represents them, it contains them; the reader or audience not only appreciates them, but suffers them, and it is not surprising that more than one critic, coming to a point of temporary resolution or of clarity in the text, sounds as if he is sharing the Dreamer's joy and relief. "So the Plowman, and after him the Saviour Himself, are sent to meet our need," says John Lawlor, who makes of the reading itself a necessary experience "of the very sense of weariness and apparent purposelessness that any stage of the journey may afford."[14]

We find this kind of difficulty and this kind of solution again if we look at the other resources of literary genre that were open to the poet. The poem can be regarded as a series of dreams or visions in allegorical form, but it is neither vision nor allegory in the conventional sense. Its deviations from the traits of genre, indeed, give us some positive indications of the ultimate quality of the poet's vision and of his historical significance.

The medieval vision—very early a vehicle for describing the afterlife—is conventionally adapted for the description of experience on a level other than that of everyday sensation. Resting firmly on the authority of biblical visions (Ezekiel, Daniel, St. John) and on a well-developed science of dreams, it was so natural a vehicle for the wonderful that even the love-poets took it up as a frame for their erotic heavens, hells, and purgatories. Both the Bible and dream-science taught that the dream or vision could be of hidden significance, and this very early led to a solid merger between dream and allegory. Allegory, highly developed in the Middle Ages as a device to explore the world of noumena—of nonsensuous moral and psychological entities— creates precisely that appearance of the strange and wonderful—of cryptic, nonnaturalistic, needing-to-be-interpreted experience—for which the dream-vision is the natural frame. Allegory has its own inner laws, chief of which is that it is habitually telling two simultaneous stories. One is fictional, rendered by the interplay of personified abstractions— like Charity and Cupidity, who may be rendered as two attractive ladies who struggle for the attention of a young man named Free Will. The other story is the simultaneous, hidden signification—let us say a moral issue in the actual world or even a crisis in the mind of a single person. The characteristic allegory keeps the two stories separate and distinct, that there be no confusion between the two worlds or two levels of reality represented. Medieval poets vary in their capacity to manage allegory, but by the time Langland wrote, the allegorical dream-vision was a venerable medieval genre whose form and tradition were known to everyone.

Langland introduces his dream-vision conventionally, with good heart, and he arouses conventional expectations. The time is May, the narrator wanders forth in the world to hear wonders; a marvel befell him, he says, almost a fairy-tale. He dreamt a marvelous dream, that he was in a wilderness; then comes mention of the allegorical tower and dungeon, and we seem indeed to have been introduced to a strange, allegorical world. But Langland makes no attempt to sustain either the sense of unfamiliarity, strangeness, or wonder sanctioned by the dream-form, nor can he for more than a few moments maintain the sense of the separateness of different levels of reality suggested by allegory. To put it another way, for him the familiar London scene is a wilderness seen in a vision. The world of moral abstractions is concrete and present, and the concrete, present, everyday world is itself an allegory, heavy with moral significance.

Turning to a description of the fair field full of folk—an allegory of the present condition of man in the world—he cannot render it schematically or abstractly, as in a vision, although he tries. "Some men put themselves to the *plow*" he says "and they played very seldom. In tilling and sowing they worked very hard, and earned what wasters destroy with gluttony. And some put themselves to *pride,* and appareled themselves accordingly; they came all decked out in the disguises of clothing." Right there in the forceful parallel between the concrete term "plow" and the abstract term "pride," as if there were not the slightest difference in kind between them, we have a small hint of the nature of Langland's vision: "plow" for him is a general moral term, "pride" is a concrete reality.[15] As his summary of the activities of man proceeds we can detect his impatience with allegory and even with mimetics. As abstraction and concreteness alternate or merge in his discourse so do the graphic and the doctrinal, description and exhortation.

Were it not too long a tale, I could tell how, again and again, Langland's sense of the present reality rends the curtain of allegory. How he brings abstractions like Meed, Reason, and Conscience before such historical figures as King Edward III at Westminster; how, in the midst of an allegorical pleading between Meed and Conscience before the King, another and much more concrete case suddenly comes up: Peace vs. Wrong. The episode amplifies for us the nature of Meed (Lucre), but its realism and color take us deep into a specific neighborhood (Passus IV, 47–109). Wrong has stolen Peace's wife, ravished a girl named Margaret, and also Rose (Reginald's sweetheart), has stolen geese and little pigs, broken the barn door and taken grain; he has even beaten up Peace and seduced his maid. Having—allegorically—the King's ear, Langland cannot refrain from inveighing against these deplorably literal results of the system of Maintenance in the countryside.

In illustration of Langland's curious way with dream-allegory I will only mention in addition his celebrated treatment of the Seven Deadly Sins. This sequence stands for a step in the process of Penance: Confession is represented by a series of confessions made by personifications of the sins. But the sins are not equal personifications, nor are their performances the least bit uniform. The names, again, are significant. Envy is called Envy, but Lechery is called Lecher (a degree less of abstraction), and Pride, even less abstractly, is represented as a girl named Peronelle Proud-Heart. Covetousness is called Sir Harvey. When Langland comes to the "confession" of Gluttony, local realism takes over completely. Glutton on his way to confession meets Betty the brewer and he is led into the tavern instead.

We have a tavern scene comparable to this in an early thirteenth-century French moral allegory, the *Songe d'Enfer,* where the Dreamer, having passed through the city of Covetousness and crossed the River of Gluttony, comes to the tavern and is welcomed by Theft. He gambles and meets with characters named Gambling, False Count, and Cheating. Then Drunkenness enters with her son Brawling, who has a fight with the Dreamer. Drunkenness takes the Dreamer via Fornication on to the brothel, which harbors Larceny and Shame, the daughter of Sin. The conduct of this earlier work is allegorically conventional and impeccable of its kind. These are the characters, and this the action we expect to find in such a setting. Although the author (like Dante) is fond of peppering his account with the names of actual people and places, such references are kept firmly within the boundaries of the moral-allegorical frame. (Thus Gambling asks the Dreamer for news of one Michiel de Treilles, but he is not confused with nor does he give up his role to the apparently notorious Michiel.) Langland's tavern, on the other hand, is incurably concrete and local:

> Thanne goth Glotoun in and grete othes after;
> Cesse the souteresse sat on the benche,
> Watte the warner and his wyf bothe,
> Tymme the tynkere and tweyne of his prentis,
> Hikke the hakeneyman and Hughe the nedeler,
> Clarice of Cokkeslane and the clerke of the cherche,
> Dawe the dykere and a dozeine other;
> Sire Piers of Pridie and Peronelle of Flaundres,
> A ribibour, a ratonere, a rakyer of Chepe,
> A ropere, a redyngkyng, and Rose the dissheres,
> Godfrey of Garlekehithe, and Gryfin the Walshe,
> And vpholderes an hepe erly bi the morwe
> Geuen glotoun with glad chere good ale to hansel.

> (B V 314–326)

> There was laughyng and louryng and "let go the cuppe,"
> And seten so til euensonge and songen vmwhile,

Tyl Glotoun had y-globbed a galoun an a Iille.
His guttis gunne to gothely as two gredy sowes;
He pissed a potel in a *pater-noster*-while,
And blew his rounde ruwet at his riggc-bon ende,
That alle that herde that horne held her nose after,
And wissheden it had be wexed with a wispe of firses.
He myƷte neither steppe ne stonde er he his staffe hadde;
And thanne gan he go liche a glewmannes bicche,
Somme tyme aside and somme tyme arrere,
As who-so leyth lynes forto lacche foules.
And whan he drowgh to the dore thannc dymmed his eighen,
He stumbled on the thresshcwolde an threwe to thc crthe.
Clement the cobelere cauƷte hym bi the myddel,
For to lifte hym alofte and leyde him on his knowes;
Ac Glotoun was a gret cherle and a grym in the liftynge,
And coughed vp a caudel in Clementis lappe;
Is non so hungri hounde in Hertford schire
Durst lape of the leuynges so vnloucly thei smauƷte.
With al thc wo of this worlde his wyf and his wenche
Baren hym home to his beddc and brouƷte hym thcrinne.
And after al this excesse he had an accidie,
That he slepe Saterday and Sonday til sonne Ʒede to reste.
Thanne waked he of his wynkyng and wiped his eyghen;
The fyrst worde that he warpe was, "where is the bolle?"

(B V 344–367)

[Then Glutton went in and Great Oaths after him. Cis the shoemaker sat on the bench, Wat the game-keeper and his wife also, Tim the tinker and two of his apprentices, Hick the horse-renter and Hugh the needle-makcr, Clarice of Cock's Lane and the clerk of the church, Davy the ditch-digger and a dozen others, Sir Piers the priest and Peronelle the Flemish whore, a fiddler, a rat-catcher, a Cheapside street-cleaner, a rope-maker, a horse-boy, and Rose the dish-seller, Godfrey of Garlick-hithe and Griffin the Welshman, and a bunch of auctioneers, early in the morning, hospitably gave Glutton a drink of good ale for luck. . . .

There was laughing and scowling and "Let go the cup," and they sat there till vespers, singing a while, till Glutton had gulped down more than a gallon. His guts began to rumble like two greedy sows. He pissed two quarts as quickly as you could say the Lord's Prayer, and blew the round bugle at the end of his backbone so that all who heard that horn

held their noses afterwards, and wished it had been stoppered with a
bunch of furze.

He could neither walk nor stand till he had his staff, and then he
moved like a (blind) minstrel's bitch, sometimes sideways and sometimes backwards, like someone laying nets to catch birds. And when he
drew near the door his eyesight dimmed; he stumbled on the sill and fell
to the earth. Clement the cobbler grabbed him by the middle to lift him
up, and he got him to his knees. But Glutton was a big fellow, terribly
heavy to lift, and he threw up a mess right in Clement's lap. There isn't
a hound in Hertfordshire hungry enough to lap up those leftovers, they
smelled so foul.

With a world of trouble his wife and his maid carried him home and
got him to bed. And after all this carousing he fell into such a stupor that
he slept all through Saturday and Sunday until sunset. Then he waked
out of his sleep and wiped his eyes. The first words that he got out were
"Where's the cup?"][16]

After the confessions of the sins, a few pages farther on, appears
Repentance, to whom Langland entrusts one of his most lofty and
touching utterances on the meaning of Christ's sacrifice—and the religious allegory is resumed until its next interruption.

Langland's unorthodox form and genre—if form and genre they
be—produce a final structural quality I want to mention: that is a peculiarity in his sense of locus or space. For while the poem goes ahead by
seemingly ordinary chronology—in seven successive visions, with
wakings in between, and with liberal use of the formula "and then,"—
the location of its characters and actions and their spatial relations are
continuously shifting.[17]

Of course we do not ask for a realistic landscape from dream-vision;
nor do the materials of allegory—the moral and psychological entities—
have natural spatial relations. Yet partly because of the logical and temporal relations among these moral and psychological entities, partly
because of the device of personification, and partly because narrative
itself connotes space as well as time, medieval visions and allegories do
generate a considerable geometry and often an elaborate geography. The
allegory as pilgrimage—the genre to which *Piers Plowman* is closest—
involves a strong sense of location and space, and this is often turned
to advantage in the allegory itself. It makes things clearer. In the *Pèlerinage de Vie Humaine,* a fourteenth-century French work of the genre,
the geography is governed by the relations of the concepts dealt with.

The Dreamer-pilgrim comes to a fork in the road; on the left is Laziness, on the right Work, and his body counsels him to take the path of Laziness, which he does. His well-wishers, Grace and Reason, tell him to leave this road and come to the other through the hedge planted by Penitence. As he is trying to find a way through the hedge, he is attacked by sins—and so forth.[18] Not a very subtle or complicated matter, no doubt, but at least this pilgrim's progress has a locus and direction.

Langland's space is surrealistic. His opening places the fair field full of folk, with clear allegorical meaning, between tower and dungeon, Heaven and Hell. And there may be a kind of allegorical logic in that no spatial relation, but only confusion, a heaping and piling of images, follows in his picture of man's activities in this wilderness earth. But artistic logic fades as one scene reels and melts into the next, as characters—sometimes whole troops of them—appear and disappear or are forgotten. Dante, at every turn of the road, can suddenly expose us to a shift of perspective, a change of scale, without this surrealist feeling. In Canto IV of the *Inferno,* in the midst of darkness, we reach all of a sudden a seven-walled castle, and within it a green field in a place "open, luminous, and high" (v. 116), where the heroes of antiquity are visible. But then we turn back with the narrator and guide to "the part where there is nothing that shines" (151)—that is, back to the spatial and locational frame that organizes the whole. In *Piers Plowman* there is no going back. The fair field and the mountain are transformed without notice into a great encampment—with ten thousand tents for all the onlookers at the marriage of Meed. We are suddenly present at the dickering over the marriage articles. Thence we go—by what road I know not—to Westminster, before the King. In the next vision we have successively Conscience preaching to the people in the field and the confessions of the Seven Deadly Sins mentioned before; then in an unspecified locus, a thousand men throng together to seek St. Truth (Passus A V, 260); they walk or ride in many lands, bustling forth as beasts over valleys and hills. After a long journey they meet a pilgrim who says he has never heard of St. Truth. At that instant "Peter!" says a plowman, "I know him" (BV, 544), and from nowhere Piers Plowman materializes into the poem. He describes to them the road, by way of meekness and conscience and the ten commandments, to where truth resides in the human heart. The next spatial reference finds them all plowing Piers' half-acre. . . . And so the poem goes, existing in no one realm of space and location, invoking successive spatial images for limited and temporary effect without tending to the relations between them.

We can trace analogies of Langland's problematical structures, his unstable allegory and his emblematic realism, his surrealistic space, in other characteristics of his art. There is surely something of the same quality in his handling of the crucial but mysterious figure of Piers Plowman himself, who has been called the "supreme example of the poem's suggestive indefiniteness"[19]—with his various identities and sudden appearances and disappearances. There is something at once strange, difficult, and characteristic in a great many of Langland's transitions: abrupt, startling, sometimes so enigmatic that the sets of material that find themselves juxtaposed seem held together only by the force of the poet's personality. Bloomfield remarks that following some of the sequences of Langland's arguments and quotations "is like reading a commentary on an unknown text."[20] Yet another set of symptoms of the same basic character are those moments in the poem where, as a recent translator good-naturedly puts it, "it is not . . . clear who is speaking, whether the poet himself, the Dreamer, or one of the characters in the dream."[21]

In either explaining or at least sensing and responding to these problematic qualities of the poem, modern criticism has tended at times to turn away from the conventions and traditions of medieval thought and literature and to seek some solution in the peculiar condition of the poet himself. But one important appeal to tradition must still be noted: the poem's relation to the sermon. To put it briefly, and omitting all the well-known resemblances between the sermon and other genres we have mentioned, we are told that medieval sermon technique justified digression; digression was one of the best known procedures of rhetoric, and it is validated further by a religious purpose. If an opportunity for edification occurs, turning aside from the argument is morally justified; the spiritual purpose has precedence over the artistic. In this manner may be explained all manner of repetitions, sudden transitions, circuitous routings of thought, and apparently otiose amplifications, which we might otherwise attribute to carelessness or lack of art.[22]

Finding connections between *Piers Plowman* and sermon tradition is entirely justified—one could not imagine Langland in a world without sermons—but the connections apply better as to subject and to incidental traits of style than as to genre. The poem is manifestly not a sermon itself, and its depth and variety of "digressiveness" can hardly be matched in any known sermon. It is rather in its appeal to the question of "spiritual" purpose over "artistic" purpose that the argument from sermon-style has its force. And here I paraphrase from recent criticism of the poem: Sermon technique is utilitarian technique, the technique of the man who cares more for the spiritual significance of his words than for their art, less for narrative causality than for a higher order of truth; and we cannot doubt that Langland is such a man. Langland manifests some uncomfortableness at being a poet and writes in a very plain style for the alliterative tradition. The poem may not even be meant as art; for poetry in those days was a convenience, used for many utilitarian purposes as well. Thus Langland is interested as much in the spiritual background as in the narratives he commences, and a great deal of his background is at any rate not irrelevant to the story to which he periodically returns. His is an art of local tactics rather than of grand strategy; his coherence is thematic rather than narrative. A reformer and satirist, his mode is digressive and disintegrative, but his norms, at least, are consistent. End of paraphrase.[23]

A bolder development of this solution is also inherent in the poem's criticism. Here again I paraphrase: Writing the poem was a process of learning by the poet himself, thus the poem must always be in the process of revision and must always be unfinished. The perplexities of the poem are the exploratory perplexities of the poet's own mind, and they become those of the audience as well: it is the kaleidoscopic, problematical record of the search for Truth which Langland pursued all during his lifetime that *is* the poem. The poem is a record of cross-purposes, of repeated failures of inquiry, of the sometimes maddening slowness of the quest. We as readers are exposed to the same experience, undergo the same pains, enjoy the same exhilaration. End of paraphrase.[24]

This is an affecting argument, and there is much truth in it. It begins to explain how a work so bereft of the traditional apparatus of unity and coherence can have commanded so much attention and respect for so long. Though most of the critics I have paraphrased would still insist on the conscious art of the poem, the drift of the argument, as I have intimated, is to see the work not as art, but as a special sort of record of experience. It tends to see the audience as reliving that experience rather than as responding to art. By implication the author himself becomes the unifying feature of the work. The poem records the thoughts and feelings of a quite extraordinary man, passionate, moral, tender, humorous, dogged, and above all sincere. (The theories of a fictional Dreamer as unifying the poem simply melt in the felt heat of the poet's personality.) It is *his* earnestness and *his* plight that command our sympathy and retain our attention, even over the most difficult stretches of the work. *Piers Plowman* in this reading becomes, rather than a self-contained consciously wrought work of art, an intensely moving record of a man who wrote a lot of poetry in the midst of a prolonged spiritual struggle.

Whether we regard the problematic qualities of the poem's structure as arising from artistic failure, or from an artistic plan which we still only imperfectly understand, or as not properly belonging to art at all would seem to be partly, at least, a matter of attitude. For the critics agree remarkably on the describable qualities of the poem's structure, and in large part its artistic effect is independent of whether we think of it as proceeding from "art" or not. But as much as we should hesitate to find "defects" in a great monument of culture when the fault is likely to be in our own perception, it is difficult to stop looking at *Piers Plowman* as art. In the first place, to refuse to recognize what may be an artistic breakdown would be to refuse to listen to something fundamental about the artist and his epoch that the work is telling us. In the second place, quite simply, the poet was incontestably an artist. Even though that fact may not have dominated his intentions, his work raises the issue. The question of artistic structure is raised by great fragments of structural material disposed throughout the poem; the question of literary genre, by the unmistakable beginnings in it of half a dozen literary genres; the question of narrative art, by such famously successful episodes as the field full of folk (Prologue), the debate with the Doctor (Passus XIII), and the harrowing of Hell (Passus XVIII).

The issue is raised yet again, and settled, I think, when we consider the poem's poetic texture.[25] Here I shall review some of its most obvious stylistic traits in order to show that we are dealing with a poet of great power, whose local style is of a piece with the structure of his poem.

The poet has an enormous range of tone—as great as Chaucer's. One extreme of it derives from his rich, easy capacity to render the familiar and concrete. I have already quoted one of the famous passages in which he creates a grotesque ugliness for satiric effect. He can use a version of this familiar style with penetrating sympathy as well:

The most needy aren oure neighebores, and we nyme good hede,
As prisones in puttes and poure folke in cotes,
Charged with children and chef lordes rente;

That thei with spynnynge may spare, spenen hit in hous-hyre.
Bothe in mylk and in mele to make with papelotes,
To a-glotye with here gurles that greden after fode.
Al-so hem-selue suffren muche hunger,
And wo in winter-tyme with wakynge a nyghtes
To ryse to the ruel to rocke the cradel,
Bothe to karde and to kembe, to clouten and to wasche,
To rubbe and to rely, russhes to pilie,
That reuthe is to rede othere in ryme shewe
The wo of these women that wonyeth in cotes. . . .

(C X 71–83)

[The neediest people are our neighbors, if we pay some attention, like the prisoners in dungeons and poor folk in shacks, burdened with children and landlords' rent. Whatever they can save by spinning they spend for rent, and for milk and meal to make porridge to fill up their children who cry for food. They themselves endure much hunger, and pain in winter; they have to get up to rock the cradle alongside the wall, to card and comb wool, to mend and wash, to rub, and wind yarn, and peel rushes—it is pitiful to read or tell in verse of the misery of these women who live in shanties.]

The other extreme limit of his tone is supported by perhaps his most notable gift as a poet: his capacity to express the most elevated of religious feelings in the simplest terms. He is one of the few medieval poets besides Dante to have felt his way successfully back to the "incarnational" style, the *sermo humilis* that reaches sublimity of feeling without elaborate dependence on the "high style" of rhetorical tradition.[26]

"And sith with thi self sone in owre sute deydest
On godefryday for mannes sake at ful tyme of the daye,
There thi-self ne thi sone no sorwe in deth feledest;
But in owre secte was the sorwe and thi sone it ladde,
  Captiuam duxit captiuitatem.
The sonne for sorwe ther-of les syʒte for a tyme
Aboute mydday whan most liʒte is and mele tyme of seintes;
Feddest with thi fresche blode owre forfadres in derknesse,
  Populus qui ambulabat in tenebris, vidit lucem magnam;
And thorw the liʒte that lepe oute of the Lucifer was blent,

And blewe alle thi blissed in-to the blisse of paradise."

(B V 495–503)

["And then, (God), with your own son clothed in our flesh you died on Good Friday for man's sake at high noon, and neither you nor your son felt the least pain in death. Rather the pain was in our flesh, and your son led it captive: "he led captivity captive." The sun (son) out of sorrow became blinded for a while, about midday, when there is the most light and it is the mealtime of saints; then you fed with your fresh blood our forefathers who were in darkness: "The people who walked in darkness have seen a great light." And through the light that leaped out of you Lucifer was blinded, and you blew all your blessed into the bliss of Paradise."]

The sequence describing the harrowing of Hell couples this sublime simplicity with flashes of the poet's dramatic powers:

Efte the liȝte bad vnlouke and Lucifer answered,
"What lorde artow?" quod Lucifer "*quis es iste?*"
"*Rex glorie*" the liȝte sone seide,
"And lorde of myȝte and of mayne and al manere vertues;
  dominus virtutum;
Dukes of this dym place anon undo this ȝates,
That Cryst may come in, the kinges sone of heuene."

(B XVIII 313–318)

[Again the light commanded them to unlock, and Lucifer answered, "What lord are you?" "Who is this man?" said Lucifer. "The King of Glory," the light at once replied, "and lord of might and power and of every goodness; 'The lord of virtues.' Dukes of this dark place, unlock the gates at once, that Christ may come in, the son of the King of Heaven."]

Christ's speech to Lucifer is perhaps the poetic highpoint of the poem:

"For I, that am lorde of lyf, loue is my drynke,
And for that drynke to-day I deyde vpon erthe.
I fauȝte so, me threstes ȝet for mannes soule sake;
May no drynke me moiste ne my thruste slake,
Tyl the vendage falle in the vale of Iosephath,

128

That I drynke riʒte ripe must *resureccio mortuorum,*
And thanne shal I come as a kynge crouned with angeles,
And han out of helle alle mennes soules."

(B XVIII 363–370)

["For I, the Lord of Life, drink only love, and for that drink today I died
on earth. I fought so, that I am thirsty yet for man's soul's sake. No drink
can refresh me nor slake my thirst till vintage-time comes in the valley
of Jehoshaphat, and I drink the fresh new wine of the resurrection of the
dead. Then shall I come as a King, crowned with angels, and fetch out
of hell all men's souls."]

The poet's work is marked by another rare quality, his gift for the
arresting image, that supports effects ranging from incongruity and surprise to the profoundest metaphorical illumination of the subject. I can
quote only a few of the examples familiar to every reader. Langland
congenitally disliked lawyers:

Thow myʒtest better mete the myste on Maluerne hulles,
Than gete a momme of here mouthe but money were shewed.

(B Prol. 214–215)

[You could sooner measure the mist on the Malvern Hills than get a
word out of their mouths before showing your money.]

and timeservers:

. . . ful proude-herted men pacient of tonge,
And boxome as of berynge to burgeys and to lordes,
And to pore peple han peper in the nose. . . .

[B XV 195–197)

[. . . very proud men who are humble in speech, submissive in their conduct toward important citizens and noblemen, but to the poor (as snob-
bish) as if they had pepper in their noses.]

and the rich:

Clerkes and kniʒtes welcometh kynges ministrales,
And for loue of the lorde litheth hem at festes;

Muche more, me thenketh, riche men schulde
Haue beggeres byfore hem, the whiche ben goddes ministrales,
. . .
For-thi I rede ʒow riche, reueles whan ʒe maketh,
For to solace ʒoure soules suche ministrales to haue;
The pore, for a fol sage syttynge at the heyʒ table,
And a lered man, to lere the what oure lorde suffred,
For to saue thi soule fram Sathan thin enemy,
And fithel the, with-out flaterynge, of gode Friday the storye. . . .

(B XIII 437–440, 442–447)

[Clerks and knights welcome the king's minstrels, and out of respect for their master they listen to them at feasts. There is more reason, I think, for rich men to have at table beggars, who are God's minstrels. . . . So I advise you rich men to have minstrels like these to care for your souls when you make your revels—the poor rather than a wise fool sitting at the high table, and a learned man to teach you what our lord suffered to save your soul from Satan, your enemy, and to fiddle you without flattery the story of Good Friday.]

Defective clerics brought out some of his most striking imagery:

Thus thei dryuele at her deyse the deite to knowe,
And gnawen god with the gorge when her gutte is fulle.

(B X 56–57)

[Thus they drivel at the high table as if they knew the Deity, and when their guts are full find God in their gullets.]

"I shal Iangle to this Iurdan with his Iust wombe. . . ."[27]

(B XIII 83)

["I shall dispute with this pot-bellied jordan. . . ."]

I rede eche a blynde bosarde do bote to hym-selue. . . .

(B X 266)

[I advise each of these blind buzzards to look after himself. . . .]

In passages dealing with ordinary matters of faith and doctrine, the

130

apparent ingenuousness of the imagery is sometimes highly arresting. Thus God "may do with the day-sterre what hym deore lyketh" (A VI 83), "Adam and Eue eten apples vnrosted" (B V 612), and Soul is described as "a sotyl thinge with-al, one with-outen tonge and teeth" (B XV 12–13). Regarding the salvation of the poor,

> . . . none sonner saued ne sadder of bileue,
> Than plowmen and pastoures and pore comune laboreres,
> Souteris and shepherdes; suche lewide Iottis
> Percen with a *pater-noster* the paleis of heuene. . . .
>
> (B X 458–461)

[. . . none are more likely to be saved nor steadier in their faith than plowmen and herdsmen and poor common laborers, cobblers and shepherds; such ignorant nobodies can pierce the palace of heaven with the Lord's Prayer . . .]

On wasting words, the poet writes:

> Lesynge of tyme, treuthe wote the sothe!
> Is moste yhated vp erthe of hem that beth in heuene,
> And sitthe to spille speche, that spyre is of grace,
> And goddes gleman and a game of heuene;
> Wolde neuere the faithful fader his fithel were vntempred,
> Ne his gleman a gedelynge, a goer to tauernes!
>
> (B IX 98–103)

[Wasting of time, God knows, is the thing on earth most hated by those in heaven, and next is wasting of speech, that is the sprout of grace and God's minstrel and a pastime of heaven; the faithful Father never meant his fiddle to be untuned, nor his minstrel to be a scoundrel, a goer to taverns!]

The indispensable nature of charity brings out two memorable similes in half a dozen lines:

> For thouȝ ȝe be trewe of ȝowre tonge and trewliche wynne,
> And as chaste as a childe that in cherche wepeth,
> But if ȝe louen lelliche and lene the poure,
> Such good as god ȝow sent godelich parteth,

Ʒe ne haue na more meryte in masse ne in houres
Than Malkyn of hire maydenhode that no man desireth.

(B I 177–182)

[For though you be true of tongue, and earn your living honestly, and be
as innocent as a child that weeps in church, unless you are sincerely
charitable, and give to the poor, properly sharing the goods that God has
sent you, you will get no more credit from attending masses and services
than Molly from her maidenhead that nobody wants.]

The Trinity of course evoked the poet's powers of analogy. During a
complex comparison between the Trinity and a torch, he takes up the
gift of the Holy Ghost:

And as glowande gledes gladieth nouƷte this werkmen,
That worchen and waken in wyntres niƷtes,
As doth a kex or a candel that cauƷte hath fyre and blaseth,
Namore doth sire ne sone ne seynt spirit togyderes,
Graunteth no grace ne forƷifnesse of synnes,
Til the holi goste gynne to glowe and to blase.

(B XVII 217–222)

[And just as glowing coals do not cheer those workmen who stay up and
work on winter nights as much as does a torch or a candle that has been
lit and burns with a flame, so neither the Father, nor the Son, nor the
Holy Spirit together will grant anyone grace or forgiveness of sins until
the Holy Ghost begins to burn and to blaze.]

The most striking imagery in the poem comes perhaps in Passus I, in
reference to the Incarnation:

For trewthe telleth that loue is triacle of heuene;
May no synne be on him sene that vseth that spise,
And alle his werkes he wrouƷte with loue as him liste;
. . .
For heuen myƷte nouƷte holden it, it was so heuy of hym-self,
Tyl it hadde of the erthe yeten his fylle;
And whan it haued of this folde flesshe and blode taken,
Was neuere leef vpon lynde liƷter ther-after,
And portatyf and persant as the poynt of a nedle,

132

That my3te non armure it lette ne none hei3 walles.

(B I 146–148, 151–156)

[For it is God's truth that love is the sovereign medicine of heaven; there is not a sin to be seen on him who uses that kind. And God made all his works with love, as it pleased him; . . . For heaven could not hold it, it was so heavy in itself, until it had eaten its fill of this earth. And after it had taken on flesh and blood of this world, there was never a leaf on a linden tree more light; it was as delicate and piercing as the point of a needle. No armor or high walls could keep it out.]

There is another dominant trait of his style that is related to the surprise effect of his imagery: the line or half line that suddenly turns the mood or thought around, often with a satiric snap:

Pilgrymes and palmers pli3ted hem togidere
To seke seynt Iames and seyntes in Rome.
Thei went forth in here wey with many wise tales,
And hadden leue to lye al here lyf after.

(B Prol. 46–49)

[Pilgrims and palmers joined together to visit the shrines of St. James in Compostela and of the saints in Rome. They made their way there with a lot of smart talk and felt free to tell lies about it for the rest of their lives.]

Persones and parisch prestes pleyned hem to the bischop,
That here parisshes were pore sith the pestilence tyme,
To haue a lycence and a leue at London to dwelle,
And syngen there for symonye, for siluer is swete.

(B Prol. 83–86)

[Parsons and parish priests complained to the bishop that their parishes had been poverty-stricken since the time of the plague—just to get permission to live in London and sing masses there for profit, for silver is sweet.]

And that is the professioun appertly that appendeth for kny3tes,
And nou3t to fasten a Fryday in fyue score wynter. . . .

(B I 98–99)

[And that is obviously the proper activity for knights, and not to fast one
Friday in a hundred winters. . . .]

Langland has no inhibitions about colloquial language. Here Learning
describes a Chaucerian monk:

A priker on a palfray fro manere to manere,
An heep of houndes at his ers as he a lorde were.

(B X 308–309)

[A galloper on horseback from manor to manor, with a bunch of dogs at
his ass as if he were a lord.]

Learning's cousin, Lady Study, feels strongly about intellectual pretentiousness:

Wilneth neuere to wite whi that god wolde
Suffre Sathan his sede to bigyle,
Ac bileue lelly in the lore of holicherche,
And preye hym of pardoun and penaunce in thi lyue,
And for his moche mercye to amende ȝow here.
For alle that wilneth to wyte the weyes of god almiȝty,
I wolde his eye were in his ers and his fynger after. . . .

(B X 117–123)

[Never try to find out why God would let Satan deceive his children, but
believe faithfully in the teaching of Holy Church, and pray God for pardon, and to let you do penance while you are alive, and out of his great
mercy to correct you on earth. As for anyone who wants to pry into the
ways of God almighty, I wish his eye were up his ass and his finger after
it. . . .]

Langland's poetic rhythms would be at best difficult to deal with,
and in small compass I cannot attempt it. But I must advert in passing
to a rhythmical trait that seems to be characteristic of his work both in
large and small: its continual susceptibility to irruptions—whether in
the poetic line or in the narrative. Some of the poetic texture—the
metaphorical or referential surprise described above—contributes to
this rhythm. In addition the reader soon learns to recognize as part of

Langland's style the sharp transitions between scenes and the sudden appearances of characters, sometimes with interjectional force:

"Peter!" quod a plowman and put forth his hed. . . .

(B V 544)

"3ee! baw for bokes!" quod one was broken out of helle,
Hi3te *Troianus*. . . .

(B XI 135–136)

["Yeah! Bah for books!" said a man named Trajan, just broken out of hell. . . .]

"3e, bawe!" quod a brewere, "I will nou3t be reuled. . . ."

(B XIX 394)

Rhythmically of a piece are the occasional dramatic irruptions of "pure tene," sheer anger. Those of Piers the Plowman himself seem to set an exemplary tone of divine impatience for the poem as a whole:

"Now, bi the peril of my soule!" quod Pieres al in pure tene. . . .

(B VI 119)

And Pieres for pure tene pulled it atweyne. . . .

(B VII 116)

(thus suddenly setting off the most difficult of the poem's puzzles);

And Pieres for pure tene that o pile he lau3te,
And hitte after hym, happe how it my3te. . . .

(B XVI 86–87)

[And Piers in sheer anger seized one of the staffs and swung at him, whatever might happen. . . .]

There are yet other sources of periodic and often unpredicted interruptions of the poem's rhythms: the shifts of focus from individual to scene, well described by John Lawlor; the frequent changes of the narrative's apparent pace—what Rosemary Woolf has termed "an alternate dawdling and darting movement;"[28] the actual suspensions of the narrative with direct address by the narrator to the audience; and doubtless others yet to be identified. While the poem contains many comfortingly repeated motifs,[29] and great stretches of relatively stable didactic utterance—enough for Morton Bloomfield to have found in its tone and diction a source of what "stability" it has[30]—we still come away from it with something of the feeling that in it anything might have happened.

The artistic character of *Piers Plowman,* when it is viewed as a whole as we are attempting to view it now, has a strange integrity and coherence. Many of the formal and stylistic traits we have observed can be found in other respectable medieval poems. I venture to say that no other work of the Middle Ages has them all. Together they are quite distinctive, but they are also peculiarly harmonious. Even the poem's seemingly most disparate traits have a common basis. It is not only that "there is a consistency in the very lack of consistency," as Talbot Donaldson has remarked of the art of the C-reviser;[31] the poet does not seem to have been aware of inconsistency as a problem. Thus the ease with which the poem can at one moment evoke simultaneously the realistic and the sublime seems to issue from the same mentality, the same sensibility, that produces the violent transitions and the equivalences that seem startling. It is as if the poet felt none of his disjunctures as such because to him the concrete and the abstract, the actual and the moral had themselves taken on a special sort of equivalence. I say a special sort, because the capacity to see the spiritual in the concrete and to aver the reality of the spiritual and moral realms were hallmarks of medieval mentality in general. In *Piers,* however, they are not only equivalent, but mingled; the borders and distinctions have melted or collapsed.[32] This, as it seems to me, is the import of the artistic character of the poem. The obscurity of the larger plan, the seemingly capricious interplay of debate, pilgrimage, and quest, and of mimetics and didacticism; the periodic establishment and collapse of the dream-frame; the shiftiness of space; the paradox of graphic power and pictorial diffuseness;[33] the alternations within a great range of tone and temper; the shiftiness of rhythm—all these produce a curiously homogeneous artistic effect that for lack of a better term I have called surrealistic.

The art of *Piers Plowman* is assuredly the creation of a quite remarkable personality, but it is also a response to a cultural situation. Viewed in this way, the form and style of the poem seem to be saying something more than do its overt arguments. In the sequence of his arguments, Langland seems to me finally to lead us, on some level, toward the

Truth he sought. The uncontroverted advice of Holy Church, the consistent recommendation of natural wisdom, and the triumphant vision of the Passion and the harrowing of Hell are the most obvious controlling points of the poem's motion; and there is an aura of a new understanding, if not a final resolution, in the closing scenes which, drawn from life in fourteenth-century England, suggestively parallel the opening scenes of the poem. But nevertheless, the more that criticism reveals the manifold, intricate filiations between the thought of the poem and orthodox medieval doctrine, and the closer we are brought to sensing the intended directions of its argument,[34] the more the form and style of the poem seem to envelop it in a sort of pathos. For if the thought of the poem is orthodox, Christian, and hopeful, its art suggests instability: the imminent collapse of orthodoxy and failure of hope. The great artistic schemes that Langland attempts and abandons had all been adapted before him to expressing the security of the medieval Christian vision. His failure with them, his failure to organize and "see" by means of them, suggests that for a man of his sensitivity, responding to the culture around him, those schemes had lost their meaning. For him, the road to the New Jerusalem has become newly devious, the structure of the moral world newly problematical. His passionate criticisms, his earnest exhortations, seem all the more urgent for issuing from within this strange, surrealistic structure. The range and texture of his style have the same ring: urgent, sincere, and somehow pathetic, as if marshalled desperately against some unavoidable crisis. The poem has been well called "the epic of the dying Middle Ages,"[35] but it carries the instability of the epoch in its very structure and style as well as in its argument.

If we are to see a cultural significance in the art of *Piers Plowman,* we should be able to compare it with the art of some of his contemporaries. It would be particularly comforting to find, for instance, a well-developed tradition of "surrealism" in late medieval England. Unfortunately, the analogies to Langland's art that I have so far been able to trace are rather far afield. There is assuredly something surrealistic in late-medieval pictorial art; we see it everywhere in the margins of manuscripts, and I am not the first whom Langland's style has reminded of that of Hieronymus Bosch.[36] Closer to Langland in time is a group of Tuscan painters in the generation after the Black Death, in an atmosphere of guilt and fear, whose style can be described in terms that are like those I have used to describe *Piers Plowman.* They turn from the current of realism stemming from Giotto, to a style more rigid, formalistic, pious, and mystical. They reject perspective and are full of paradox, particularly in the sense of space. A St. Matthew by Orcagna is described by the art historian Millard Meiss as exhibiting a tension incapable of resolution, "Arising as it does from an interpenetration of the natural and unnatural, the physical and the abstract." Meiss suggests that this quality of the painting reflects a polarization in the society between strenuous religiosity on the one hand and moral and religious dissidence on the other.[37]

Though Langland is also a post-Plague artist—he continually insists on the moral import of pestilence—important parallels to the corresponding quality of his style are not obvious in England, whether in painting or in literature. The strongest resemblance is to be found in Chaucer's *House of Fame,* but that work is by far Chaucer's most puzzling one. Even the complex, ironic structuring of so variegated a satire as the *Nun's Priest's Tale* produces a sense of assurance and security quite foreign to *Piers Plowman.*

If we lack satisfying contemporary analogues to the art of *Piers Plowman,* we can still learn something by contrast. *Pearl* and *Sir Gawain* are also searches for salvation and for perfection, and are also conducted by a man who was at once a moralist and artist. The distance between them is instructive. It is almost the extreme range in form and style that contemporaneous works of art, in the same stream of history, could be imagined to produce. On the one hand an almost obsessive unity, an overpowering devotion to artifice, as if the work of art were in itself an assertion of the truths it was testing, and the creation of the work, not a denial of crisis, but at most expressing it obliquely and at a remove. On the other hand, a direct facing, an immersion in the problematic character of the times, to the point where the poem with the poet, having together been submitted to the crisis itself, seem to have become in part its victims.

CHAUCER: IRONY AND ITS ALTERNATIVES

It is perhaps no coincidence that Langland's *Piers Plowman* reached its full scope in the same decade as Chaucer's *House of Fame.* The *House of Fame* is Chaucer's most flamboyant and puzzling work, also an unconventional dream-allegory, capricious, varied to extremes, shifting in tone and structure, strung out between serious formality and comic realism. If these works show both poets confronting the same cultural situation with a similar variety of formal and stylistic resources, Chaucer's later career shows that he came to a different and more peaceful conclusion. In the *Canterbury Tales* he uses the pilgrimage form to enclose and control a wide range of experience. The variety of texture in the *Tales* and in the *Troilus*—a matter of exquisitely adjusted and contrasting patches of value—is a source of irony, a controlled irony. And in our perspective, at least, it is irony, comic or grave, that is Chaucer's characteristic response to the fourteenth-century dilemma.[1] His irony, if it does not resolve the contradictions and disparities of late-medieval life, embraces, displays, enjoys, and makes capital of them. The great virtues that Chaucer teaches are perception and tolerance. The disparity between what men might be and what they are fascinated the *Pearl* poet as well, and also produced a certain irony in his works. But he is not nearly so tolerant or liberal as Chaucer, for whom ironic appreciation of what life has to offer is almost a norm. Langland, too, is a respectable ironist, but even less ultimately one. Langland is equipped with a sense of the facts of life equal to Chaucer's, but with a moral idealism so urgent and so powerful that it continually threatens to yank irony, or any other complex or tentative view, out of the question.

Chaucer's irony must impress us with its depth and congeniality. It is not only a literary and structural device, but a personal propensity. There is in Chaucer's basic habits of discourse already a mixture of relaxation and intensity, naturalness and artifice, familiarity and distance, colloquialism and learned sophistication—a mixture ready at any moment to explode with ironic effect. His development as a poet may be viewed, in fact, as a progressive discovery and exploitation of this propensity.[2]

It would be safe, therefore, to imagine that the mature Chaucer, the Chaucer of *Canterbury Tales* Fragment A (the *General Prologue,* the Knight's, Miller's, Reeve's and Cook's tales) for instance, actually came to feel this as his very own mode, if not consciously, then by instinct and experience. For the scheme of the *Canterbury Tales* could not be improved upon, with its built-in sequence of tales, not only to create a structural irony in the juxtaposition of the tales to be written, but, once it had accommodated some of the older things already in Chaucer's desk, to confer on those, too, an ironic character with which they had not originally been invested. The structure of the *Tales,* then, actually masks the observation, readily apparent in the *House of Fame,* that Chaucer was not always an ironist, was sometimes not at all in that mood, and may for a long time not even have felt irony to be his "solution."

The Chaucer of the *Retractation,* perhaps facing his death, undoubtedly felt himself to be, if not first then last, a Christian, and there is an unwaveringly orthodox profession of faith in other of Chaucer's endings—as of his *Troilus* and his *Nun's Priest's Tale.* The logic of his ironic structure, pushed toward a consideration of ends, ultimate realities, provided in fact a justification of orthodox faith. Serious irony can be made finally to expose the instability of this brittle world and by implication to turn our attention to a stable world of faith in God. Chaucer was always a Christian, then, and that solution for Chaucer lay beyond irony. The faith of the *Retractation,* of the *Troilus* Epilogue, of even the *Nun's Priest's Tale,* is a grand and final thing, and it is validated by the rich experience that has gone into the ironic vision even as the latter is finally transcended. This, then, I should call not so much a working alternative to irony as a final consequence of it.

I am laboring here to mark out this source, this location, this kind of religiosity for a number of reasons. First, to anticipate the reader's natural objections to my suggesting that irony was close to being Chaucer's ultimate position. Second, to make clear that I do not read any of Chaucer's secular works as covert religious allegories. Third, to distinguish this solemn, ultimate religiosity—perhaps we might call it eschatological faith—from a different current of religious feeling in Chaucer's works: that is, the religiosity around which are clustered feelings of tenderness and pathos, and which is often associated with motherhood, little children, and the cult of the Virgin Mary. If we take Chaucer's *ABC* to be an early work, as it may well be, we can see that this current of religious feeling must have been for quite a long time for Chaucer a major alternative to irony. The character and implications of this whole vein in Chaucer's work will occupy a good deal of our attention in this chapter. But before we turn to them, we must first make a survey of some other of Chaucer's alternatives.

Even had we no *House of Fame,* a line drawn from the *Book of the Duchess* through the *Parliament of Fowls* would have shown the growth of Chaucer's famous comic realism. Chaucer was capable of solemnity, but even on the solemn occasion of elegizing the Duchess of Lancaster we sense a certain restiveness in him. He cannot quite abide the idea of elegy pure and simple, and out comes the characterization of the narrator with its unmistakably Chaucerian touches of humor and naive realism. There is no victim of irony but the narrator himself, and he remains subordinate, serving only to heighten, not to complicate or qualify, the elegiac feeling; but he is there. In the *Parliament of Fowls* the lesser fowls take up the style of his strain of realism and connect it with a set of attitudes, a position. But by now the position is already safely embraced in a larger plan, and we recognize in the *Parliament*'s ironic balance between realism and idealism in love a perfect foretaste of Chaucer's classic stance.

The dramatic realism in the *House of Fame,* by which I mean Chaucer's characterization of the loquacious and pedantic Eagle, is not similarly held firm in an ironic balance with something else. It floats almost free, almost an end in itself. With its technical brilliance, which conveys a palpable joy in the characterization, it suggests strongly that at one moment Chaucer might have given himself up to the dramatic-realistic mode and finally to the implications of attitude that would inevitably follow from it. Indeed, a couple of times he may have come close. Pandarus, by the Third Book of the *Troilus,* has grown alarmingly vivid, alarmingly sympathetic, alarmingly real. Many a reader, I am sure, has already noticed the amount of Chaucer in him— Chaucer the court official and man of affairs, intimate of nobility, skillful, reliable, well-read, tactful agent and messenger, who knows the "olde daunce" (his sister-in-law, after all, is mistress of the greatest Duke of the realm). But no—Chaucer is also an idealist and moralist, and Pandarus is finally held firm in the larger perspective created by Troilus and by the poem's denouement.

Barely held firm, but held firm nevertheless, is also the Wife of Bath. We do not come away from a reading of her *Prologue* converted sensualists; that is proof enough of Chaucer's firm grip. But I am not certain I understand how he does it. It is not simply by impregnating the *Prologue* with ill-veiled examples of her gross misunderstanding of Scripture.[3] No one would expect her to have a theologian's understanding of Scripture. She wins the contests described in her *Prologue;* for the moment, at least, wins Chaucer; wins us (or many of us); wins the contest offered by the Clerk—that skinny scholar could never turn the world from sin; and if you look not far about you, now that love is no longer sin, you will see that she has won the contest with history. Yet Chaucer finally holds her in perspective; not solely with any a priori moral doctrine, nor with any single counterbalancing character or tale, but perhaps with the cumulative wisdom of all of them. "I have had my world as in my tyme" is a compelling motto; but Chaucer feels, and makes us feel, ultimately, that it is not enough. If anything, it lacks irony.

There is yet another serious brush that Chaucer has with the implications of dramatic realism, serious not in extent, but in depth. I refer to the bottomless pool we may be looking into toward the end of the *Pardoner's Tale*. The Pardoner is, like Pandarus, something akin to Chaucer himself, in this case akin as rhetorician and storyteller. He is the most accomplished literary artist among Chaucer's characters. It is interesting to speculate whether there is any connection between the almost grotesque perversity of his description—he is the most "unnatural" of the Canterbury pilgrims—and some special baseness Chaucer may feel in the perversion of his talent. At the end of the tale there does seem to be an odd and special contact between Chaucer and his Pardoner. As a good many people read it, the Pardoner's demonstration sermon ends with a last blast of rhetorical fireworks, followed by a sales pitch to his imagined demonstration audience, followed by a brief explanatory address to his new friends the Canterbury pilgrims. This brief address, beginning "And lo, sires, thus I preche," has an exquisite human interest, for in it the practised and hardened confidence man for once puts by his cynicism—warmed perhaps by friendship and ale— and invokes, not his own pardon for his companions, but Christ's, "for that is best." Let me quote the passage:

"O cursed synne of alle cursednesse!
O traytours homycide, O wikkednesse!
O glotonye, luxurie, and hasardye!
Thou blasphemour of Crist with vileynye
And othes grete, of usage and of pride!
Allas! mankynde, how may it bitide
That to thy creatour, which that the wroghte,
And with his precious herte-blood thee boghte,
Thou art so fals and so unkynde, allas?
   Now, goode men, God foryeve yow youre trespas,
And ware yow fro the synne of avarice!
Myn hooly pardoun may yow alle warice,
So that ye offre nobles or sterlynges,
Or elles silver broches, spoones, rynges.
Boweth youre heed under this hooly bulle!
Cometh up, ye wyves, offreth of youre wolle!
Youre names I entre heer in my rolle anon;
Into the blisse of hevene shul ye gon.
I yow assoille, by myn heigh power,

Yow that wol offre, as clene and cck as cleer
As ye were born.—And lo, sires, thus I preche.
And Jhesu Crist, that is oure soules leche,
So graunte yow his pardoun to receyve,
For that is best; I wol yow nat deceyve."

(895–918)

Not one of the pilgrims responds. Rather, the Pardoner begins again, with a crude and cynical sales pitch addressed directly to them: "But, sires, o word forgat I in my tale. . . ."

At this point variant interpretations are possible. We need stage directions and there are none. Why does the Pardoner so abruptly change his tack? Is he serious, or patently joking? Reading the analogous passage in the *Roman de la Rose*—where the character Faus-Semblant admits to his hearers at the end of his confession that despite his present candor he would trick them if he could[4]—I am led to think that the Pardoner is meant to be serious. If he is, the sequence of candor, of honest piety, and then of redoubled cynicism in this reading is almost terrifying in its moral range. Harry Bailly thinks he is serious, and replies with obscene directness. But either way, the Canterbury pilgrims must be imagined to have been left thunderstruck by the sermon, as affected as any of the Pardoner's provincial audiences. It is a moment of extraordinary psychological complexity; and with Harry Bailly's response to the Pardoner we are for a moment absorbed in the interest of the Pardoner's personality. Chaucer's crucial leaving-out of the stage directions here makes everything depend on the sheer dramatics of the reading; it is a moment almost unique in his works. Behind it we glimpse, possibly, a man like the Pardoner possessed by pride in his own technique, but both he and the Pardoner pass from sight at the next moment. Chaucer may have flirted with, but was never captured by, an absorption with either human personality or artistic technique.

Turning to yet another of Chaucer's alternatives to irony, we can see clearly that French courtly idealism, with the rather fragile poetry it generated, could not become a major solution for Chaucer any more than could realism. Like realism it early and importantly enters into, and its ideals are qualified by, the ironic configuration. Yet for a considerable while Chaucer seems nevertheless to have felt the pull of an unqualified secular idealism. The composition and revision of the *Legend of Good Women* in the late 1380s and '90s, after the fully ironic position of the *Troilus* had been achieved, must be a symptom of a periodic resurgence of a mood of idealism that is otherwise registered in the *Anelida and Arcite,* the *Knight's Tale* and the *Franklin's Tale.* The *Anelida* and the *Knight's Tale,* along with some framing passages of the *Troilus,* show Chaucer furthermore experimenting with a heroic style. In this, Chaucer seems to be attempting to overcome a certain deficiency of expressiveness in the French courtly tradition while adhering to the chivalric and erotic ideals it represents. He is reaching back, as did in some sense every generation of English poets after him for centuries, reaching back to the heroic classics—in this case Virgil and Statius—and like some later generations, coming up not so much with the classics as with the Italians.

The epic-sublime style of Vergil was for a long time beyond the art of the Middle Ages except in such direct imitations as Joseph of Exeter's *De Bello Troiano.*[5] It is curious that the vernacular French courtly tradition represented by the *Book of the Duchess,* by Deschamps, Machaut, Froissart as poet, Guillaume de Lorris, and even Chrétien de Troyes, almost totally lacks the epic and heroic note. Chaucer heard echoes of Anglo-Saxon epic style in some second- and third-rate English romances of his own times; and early French romance, in the decades when it is still not certain of itself, not certain whether it is romance or epic, has a martial note related to that of the *chanson de geste.* But as soon as the connection between chivalry and courtly love is firmly made, the iron goes out of medieval narrative style, no matter how many hand-to-hand combats remain. The recapturing of "classical" epic style in the vernacular before Milton is largely the work of the Italians of the Middle Ages and early Renaissance— from Dante and Boccaccio through Ariosto and Tasso—and to this labor Chaucer seems to have lent himself for perhaps a decade in the 1370s and '80s.

The role of the Italians in guiding Chaucer's stylistic experiment was long ago noted by Root:

> From Italy, and primarily I think from Dante, came the inspiration to tell the story of Troilus in the *bel stilo alto;* to write in the vernacular with the dignity and elevation which mark the great ancients. . . . Similar in character to his debt to Dante is Chaucer's debt to the *Teseide* of Boccaccio, a poem in its style as ornate and elevated as the *Filostrato* is simple and direct.[6]

The *Teseida,* full of reminiscences of the *Divine Comedy,* the *Aeneid,* and *Thebaid,* was in fact quite self-consciously designed to revive the epic style. Boccaccio announces in its final stanzas that virtue and love, two of the three great poetic subjects (defined by Dante in the *De Vulgari eloquentia*), have already been treated by vernacular poets "con bello stilo"; and he makes invocation to his own book, which will be first to sing of the third subject, arms:

ma tu, o libro, primo a lor cantare
di Marte fai gli affanni sostenuti,
nel volgar lazio più mai non veduti.[7]

[But you, my book, will be the first to sing to them of the painful labors undergone in war, hitherto unheard of in the vulgar tongue.]

As Root suggests, Chaucer clearly felt the pull of the classical-sublime in Dante's style; and as a close reader of the *Teseida* he was surely aware of Boccaccio's stylistic program as well. But if the *House of Fame* is any indication (and if we have the sequence of his works here correctly), Chaucer's earliest contact with the Italians did not at once suggest that they could teach him how to do epic style in the vernacular. As with almost all the other sources or inspirations behind the *House of Fame,* Chaucer here seems stimulated by the Italians without being directed by them. The long summary of the *Aeneid in House of Fame,* Book I, does not in the slightest suggest epic style. Chaucer rather, with the lion's share of the summary given to the Dido episode, falls back toward the French and Ovidian mode, the mode of pathetic female complaint, pointing along the axis of the *Legend of Good Women* and Dorigen at the seashore. Chaucer does make epic invocation to Cipris and the muses at the opening of Book II, in a passage mingling reminiscences of Dante and Boccaccio, but precedes it with a handful of verses so un-epic that the passage must be heard to be believed:

Now herkeneth, every maner man
That Englissh understonde kan,
And listeneth of my drem to lere.
For now at erste shul ye here
So sely an avisyon,
That Isaye, ne Scipion,
Ne kyng Nabugodonosor,

Pharoo, Turnus, ne Elcanor,
Ne mette such a drem as this!
Now faire blisfull, O Cipris,
So be my favour at this tyme!
And ye, me to endite and ryme
Helpeth, that on Parnaso duelle,
Be Elicon, the clere welle.
O Thought, that wrot al that I mette,
And in the tresorye hyt shette
Of my brayn, now shal men se
Yf any vertu in the be,
To tallen al my drem aryght.
Now kythe thyn engyn and myght!

(509–528)

Chaucer does connect the Italians and an epic style in the unfinished *Anelida and Arcite;* apparently he had both the *Teseida* and the *Thebaid* before him as he wrote the first seventy lines. The remainder of the poem, except for its complex metrical form, could well have been included in the *Legend of Good Women,* where it would have ranked among the less interesting pieces in that rather bland collection. But the opening of the *Anelida* is important and fascinating, being Chaucer's first sustained passage in the epic mode. It is full of his sense of its importance, with its multiple invocations, its citations of antiquity and authority, and then its beginning of the narrative in the highest of the high style. Every student of Chaucer's art should ponder the comparison between the quite respectable martial poetry of his description of Duke Theseus here with its later perfection in the *Knight's Tale.* I quote only a few lines of each; here *Anelida:*

Beforn this duk, in signë of victorie,
The trompes come, and in his baner large
The ymage of Mars; and, in token of glorie,
Men myghte sen of tresour many a charge,
Many a bright helm, and many a spere and targe,
Many a fresh knyght, and many a blysful route,
On hors, on fote, in al the feld aboute.

(29–35)

And here the *Knight's Tale:*

146

The rede statue of Mars, with spere and targe,
So shyneth in his white baner large,
That alle the feeldes glyteren up and doun;
And by his baner born is his penoun
Of gold ful riche, in which ther was ybete
The Mynotaur, which that he slough in Crete.
Thus rit this duc, thus rit this conquerour,
And in his hoost of chivalrie the flour. . . .

(975–982)

The epic mode in *Anelida,* from what we can tell, remains decoration; Chaucer does not yet suggest a reconnection of love and heroism.
But he is already using the mode as a kind of framing device, as he does
in the *Troilus* and the *Knight's Tale.* In the *Troilus* the passages of epic
style have a number of functions; one is to connect Troilus' valor in war
with his worthiness for love. Here is the heroic Troilus seen by
Criseyde:

This Troilus sat on his baye steede,
Al armed, save his hed, ful richely;
And wownded was his hors, and gan to blede,
On which he rood a pas ful softely.
But swich a knyghtly sighte, trewely,
As was on hym, was nought, withouten faille,
To loke on Mars, that god is of bataille.

So lik a man of armes and a knyght
He was to seen, fulfilled of heigh prowesse;
For bothe he hadde a body and a myght
To don that thing, as wel as hardynesse;
And ek to seen hym in his gere hym dresse,
So fressh, so yong, so weldy semed he,
It was an heven upon hym for to see.

His helm tohewen was in twenty places,
That by a tyssew heng his bak byhynde;
His sheeld todasshed was with swerdes and maces,
In which men myght many an arwe fynde
That thirled hadde horn and nerf and rynde;
And ay the peple cryde, "Here cometh oure joye,

147

MEDIEVAL LITERATURE, STYLE, AND CULTURE

And, next his brother, holder up of Troye!"

(II, 624–644)

But the heroic Troilus is ironically exposed to the perspective of Pandarus' realism. Here is the same hero as seen by his friend:

> This Pandarus com lepyng in atones,
> And seyde thus, "Who hath ben wel ibete
> To-day with swerdes and with slynge-stones,
> But Troilus, that hath caught hym an hete?"
> An gan to jape, and seyde, "Lord, so ye swete!"

(II, 939–943)

Elsewhere the epic style helps to link the fate of the lovers with the fate of Troy:

> Yt is wel wist how that the Grekes, stronge
> In armes, with a thousand shippes, wente
> To Troiewardes, and the cite longe
> Assegeden, neigh ten yer or they stente,
> And in diverse wise and oon entente,
> The ravysshyng to wreken of Eleyne,
> By Paris don, they wroughten all hir peyne.

(I, 57–63)

> Liggyng in oost, as I have seyd er this,
> The Grekys stronge aboute Troie town,
> Byfel that, whan that Phebus shynyng is
> Upon the brest of Hercules lyoun,
> That Ector, with ful many a bold baroun,
> Caste on a day with Grekes for to fighte,
> As he wont, to greve hem what he myghte.

> Not I how longe or short it was bitwene
> This purpos and that day they fighten mente;
> But on a day wel armed, brighte, and shene,
> Ector and many a worthi wight out wente,
> With spere in honde and bigge bowes bente;
> And in the berd, withouten lenger lette,
> Hire fomen in the feld anon hem mette.

148

The longe day, with speres sharpe igrounde,
With arwes, dartes, swerdes, maces felle,
They fighte and bringen hors and man to grounde,
And with hire axes out the braynes quelle.
But in the laste shour, soth for to telle,
The folk of Troie hemselven so mysledden
That with the worse at nyght homward they fledden.

(IV, 29–49)

The heroic vision is thus in this poem exposed to and limited by the tragic perspective of human history.

In the *Knight's Tale* the epic style and its concomitant ethos have their freest expression in Chaucer. Here Chaucer for once subordinates the courtly-love motif to the epic.[8] There are good reasons to believe that the tale was composed in substantially its present form, as a separate work, before the *Canterbury Tales*. If so, it was Chaucer's only complete, free-standing, unqualified treatment of the noble life, comparable to *Sir Gawain and the Green Knight*. If there is some doubt as to how seriously Chaucer takes the two young rivals Palamon and Arcite, there is no question that he takes Theseus seriously. The poem is a statement of ultimate belief in royal government and in the higher order of which it is a copy. "What maketh this but Juppiter, the kyng, / That is prince and cause of alle thyng . . . ?" (3035–3036).

By putting it at the head of the *Canterbury Tales* Chaucer shows how deeply his own sympathies—or his sense of respect—were ultimately bound up with its ethos. But he put it into the *Canterbury Tales* nevertheless, and at that point may have added some of the flickerings of irony which critics persist in finding in it. In any event, the damage was done. The meaning of the tale is qualified in the new context. Apart from the juxtaposition of tales, a powerful basis for irony in the form of the *Canterbury Tales* is that it is a series narrated by different characters. The meaning of each tale is thus potentially qualified by our consideration of the special leanings and interests of the teller. The tale of Palamon and Arcite is assigned to a "verray, parfit, gentil knyght," a noble man of mature years, which both fixes its class orientation and suggests a certain nostalgia. It is followed by the disrespectful tales of the Miller and the Reeve, which in some ways parody it. They come nowhere near damaging it, but, permanently connected to it, they do not leave it the same.

Chaucer does not go back to romantic epic or epic romance after the

Troilus and the *Knight's Tale* except in parody, but he does have a fling at a related mode: the romance, Arthurian or oriental, of magic and marvels. To look back at the multifariousness of the *House of Fame* once again, one would have imagined that Chaucer could well have given himself up to this mode. The *House of Fame* is full of marvelous gimmicks, hugely enjoyed. What more magic steed than the Golden Eagle with its promise of love-tidings? What more exotic and enchanted places than the successive settings of that poem: the temple of glass, the mysterious desert, the hill of ice, the pinnacled abode of Fame, made all of beryl, and the revolving house of rumor, made all of varicolored twigs? Chaucer seems to have followed out later every one of the starts made in the *House of Fame,* but the results with this one are surprisingly meager. There is some magic, but not much of an atmosphere of the magical, in the *Franklin's Tale.* The *Wife of Bath's Tale* makes touching use of the idea of magic. In the context of the teller's sense of the loss of her youth and beauty, the magic transformation of the old hag into a young and fair lady is very gently suggested to be wish-fulfillment. But otherwise Chaucer is almost fidgety about the Celtic fairy atmosphere. His charming opening picture of the elf-queen and her jolly company is soon rent by the joking at the expense of begging friars. The rest of the fairy story is weighed down with the hag's Ovidian exemplum and sententious lecturing on *gentillesse* and poverty—which the tale survives very well, but not the magic nor the marvelous.

Chaucer seems even less at home in the Eastern atmosphere of the *Squire's Tale.* Had Milton's *penseroso* been able to

> . . . call up him that left half told
> The story of Cambuscan bold,

he might have found Chaucer quite unwilling to go on with it. The poem begins attractively enough, though the inordinate space given to repeated self-conscious remarks about rhetoric might give us pause. What is the meaning of this much interruption of the narrative? As the poem progresses, propelled by the exotic interest of the knight's arrival on his flying steed of brass, with his magic gifts, we are nevertheless aware that it is proceeding against some resistance. There is a certain woodenness in the endstopped lines, the repetitive and sententious character of passage after passage, as in fact the plot limps to a standstill (about verse 189) and then takes no significant turn for some hundreds of verses. At length Canacee finds her falcon and begins to listen to her story of unfaithfulness in love. We are, in short, out of the magical realm, and back to what, for Chaucer-lovers, is almost too familiar: Dido's lament in the *House of Fame,* the complaint of *Anelida,* and the romantic pathos of the legends of *Good Women.* Chaucer's odd confusion of the characters' names at the end of the fragment may be the final symptom of his dying interest. The peculiar clumsiness with which this oriental romance is handled by a great artist has prompted a number of comic interpretations at the expense of the tale's teller, abetted as usual by the Canterbury context.[9] Whether or not Chaucer's failure to complete the tale can be blamed on the Squire, the fact remains that the exotic magic leaks out of it early; oriental romance finally succumbs either to irony or to boredom.

In tracking out and sorting the varieties of Chaucer's romances we have come again and again upon the note of pathos. It is a subject which has been widely observed and admired in Chaucer, but it has not been adequately studied. Yet it must be by all odds the most persistent alternative to irony that Chaucer felt, so persistent that no account of Chaucer's character and stance would be complete without recognizing it. But dealing critically with pathos is a tricky business, since pathos is, to an extraordinary degree, relative to individual taste and sensibility.[10] One man's tenderness is another man's mawkishness. One generation is taught to weep, another to hold back the tears.

How shall we interpret and evaluate the pathetic Chaucer? Ideally we need first a consecutive account of the pathetic mode in earlier poetry, both religious and secular, Latin and vernacular, against which we might measure, at least comparatively, the quality and intensity of Chaucer's feeling. Pathos is a latent possibility, at least, in most periods and genres of literature; it is a presence in medieval literature as early as the time of Anselm of Canterbury and Bernard of Clairvaux. Considering the openings for it in pious subject matter—the sacrifice of Isaac, the slaughter of the Innocents, the Nativity, the Passion, the life and miracles of the Virgin Mary, the legends of such saints as Elisabeth and Paula—early medieval literature has relatively few heavily pathetic passages.[11] But there is a real shift of sensibility—of which the rise of Franciscanism may be more a symptom than a cause—toward the middle of the thirteenth century; we need particularly a close study of the change in religious feelings that produces in this period the fully pathetic version of the life of Christ found in the iconography traced by Mâle and in the *Meditations* of the pseudo-Bonaventura.[12] We would

find Chaucer, I think, in the full tide of this typically late-medieval sen-
timentalization of religious feeling, and it is possible that for the England of his time, and for some centuries thereafter, he is a cultural
landmark in the breadth and depth to which the feeling runs.[13]

For our present purposes, we shall have to be content with the more
limited appraisal of Chaucer's pathos that we can get from comparing
his different works. Pathos falls across both his romantic and religious
poems, and no doubt its powerful expression in such works as the
Clerk's Tale derives from the fusion of both streams. Griselda is both a
Christian mother and a legendary heroine. It is interesting to observe,
then (assuming always that our rough chronology is correct), that
Chaucer's early works in both genres do not show anything suggesting
extremes of pathos. *An ABC* is a translation from De Deguileville, and
both the choice of the piece and the closeness of the translation may
indicate some tendency on Chaucer's part, before the *Canterbury Tales*
years, to lean toward a mariology that is reverent and tender but not sentimental. The crucified Jesus and sorrowing Mary have little space in
An ABC; what pathos there is, rather, is generated more by the sinning
speaker's own stance as an erring child of God:

> Glorious mayde and mooder, which that nevere
> Were bitter, neither in erthe nor in see,
> But ful of swetnesse and of merci evere,
> Help that my Fader be not wroth with me.
> Spek thou, for I ne dar not him ysee,
> So have I doon in erthe, allas the while!
> That certes, but if thou my socour bee,
> To stink eterne he wole my gost exile.

> (49–56)

The *Second Nun's Tale,* similarly a close translation, is even more continent, and asks of us neither sigh nor tear as we witness the martyr St.
Cecelia's perfection both in courage and in doctrine.

I have several times mentioned the long lament of Dido in the *House
of Fame.* It is by no means certain why Chaucer made it so long; it can
be read as merely a rhetorical exercise, perhaps meant to be comic.[14]
Within it is practice in the love-complaint mode and surely an attempt
at pathos:

> "Allas!" quod she, "my swete herte,

Have pitee on my sorwes smerte,
And slee mee not! goo noght awey!
O woful Dido, wel-away!"
Quod she to hirselve thoo.
"O Eneas, what wol ye doo?
O that your love, ne your bond
That ye have sworn with your ryght hond,
Ne my crewel deth," quod she,
"May holde yow stille here with me!
O haveth of my deth pitee!
Iwys, my dere herte, ye
Knowen ful wel that never yit,
As ferforth as I hadde wyt,
Agylte [I] yow in thoght ne dede.
O, have ye men such godlyhede
In speche, and never a del of trouthe?
Allas, that ever hadde routhe
Any woman on any man!
Now see I wel, and telle kan,
We wrechched wymmen konne noon art;
For certeyn, for the more part,
Thus we be served everychone.
How sore that ye men konne groone,
Anoon as we have yow receyved,
Certaynly we ben deceyvyd!
For, though your love laste a seson,
Wayte upon the conclusyon,
And eke how that ye determynen,
And for the more part diffynen."

(315–344)

Whatever Chaucer's intent here, the mixture of other modes in the speech, especially the scholastic, squelches whatever sympathy is generated. Furthermore we see here a hint of a quality that may be found in other specimens of Chaucerian pathos—a lack of background, of context, within which the powerful feeling might have taken on more local solidity and justification.

The occasions for pathos are multiplied by as many good women as there are in the *Legend of Good Women,* but here again we find remarkably little sustained pathos, either achieved or attempted. There are a few tentative fingerings of the theme of suffering children, which will later become a very fount of Chaucerian tenderness. Thus Tisbe apostrophizes her father before she kills herself:

"And now, ye wrechede jelos fadres oure,
We that whilom were children youre,
We preyen yow, withouten more envye,
That in o grave yfere we moten lye,
Sith love hath brought us to this pitous ende.
And ryghtwis God to every lovere sende,
That loveth trewely, more prosperite
Than evere yit had Piramus and Tisbe! . . ."

(900–907)

In the legend of Dido, Chaucer picks up the Ovidian suggestion that Dido was pregnant:

"I am with childe, and yeve my child his lyf!
Mercy, lord! have pite in youre thought!"

(1323–1324)

In the legend of Hypermnestra, the daughter is made the victim of her wicked father. In the characterization of Lucrece we can see touches of the Griselda type of humble, wifely chastity; but she accepts the violence done her with Roman stoicism. Her account of the rape is told almost entirely in indirect discourse, so that although Chaucer tells us that

Al hadde folkes hertes ben of stones,
Hyt myght have maked hem upon hir rewe. . . .

(1841–1842)

the account is too masked and compressed to summon our tears. The rape of Philomela leads to similarly condensed pathetics.

The note of pathos in most of these accounts is summoned by Chaucer not only for unrequited love—the conventional cue for complaint—but more often for defenseless weakness against a brutal, masculine world. Without a rich context, these anecdotes seem to be drawing in part on stock response, on some easy source of feeling in the audience—"pitee renneth soone in gentil here." When Chaucer provides such passages an adequate context, however, they draw from deeper wells of feeling and take on deeper meaning. One of the most successful touches of pathos in Chaucer, both poetically and strategically, is the beginning of the death speech of Arcite in the *Knights' Tale:*

> Naught may the woful spirit in myn herte
> Declare o point of alle my sorwes smerte
> To yow, my lady, that I love moost;
> But I biquethe the servyce of my goost
> To yow aboven every creature,
> Syn that my lyf may no lenger dure.
> Allas, the wo! allas, the peynes stronge,
> That I for yow have suffred, and so longe!
> Allas, the deeth! allas, myn Emelye!
> Allas, departynge of oure compaignye!
> Allas, myn hertes queene! allas, my wyf!
> Myn hertes lady, endere of my lyf!
> What is this world? what asketh men to have?
> Now with his love, now in his colde grave
> Allone, withouten any compaignye.
> Fare wel, my sweete foo, myn Emelye!
> And softe taak me in youre armes tweye,
> For love of God, and herkneth what I seye. . . .
>
> (2765–2782)

Here the powerful feeling is contained, both fore and aft, by the narrator's prosaic and medical acceptance of Arcite's death. Meanwhile we have been exposed to a pathos as deep as human doubt can go. "What is this world, what asketh men to have?" The fact that the whole of this rich poem devotes itself to finding an acceptable answer to the question somehow validates the feeling and supports us in our temporary surrender.

But the glimpse of man "in his colde grave" should remind us that not all such feeling in the late Middle Ages was so contained and supported in its pathos. Huizinga remarks that the new preoccupation with Death in the period is not a form of asceticism or religiosity, but rather the reverse.[15] It presumes a worship of the living flesh and a desperate pessimism as to the hereafter. It proclaims the weakening of faith. Chaucer never falls into the blacker stages of the fifteenth-century mood (though he approaches them in the plague and murder scenes of the *Pardoner's Tale*). But I wonder whether the extreme pathos of the Hugelino episode, of the *Clerk's, Physician's, Prioress's,* and *Man of Law's Tales*— if we set them beside the confident dignity of *An ABC* and the *Second Nun's Tale*—do not show a wavering of morale along with the undeniable increase in poetic power and religious feeling. For the pathos of defenseless weakness can be based on a kind of pessimism that sees in the world malignity without cause and without cure; justice perverted; protection uncertain. The miracle of the Blessed Virgin, the need for divine intercessory tenderness, long antedates Chaucer's time. But when it comes as relief from a strain that has begun to grow intolerable, it brings a new accession of pathos.

The whole subject of suffering children is introduced between the two groups of poems we are comparing. The turning of the mature Chaucer to the subject of children is itself a symptom of something. Children, to all intents and purposes, were not recognized in art or literature until the late thirteenth century,[16] and their discovery is coincident with the shift in religious feeling we have noted above. In the absence of statistics we cannot attribute it to a lessening of infant mortality—more likely there was a rise, in a period of plague, famine, war, and depression. In fact, nearly all of Chaucer's children exist, not to live out their childlike lives, but to suffer death, or the threat of death. It is true, as D. S. Brewer points out, that this is a fact of fourteenth-century life;[17] but it was also a fact of thirteenth-century life, and that century was peculiarly untroubled by death. The direction in which this sentiment is moving is well illustrated in the fifteenth century in Antoine de la Sale's *Le Réconfort de Madame du Fresne:*

> But the child, who thought, after the guards' consoling words, that he was being taken toward the fortress, when he saw that they were going toward Mont Réont, was frightened more than ever. He now began to weep and despair and said to Thomas, the leader of the guards: "Oh, Thomas, my friend, you take me away to die, you take me away to die. Alas, you take me away to die, Thomas, you take me away to die. Alas, my lord father, I shall die. Alas, my lady mother, I shall die. I shall die! Alas, alas, alas, I shall die, die, die, die!" And crying thus and weeping, looking before and behind and around him, he saw me, woe unto me!, with your coat of arms which I wore, and when he saw me, he called aloud, as loud as he could. And he said to me: "Ah, Chastel, my friend, I shall die! Alas! My friend, I shall die!" And when I heard him cry thus,

then like dead I fell to the ground. And according to orders I was carried after him and there by many men was held until he met his end. And when he was set down on the mount, there was there a friar who, by beautiful words of hope in the grace of God, little by little confessed him and absolved him from his little sins. And because he could not take death willingly, they had to hold his head and bind his arms and legs so that the legs were bruised by the iron down to the bones. . . .[18]

Chaucer does not go this far, of course, yet it is worthwhile plotting his position on the curve. Theodore Spencer, in a paper that deserves to be better remembered, has already called our attention to the comparison between Chaucer's and Dante's renderings of the Ugolino episode (*Inferno* XXXIII).[19] If Dante's generates pity and terror, Chaucer's generates only pity. A softness has entered in. Comparatively, Chaucer is sentimental. Where Dante's Ugolino feels a grief so stonily deep that it cuts off both speech and tears,

Io non piangeva, si dentro impietrai. . . .

(49)

[I did not weep; inside I turned to stone]

Chaucer's Hugelino complains and weeps:

"Allas!" quod he, "allas, that I was wroght!"
Therwith the teeris fillen from his yen.

(*Monk's Tale* 2429–2430)

The following stanza is Chaucer's addition:

His yonge sone, that thre yeer was of age,
Unto hym seyde, "Fader, why do ye wepe?
Whanne wol the gayler bryngen oure potage?
Is there no morsel breed that ye do kepe?
I am so hungry that I may nat slepe.
Now wolde God that I myghte slepen evere!
Thanne sholde nat hunger in my wombe crepe;
There is no thyng, save breed, that me were levere."

(2431–2438)

157

The iron terror of Dante's concluding line—*poscia, più che il dolor, potè il digiuno,* "then fasting had more power than grief"—is lost in Chaucer's conclusion: "Hymself, despeired, eek for hunger starf."

Of the remaining four pieces that concern us, one needs little discussion. The *Physician's Tale* has not been widely praised in recent years, partly because of the hard-boiledness of our taste, but also because the tale lacks adequate underpinnings for the extremes of pathos that it attempts to engage us in. We know nothing of the Physician that would attract us to joining his feelings, and the tale generates neither the characterization nor the sense of a cosmos that in the *Troilus* or the *Knight's Tale* make the pathos acceptable. It is the gratuitousness of it that finally palls. The heroine is a textbook example of medieval secular virtue and she is done in by an equally pure vice:

> "O mercy, deere fader!" quod this mayde,
> And with that word she bothe hir armes layde
> Aboute his nekke, as she was wont to do.
> The teeris bruste out of hir eyen two,
> And seyde, "Goode fader, shal I dye?
> Is ther no grace, is ther no remedye?"
> "No certes, deere doghter myn," quod he.
> "Thanne yif me leyser, fader myn," quod she,
> "My deeth for to compleyne a litel space;
> For, pardee, Jepte yaf his doghter grace
> For to compleyne, er he hir slow, allas!
> And, God it woot, no thyng was hir trespas,
> But for she ran hir fader first to see,
> To welcome hym with greet solempnitee."
> And with that word she fil aswowne anon,
> And after, whan hir swownyng is agon,
> She riseth up, and to hir fader sayde,
> "Blissed be God, that I shal dye a mayde!
> Yif me my deeth, er that I have a shame;
> Dooth with youre child youre wyl, a Goddes name!"
>
> (231–250)

To make matters worse, the narrative style has such an unwonted flaccidity and the few essential details of plot are handled so vaguely[20] as to rob the tale further of any power it might have had to make us suspend disbelief.

The *Prioress's Tale,* on the other hand, is one of Chaucer's most moving poems. Some of its power must be due to the fact that the pathos is extraordinarily well enfolded in the characterization of the Prioress and allows even the most hard-boiled of us to take just as much of it as he wishes.²¹ The rest can be attributed to the delicate, feminine, maternal nun who tells the tale. This characterization, however, does not depend entirely on pilgrimage dramatics, on our knowing the Prioress from Chaucer's *General Prologue;* it is woven deeply into the style of the tale: in the consistent self-identification of the speaker with childlikeness; the repeated emphasis on weakness, simplicity, and on the diminutive (a *litel child,* a *litel scole,* his *litel book,* his *litel body*); the adoption of a simple diction and syntax for the narrator as well as for the child; the use of repetitions in passages and within phrases, giving the effect of simplicity; the use, repeatedly, of simple contrasts and distinctions to the same effect. Like the *Physician's Tale,* the poem turns on an elementary contrast between tenderness and violence, but the feel of tenderness is made far more substantial and appealing. Furthermore, the element of violence, the malignity and punishment of the Jews, instead of standing quite apart from tenderness, is hinged to it in the emotional system of the tale: in one stanza the image of the child's body thrown in the privy, in the next stanza the procession of the white Lamb celestial; in the same three verses the provost

. . . herieth Crist that is of hevene king,
And eek his mooder, honour of mankynde,
And after that the Jewes leet he bynde.

(618–620)

In four successive verses spanning a stanza break:

Therfore with wilde hors he dide hem drawe,
And after that he heng hem by the lawe.

Upon this beere ay lith this innocent
Beforn the chief auter, whil masse laste. . . .

(633–636)

I do not wish to enter the controversy over the Prioress's anti-Semitism or other alleged flaws in her character. But surely Chaucer is touching something true here, in these contrasts, about the kinship of pathos and violence as extremes of feeling. Their coupling, whether or not it seems grotesque, adds validity to each; and this may be, at least in part, why the poem can be read both as successful pathos and as an exposure (conscious or unconscious) of the brutality which lies beneath it.

If the success of the pathetic style in the *Prioress's Tale* is a matter of total fitness, total decorum, perhaps what bothers some readers of the *Clerk's Tale* is not the relatively restrained pathos it employs, but that pathos threatens not to fit. The poem is extremely dense and powerful in its design and extremely well fitted to the ethos of the speaker. But the speaker is a lean, philosophical man, and the design is clear, sharp, and uncompromising.[22] The uncompromising virtue of Griselda (even with her resemblances to Lucrece and Virginia) fits this design better than do the extremes of pathos. Fortunately the few stanzas of it, centering mostly around the loss and recovery of her children, hardly mar the poem.

The case is far worse in the *Man of Law's Tale;* after the *House of Fame* this is surely Chaucer's most tantalizing and exasperating poem. Tantalizing because it contains individual passages of the most affecting beauty; exasperating because so much of the rest of its feeling is unavailable except to the most willing hearts. This is not to say that the *Man of Law's Tale* would not have been prized by Chaucer's contemporaries. It must be included in that roll of serious and elevating works in the high style on which Chaucer's reputation was largely to rest in the next two centuries. Yet it has not survived as well as have other of the pious tales of the same drift, and some answer must be sought in the tale itself.

Unlike the *Prioress's* and *Clerk's Tales,* the *Man of Law's Tale,* although suitable to him, has no deeply necessary congruity with what we know of the character of the speaker. It cannot be said to represent anything that confirms or combines richly with his nature; it shows, indeed, some sign of having been assigned to the Man of Law at the last minute. If its barren stretches illustrate Chaucer's observation that the Man of Law "semed bisier than he was," the joke is a heavy one at best. Chaucer heightened the religious flavor and suppressed some of the melodrama found in the story he was adapting, and it looks as if he originally intended it to stand on its own feet, without a framing of dramatics or irony, as a kind of saint's legend.

Professor Alfred David has put his finger on an essential difference between the pessimism of the *Man of Law's Tale* and that of the *Knight's Tale:* "The dominant philosophical influence" on the former "is not *De consolatione philosophiae* but *De contemptu mundi.*"[23] Thus the religiosity of the *Man of Law's Tale* is deeper, and it makes a more naked, more naive, less philosophical appeal when it invokes divine providence. As art it calls for a far greater initial contribution of stock response from its audience. Like the *Clerk's Tale,* its plot is repetitive; but somehow its power is not cumulative. Like the *Prioress's Tale,* its color is black and white, but the contrasts are not arranged in any convincing pattern. The rhetoric of the poem is put out at a pressure that in this context would require the Pardoner's skill to bring off. Some of its flights rise so suddenly out of the mediocre recital of the plot as to suggest that the poet is coming to the rescue, sensing that the narrative itself is not pulling its own weight.[24] Then we come upon a passage like Constance's prayer on the beach, with its climactic invocation to the Virgin Mary:

> Wepen bothe yonge and olde in al that place
> Whan that the kyng this cursed lettre sente,
> And Custance, with a deedly pale face,
> The ferthe day toward hir ship she wente.
> But nathelees she taketh in good entente
> The wyl of Crist, the knelynge on the stronde,
> She seyde, "Lord, ay welcome be thy sonde!

> "He that me kepte fro the false blame
> While I was on the lond amonges yow,
> He kan me kepe from harm and eek fro shame
> In salte see, althogh I se noght how.
> As strong as evere he was, he is yet now.
> In hym triste I, and in his mooder deere,
> That is to me my seyl and eek my steere."

> Hir litel child lay wepyng in hir arm,
> And knelynge, pitously to hym she seyde,
> "Pees, litel sone, I wol do thee noon harm."
> With that hir coverchief of hir heed she breyde,
> And over his litel eyen she it leyde,
> And in hir arm she lulleth it ful faste,

And into hevene hire eyen up she caste.

"Mooder," quod she, "and mayde bright, Marie,
Sooth is that thurgh wommanes eggement
Mankynde was lorn, and damned ay to dye,
For which thy child was on a croys yrent.
Thy blisful eyen sawe al his torment;
Thanne is ther no comparison bitwene
Thy wo and any wo man may sustene.

"Thow sawe thy child yslayn bifore thyne yen,
And yet now lyveth my litel child, parfay!
Now, lady bright, to whom alle woful cryen,
Thow glorie of wommanhede, thow faire may,
Thow haven of refut, brighte sterre of day,
Rewe on my child, that of thy gentillesse,
Rewest on every reweful in distresse."

(820–854)

The passage can hardly be read with a dry eye. It is one of the greatest of Chaucer's lyrics, and we remain grateful to him—even in the following stanza, where he makes a palpable effort to squeeze for even more tears.

The pathos in Chaucer, hedged about by its pious associations, is almost totally exempt from overt irony, except perhaps that of a cosmic kind, as in the *Troilus,* which reminds us that even this ineffable sadness and pity we feel is an attachment to the world. Perhaps that is why, finally, so much pathos is contained within the enveloping structure of the *Canterbury Tales.*

In dealing with Chaucer I have followed a method quite different from that in the two previous discussions, and I hope not to be misunderstood—particularly by readers new to Chaucer. I have not given due attention here to Chaucer's main achievements, for lack of space and because they have in any case been well celebrated elsewhere. Our rapid survey of some Chaucerian excursions outside of irony has, however, a celebratory effect: to confirm that Chaucer's crowning ironic stance, though highly original, was not inevitable but emerges from a lifetime of feeling and of coming to grips with the alternative value systems that his culture offered. He tried, he tested, he experimented, he compromised, and even had moments of pessimism and failure. We see

162

that some moods came on him late, and others were abandoned early; that he may have been tempted here, and that he resisted temptation there. Apart from his perception and sympathy with life, Chaucer's great virtue is morale. It is a morale that is based, not on a doctrinaire conservatism, but on a felt acquaintance with all the alternatives.

"Poetry," as Frederick Pottle says, "cannot go wrong."[5] It is always related to history, for it is the very truest record of human sensibility. So poetry is always relevant. The question is, how does it connect? In making our survey of three poets at the same moment of history, we have found not only three different responses, but also three rather different ways in which poetry can relate to history, three kinds of relatedness between poetic art and a culture in crisis. One poet refines out, in his art, all of the contemporary except the ultimate moral issues, and reclothes them in terms that defend them from the accidental and the local. Another poet immerses himself and his poem in the moving current of history, from which both emerge with the marks of crisis upon them. The third is somewhere in between, involved yet objective, detached yet sympathetically moved. These three are great poets, and their response to their own culture is deeper and truer than other men's. Studying through them the relation of poetry to history, we learn something about the responses of men to history as well.

THE FABLIAUX

Concerning the origins of the fabliaux, Knut Togeby has observed: "The only firm date is that of the death of Jean Bodel in 1210, . . . before which he had written at least eight fabliaux" ("Les fabliaux," p. 89). Togeby offers good reasons for regarding Bodel—popular poet of Arras and author of the comic and religious drama *Le jeu de saint Nicolas* (*The Play of Saint Nicholas*) and the epic *Chanson des Saisnes* (*Song of the Saxons)*—as the father of this genre of realistic and mostly comic tales in verse. At any rate, it is very much a genre of the thirteenth century; although few can be securely dated, it is clear that most of the 150–odd fabliaux that have survived were written between 1200 and 1340.

They seem to have been primarily an "after dinner" genre, told for amusement, in a mood of relaxation and confidence, and, despite their frequently bawdy subject matter, in mixed company. They were composed and recited both by jongleurs—professional entertainers—and by amateurs; thus a traveling clerk might pay a family for his meal and night's lodging by reciting a couple of fabliaux. Clerks, indeed, are so often the erotic heroes in fabliau triangle plots that it is likely that many of these poems were composed as well as recited by clerks. Individual fabliaux were freely copied and often re-edited to suit different audiences during this period, but the general absence of immediate literary precursors—although they have many analogues in folklore from antiquity to the present—indicates that most of the stories were taken from oral tradition. Garin, the author of *La grue* (*The Crane*), says that he is using material he "heard tell about at Vézelay in front of the Exchange" (Montaiglon and Raynaud, *Recueil général,* 5:151).

Although there has been some disagreement as to precisely which poems to include in the canon, the general character of the genre is reasonably secure. Over sixty of the fabliaux are so labeled in medieval texts (the word is Picard dialect for "fable," plus a diminutive ending), and another ninety can be admitted to the canon without debate. Still, they are diverse lot. In length they range from a few dozen verses to more than a thousand. There are small masterpieces of plotting and characterization—such as *Le boucher d'Abbeville* (*The Butcher of*

164

Abbeville), *Boivin de Provins*, *La bourgeoise d'Orléans* (*The Townswoman of Orléans*), and *Auberée de Compiègne*—and such remarkably inept productions as the four by the scribbler Haiseau, who touched nothing that he did not damage. There are texts of almost courtly delicacy, and a few almost combatively disgusting. Some are wildly funny, others marginally solemn, hardly different from moral exempla. But all have a certain realism—of style, tone, or ethos—that sets them off from other genres of the period.

The stylistic realism of the fabliau is the realism of comedy. "A comic subject," wrote the medieval rhetorician Geoffrey of Vinsauf, "rejects artfully labored diction. It requires plain words only" (*Poetria Nova*, p. 255). This style freely admits comic exaggeration, grotes-querie, and caricature, but its basic world is determinedly the familiar and the local. Its imagery, though not always dense, is overwhelmingly mundane and concrete; it is a world of things, as the fabliau titles make clear: *Les braies au Cordelier* (*The Friar's Breeches*); *Brunain, la vache au prêtre* (*Browny, the Priest's Cow*); *Le chevalier à la corbeille* (*The Knight with the Basket*); *La crotte* (*The Turd*); *Le cuvier* (*The Tub*); *Le prévôt à l'aumusse* (*The Provost with the Hood*); *La sourisette des étoupes* (*The Mouse in the Tow*). The plots of about a third of the poems are closely bound up with such images.

Furthermore, a good deal of this imagery seems to exceed the demands of the plot, as if included for its own sake. The fabliaux occa-sionally parody courtly style, and in doing so present some descriptions of superlative places and things. But most often their descriptions evoke the texture of ordinary life, as in the proud inventory of pots, pans, and bedclothes in *La veuve* (*The Widow*), the hilariously padded bill for dinner and lodging in *Le prêtre et le chevalier* (*The Priest and the Knight*), the delighted descriptions of a peasant disguise in *Boivin de Provins*, and of a poor minstrel's rags in *Le prêtre et les deux ribauds* (*The Priest and the Two Rascals*). An obvious savoring of this texture, a sometimes ironical recognition and enjoyment of how things really are, explains the attractions of the many poems whose weak plots or otherwise meager narrative features would not alone have ensured their survival.

The fabliaux are generally too short to permit realistic characteriza-tion (which in this period would have been unusual in any case). Char-acters tend to be types—the jealous husband, the clever clerk, the gullible maiden, the faithless wife, the stupid peasant, the rich and/or lecherous priest—individualized, if at all, in single traits: a big head, a talent for theft, a taste for berries, a huge penis, an intolerance of dirty words. But although few characters are complex, they are still realistic in the sense that they come mainly from the audience's own world, and they are caught and recorded with just that shrewd, practical, reductive abbreviation typical of the conduct of ordinary life.

The realistic style of the fabliaux not only evokes a particular world but also supports a particular ethos: materialist, hedonistic, and finally ironic. The fabliaux are endlessly concerned with pleasure. They are, for instance, a compendium of medieval food and wine. A whole plot turns on the disposition of some roast partridges, another on a roast goose. Unsympathetic characters are known and judged by their diets: a peasant's son has no feeling for chivalry but loves tarts and custards; a hungry peasant is insulted by a seneschal as a "gulper of peas"; a buffoon and his new wife eat smelly sow-meat with pepper and juniper. Conversely hospitality, and especially that of satisfied love, is underlined by the sharing of splendid meals, whose menus are lovingly detailed, along with good wine—"clear as tears"—and often a warm tub.

The only rival to the pleasure of gastronomy in the fabliaux is that of sex. Sex is, as often as not, presented explicitly, almost never elaborately, but always with approval or enthusiasm. There is hardly a trace of the Christian-puritan taboo on sex for its own sake and, more remarkably, much less than one might expect of a mood of confrontation in the easy violations of that taboo. Of course, the fabliaux's ample treatment of sex among the celibate clergy always carries some satiric or ironic effect, but not at the expense of sex. Except for brushes with sadism in four or five poems, and for some comically epic instances of sexual prowess, sex in these poems is the normal, pleasurable thing; it is an apt subject of comedy for many reasons, but usually not just because the church forbids it.

The fabliaux are uninhibitedly concerned also with money. The subject is hedged about with a certain amount of mechanical moralizing—avarice is the root of evil—but their basic materialism is never threatened; they are endlessly concerned with large and small coins, profits, losses, bargains, prices, bribes, bills, gifts, and debts.

The final preoccupation of the fabliaux is with *engin* (wit, cleverness). Cleverness will get you money, food, and sex, and it is also pleasurable in itself. The fabliaux celebrate champion thieves and confidence men and, par excellence, clever women. Fabliau authors are not as antifeminist as they pretend to be. The woman who deceives her jealous husband to have a much better time with her lover is presented with admiration. Like other comic genres, the fabliaux are thus a mildly subversive literature. They favor the dispossessed, reward ingenuity at the expense of law and privilege, and suggest throughout that the conventional rules of morality and justice simply do not hold.

For all the material solidity of the fabliau, then, its plots and ethos suggest an ambiance of instability, of insecurity, surprise, and irony. This perhaps explains its taste for wordplay and double meaning; some forty-seven fabliaux or major episodes in them turn on words rather than on actions. They range from the verbal wit sustained through the whole of *Le roi d'Angleterre et le jongleur d'Ely* (*The King of England and the Minstrel of Ely*) to the central misunderstanding of *La male honte* (*Honte's Bag = Evil Shame*), to plentiful incidental punning, especially on the monosyllable pronounced *vi* (face, alive, penis) and the common prefix *con-* (vagina).

About two-thirds of the fabliaux contain some sort of moral or proverbial saying. This fact has given rise to the unlikely theory that the genre itself somehow evolved from the moral fable. But for the most part these prefatory or terminal or inserted "morals" rarely have a close connection with the actions of the tales they comment upon. They seem to have been included partly in response to the familiar medieval notion— based on St. Paul— that there is profitable doctrine in every text; partly as a reflex of the common rhetorical teaching that beginnings and endings call for a proverb; partly as play with the medieval habit of sententiousness itself; and perhaps partly as a means of protection from puritanical criticism. In one sense, however, they provide valuable insight into the fabliau ethos: if they do not comment directly on the tales, they mirror through their very commonplaceness the everyday wisdom of their audience.

This wisdom is almost never specifically Christian; it is overwhelmingly practical—and ironic: "Don't behave against your nature." "A fool never gives up." "The more forbidden, the more incentive." "With a mild shepherd, the wolf shits wool." "Who goes, feasts; who sits, dries up." "Troubles you can cook and eat are better than ones that give no pleasure." "Often the innocent pays the penalty." "He wiped my nose with my own sleeve." "He's a fool who believes his wife more than himself." This overt general "wisdom" ultimately harmonizes rather well with the ethos generated by the action and texture of the stories them-

167

selves. It is a wisdom of practical experience, mingling the securities of profit and pleasure with a shrewd and ironic awareness of the uncertainty of almost everything.

A central question remains: Why were these stories written up in literary form at this time? For half a century the dominant view was that of Joseph Bédier, who in 1893 identified the fabliaux as the poetry of the newly arising bourgeoisie and contrasted it with the refined literature of the courtly class: "The fabliaux are . . . the poetry of the little people. Down to earth realism, a merry and ironic conception of life, all the distinctive traits of the fabliau . . . show likewise the features of the bourgeois. On the other hand, the worship of woman, dreams of fairyland, idealism, all the traits that distinguish the lyric poetry and the romances of the Round Table, also mark out the features of the knightly class" (*Les fabliaux,* p. 371).

Bédier grants that there was some mixing of genres and classes in the 13th century, but his basic location of the origin of the genre in a specific social class commanded general assent until 1957, when Per Nykrog reopened the whole subject and led a worldwide revival of interest in the genre. His central idea is that fabliaux "were not only read and appreciated in courtly milieus, but . . . are so profoundly penetrated by the manner of thinking of these circles that to understand them well it is necessary to consider them a sort of courtly genre" (*Les fabliaux,* p. 18). Nykrog, significantly, did not challenge Bédier's theory of the class origins of the genre; but he emphatically substituted one class for another. His argument that fabliaux must have *coexisted* with courtly literature as favored entertainment for some audiences has lasting merit, and he significantly deepened our sensitivity to the element of parody in some of them—which would presuppose their audience's appreciation of courtly convention.

But thirty years of further research show that the idea of a class origin for the fabliaux will not hold. What external evidence there is indicates that they were circulated among aristocrats, the bourgeoisie, and wealthy peasants alike; and in the thirteenth century, city dwellers did not have a monopoly on tastes and attitudes that we have since come to think of as materialistic and "bourgeois." The century's economic expansion—the shift to a money economy, the weakening of social ties, the consequent weakening of fortunes based on feudal privilege, and the opening of opportunity for the newly liberated—affected all classes and is amply reflected in the fabliaux themselves. We must imagine the whole culture to have been influenced by the same climate that attended the rise of cities, the emergence of an urban middle class, and the appearance of the fabliau as a literary genre.

The fabliaux, then, are not a class literature, but reveal a stratum of sensibility that resides in the whole culture and coexists along with other strata—the courtly and the Christian, for instance—with remarkably little sense of strain or conflict. Fabliaux do contain some parody or burlesque of the courtly, and some satire of religious hypocrisy, but they do not, contrary to a common supposition, exist merely as a marginal and reactive response to establishment values. They are not a truant or temporary "carnival" literature. They express, rather, a set of cultural norms of some weight and coherence, and of great persistence.

The integrity and importance of this literature as an index of thirteenth-century sensibility is confirmed by its relatively robust survival. It is almost the only record we have of the moods of relaxed, unbuttoned, confidential conviviality in a period that tended to preserve only its "serious" and official documents. Fabliaux would always, of course, have been censored in the most puritanical of quarters. In later periods, as the newly forming genteel tradition of behavior and diction gathered strength, as fabliau language and attitudes increasingly lost their unselfconsciousness, and as the term *vulgar* took on increasingly pejorative moral and social connotations, further censorship must have ensued. In this light, the survival of 150 texts in forty-six manuscripts or fragments is impressive. In the major manuscripts, which are private literary collections, the texts exist side by side with pieces of every other kind—courtly tales, moral poems, translations from the Latin—as if to illustrate their easy naturalization within the sensibility of the time.

The fabliaux represent a mood and a set of values that in the history of culture by far antedate the courtly tradition, and indeed they reflect here and there a response to the new courtly taboos imposed on certain references and on four- (in French, three-) letter words in the thirteenth century. Their ethos probably antedates the Christian one as well. But the elaboration of a new literary genre embodying this ethos attests to a new force, or interest, or validity that a hedonistic, materialist, and ironic sensibility enjoys at this time. This stratum of sensibility is as authentic a part of the identity of the French thirteenth century as are those attested by courtly allegory, the cult of the Virgin, or the great cathedrals.

BIBLIOGRAPHY

Joseph Bédier, *Les fabliaux* (Paris: Champion, 1893).

R. H. Bloch, *The Scandal of the Fabliaux* (Chicago: University of Chicago Press, 1986).

Thomas D. Cooke and Benjamin L. Honeycutt, eds., *The Humor of the Fabliaux* (Columbia: University of Missouri Press, 1974).

Geoffrey of Vinsauf, *Poetria Nova,* in *Les arts poétiques du XIIe et du XIIIe siècles,* ed. Edmond Faral (Paris: Champion, 1924).

Robert Harrison, trans., *Gallic Salt: Eighteen Fabliaux Translated from the Old French* (Berkeley: University of California Press, 1974).

Anatole de Montaiglon and Gustave Raynaud, *Recueil général et complet des fabliaux,* 6 vols. (Paris: Librairie des Bibliophiles, 1872–1890).

Charles Muscatine, *The Old French Fabliaux* (New Haven: Yale University Press, 1986).

Willem Noomen and Nico van den Boogard, *Nouveau recueil complet des fabliaux,* 10 vols. to date (Assen: Van Gorcum, 1983–1998).

Per Nykrog, *Les fabliaux* (Copenhagen: Ejnar Munksgaard, 1957).

Knut Togeby, "Les fabliaux," *Orbis Litterarum,* 12 (1957), 85–98.

THE WIFE OF BATH AND
GAUTIER'S *LA VEUVE*

Our ideas of the sources and influences of medieval literary works are currently being modified by a number of different emphases in literary scholarship. An interest in style or genre makes possible the discrimination between stylistic sources and textual sources. Studies of oral-formulaic narrative and of folklore are making us increasingly aware of the importance of oral tradition and thus of sources and influences received by ear rather than by reading. Indeed, the general, modern sensitivity to rhetorical patterns, topoi, forms, textures, and motifs—qualities and relational elements of literary works which are not dependent for their transmission by word-for-word or line-for-line borrowings—has tended to widen our sense of the scope of literary influence.[1] Thus while the books known to have been read by such an author as Chaucer remain highly interesting to us, we cannot limit ourselves to precise verbal resemblances to them in describing the literary forces that may have shaped his work and entered into his audience's appreciation of it.[2] What Chaucer or his audience may have heard but never read—in a lifetime of listening—will have had great influence on his poems as well. Works heard as they were recited aloud may be traceable only sparsely in exact verbal reminiscences, but may still constitute "sources" or influences of genre, pattern, motif, tone, and style. This is the way in which certain scenes of Chaucer's *Troilus* must be related to fabliau tradition. In the present paper I suggest a similar relationship between Chaucer's *Wife of Bath's Prologue* and Gautier Le Leu's *La Veuve*.[3]

We are encouraged to listen for oral influences on Chaucer because we know that he had a very good ear. His style shows that either he was himself an excellent dramatic reader or he wrote with one reliably at hand. As early as the *Book of the Duchess* we find him toying with the possible dramatics of the first-person narrator's role. The progressive expansion of this role through his later works has become one of the principal topics of recent Chaucer criticism.[4] The *Canterbury Tales* is enveloped in a dramatic-narrative frame and contains half a dozen pieces ready for virtuoso oral recitation. The *Wife of Bath's Prologue* is perhaps the most brilliant of them. It is hardly unlikely that Chaucer, a master of the dramatic monologue, will have picked up some of his technique by ear.

Chaucer, of course, was also a great reader, and the *Wife of Bath's Prologue* is as learned as it is dramatic. A good deal of its contents are clearly derived from identifiable works that Chaucer read. These have been well studied; we probably have as good an account as we shall ever have of the antifeminist documents that were in his library as he wrote.[5] But our initial concern is not so much the content as the form of the *Prologue:* the dramatic monologue as genre and the particular form and texture that this particular monologue has.

Chaucer's primary debt here to Jean de Meun's *Roman de la Rose* has long been recognized. The *Roman* was constantly on Chaucer's desk, and provided both matter and manner to the Wife's *Prologue.* The dramatic monologue form—here an extended autobiographical and doctrinal discourse on love by an experienced woman—comes to Chaucer from La Vieille's discourse in the *Roman.*[6] Some of La Vieille's biography is assimilated into the Wife of Bath's, some of her nostalgic tone, and a good many of her references. But Gautier's *La Veuve* also has a group of characteristics (some of them found in the *Roman* and some not) also found in Chaucer's poem, enough of them to warrant the suggestion that reminiscences of *La Veuve* (or of a poem closely related to it) are merged with Chaucer's reading of the *Roman* and of the other antifeminist works among the literary influences on the *Wife of Bath's Prologue.*

La Veuve also delivers substantial, autobiographical speeches in dramatic form. She is not given in gross number of verses nearly as much to say as either the Wife or La Vieille, but she says quite enough to establish her personality—two hundred and seventy verses of dramatized complaint, reverie, and dramatic dialogue. Her principal speech (vv. 236–375) is a well-developed dramatic monologue, one of the earliest medieval ones extant. Furthermore, Gautier Le Leu is justly celebrated for the dramatic excellence of this speech, which in its rhythm and sequence catches beautifully the garrulousness and the wandering mentality of this speaker.[7] In this *La Veuve* displays "Chaucerian" qualities in more concentrated and consistent form than does the doctrine-ridden speech of La Vieille.

The same is true as regards imagery. One of the most striking qualities of the Wife's discourse is her heavy use of domestic imagery. She is a wealthy bourgeoise, and her speech is full of reference to domestic animals, furniture, bread, flour, bran, and the like, which give a particular flavor and authenticity to her world. Jean's La Vieille is likewise given domestic metaphor and some awareness of domestic science.[8] But although she has pillaged her lovers in the past, she is represented as a poor woman, and the texture of her speech does not convey as strong a sense of materialism as does La Veuve's:

"J'ai assés caudieres et pos
Et blanques quieltes et bon lis,
Huges, sieges et caelis. . . ."

(vv. 282–4)

"Puisque ce vient a le bescosse,
Je n'en ai cure de garbe escosse."[9]

The characterization and background of La Veuve relate her in several other ways to both Jean's and Chaucer's characters. She too has an over-developed sexual appetite, and can be by turns hypocritical or savage. She talks a lot and tells too much on herself. But she also has traits shared with the Wife of Bath that are not found in Jean de Meun at all. In a tradition so massive and pervasive as that of antifeminist satire, the single "antifeminist" trait of course counts for little in tracing influences. Almost every trait has a parallel somewhere in the tradition. That both Gautier's and Chaucer's characters (but not Jean's) are prominently represented as widows, are shown at the funeral, and then in eager remarriage, derives at least in part from the tradition of the Matron of Ephesus, and parallels can be found in such satires as the *Lamentations* of Matheolus. It is not any single trait, then, but *La Veuve's* unique combination of a number of them, that may point to its independent importance for Chaucer.

Both La Veuve and the Wife are cloth-makers (*LaV.* 312; *Gen. Prol.* 447–8). Both in their youth have had wealthy old husbands, and have married poorer, younger ones. Both prefer young men to old, and each can be too much for a husband to satisfy. Both have been in financial competition with a young husband (*LaV.* 499; *WBP* 801). La Veuve has "une parliere" to whom she tells all her business (233); the Wife correspondingly has a "gossyb" (529, 544, 548). Both are fond of walking over and talking with their gossybs. To hers La Veuve promises a Sunday picnic (369–72); with hers the Wife takes a walk in the fields in

Lent (543–49). La Veuve has her eye on a young man who lives near her gossyb, "d'autre part vo maison" (328); the Wife woos a young clerk who "Wente at hom to bord / With my gossib" (529). Both women mention dreams and enchantment (*LaV.* 66, 71ff.; *WBP* 575–82). Beside her husbands and children, La Veuve is endowed with a number of other relatives (103–4, 245, 273–4, 333, 373); the Wife is childless, but refers to her "dame" and her niece (537, 576, 583). Each is shown promenading in her finery. La Veuve is an inveterate attender of weddings (*LaV.* 142–151, 203); the Wife memorably makes "visitaciouns"

> To vigilies and to processiouns,
> To prechyng eek, and to thise pilgrimages,
> To pleyes of myracles, and to mariages. . . .
> (vv. 556–8; cf. *RR* 13523–5)

Turning now from character and background to the dramatic development of the pieces themselves, we find a noteworthy similarity in that each culminates in a fight between wife and husband and ends with peaceful reconciliation. In the *Wife of Bath's Prologue* both parties exchange blows, whereas in *La Veuve* only the woman is beaten, in exchange for an insulting tirade. Before giving her husband a final clout the Wife quite clearly pretends to be more injured than she really is; it is hard to read her speech in other than a falsetto voice:

> Til atte laste out of my swogh I breyde.
> "O! hastow slayn me, false theef?" I seyde,
> "And for my land thus hastow mordred me?"
> . . .
> "Now wol I dye, I may no lenger speke."
> (vv. 799–801, 810)

This is the very motif and tone, and close to the actual diction, of La Veuve:

> "Lere, con m'avés martirie!
> Or m'ait Dex le mort otroïe. . . ."
> Puis parole bas a fauset,
> Molt set bien faire le qauset
> Tot autresi con ele muire. . . .[10]
> (vv. 527–8, 535–7)

174

At the end both couples come together:

Puis revienent andoi ensanle. (v. 544)

We fille acorded by us selven two. (v. 812)

The Wife of Bath describes how perfect harmony followed her husband's complete surrender of sovereignty. *La Veuve* ends with the narrator's recomendation to husbands to give in.

Read side by side the *Wife of Bath's Prologue* and *La Veuve* also show many differences, and there are too few verbal resemblances between them to make it likely that Chaucer ever studied a text of the French poem. But their general correspondence in style and genre, in characterization and background, and in their culminating action—where once, perhaps, an echo of actual diction carries across—suggests that *La Veuve* was one of the poems that Chaucer did not read but heard.

THE FABLIAUX,
COURTLY CULTURE, AND
THE (RE)INVENTION OF
VULGARITY

Some years ago, in a book on the Old French fabliaux, I ventured the hypothesis that much of the fabliau diction we might now consider obscene might not have been so obscene in its own time. The fabliau language of sexuality, it still seems to me, is much of the time surprisingly free of impudence or self-consciousness. It often sounds like normal usage, the unreflective language of a culture that was relatively free of linguistic taboos, but took pleasure of various kinds in the direct verbal evocation of sexuality. It must have been the contemporaneous emergence of courtly norms of diction, I suggested, that created, invented, or perhaps reinvented, in the twelfth and thirteenth centuries a new sense of obscene or vulgar language.[1] In this essay I wish to amplify the argument for my hypothesis.

Contrary views are various, but they converge on the general idea that "obscene" fabliau diction is always obscene in the conventional sense. It is self-conscious and impudent, transgressive of accepted usage, seeking an effect of shock or parody or satire. It crosses a preexisting line of demarcation between respectability and license, calling attention to itself at the same time.[2]

One of the corollaries of this conventional view of fabliau diction is to regard it merely as a literary trait, part of the artistic aims of the authors. A typical example of this view is that of Wolf-Dieter Stempel, who approaches medieval obscenity in general as a "literary-aesthetic problem."[3] Seen as such, obscenity has to be accounted for. Why, the critic asks in any given case, does a knowing and relatively sophisticated author *use* obscenity? The answer must be something like: "for shock, or parody, or satire." This judgment is strengthened in proportion to the degree of sophistication that can be imputed to the author of the obscenity. In the case of the fabliaux, if the genre is regarded as sub-

176

stantially a product of the courtly class, the conventional view becomes almost mandatory. The meaning of fabliau obscenity must depend on, and may even be generated by, its courtly opposite.[4]

But the issue refuses to remain merely a literary one, a debate about genre. Pushed a little further, it has implications well beyond the fabliau and into the nature of medieval culture itself. For the conventional view has a certain sanitizing effect. Making so-called obscenity merely literary both cleans it up and marginalizes it. The consequences for our idea of the culture are obvious.

Some holders of the conventional view seem to hold *a priori* the general attitude that linguistic taboo is a given in culture and that the medieval period is no exception. Without solving the problem of the prevalence in culture of any sort of linguistic taboo, one can confidently affirm that obscenity and propriety with words are as relative as they are with acts. We learn from anthropologists that in Tahitian culture eating can be an obscene act when performed in the presence of other people or in public, and that "the same Tahitians who copulated in public would eat separately and privately."[5] In Lesu, "a community in New Ireland, in the southwestern Pacific, there is keen enjoyment in sexual intercourse, which begins almost immediately after puberty, and which is indulged in rather freely." The community "has no idea of the need for concealing sex and stories of a sexual content are freely told."[6] Some cultures, such as the Hopi, have "no 'proper' versus 'obscene' words. All words are on the same mundane, matter-of-fact level."[7] In such modern African languages as Yoruba and Akan, there exists only one term each for vulva, urinate, and defecate.[8] Conversely, in puritanical Dobu (near Papua) "there are no proper terms"—but only obscene ones—"for referring to the sex organs or their function."[9]

As we all recognize, where distinctions do exist between proper and obscene words, they are almost always situational, relative to the context, including the identity and social status of the speaker. A linguist studying the language of Tonga (in the South Pacific) reports that, in spite of the Wesleyans and other missionaries, the culture has preserved a vigorous tradition of *kapekape*, or crude and ribald sex talk. But the impressively rich and imaginative vocabulary of *kapekape* is strictly limited to certain situations: "these range from contexts where *kapekape* is virtually compulsory to those where it is shocking, if it ever occurs at all."[10] *Kapekape* is freely enjoyed at male drinking parties and club meetings, and also in work groups, including office workers of both sexes. In more public situations, such as in banks and post offices, it is severely curtailed; and between or in the presence of brothers and sisters, it is forbidden on pain of extreme violence.[11]

The anthropological evidence is plentiful; we should have no trouble in accepting cultural relativism as regards obscene speech. Indeed, we hardly need anthropological examples—especially since the 1960s—to tell us that some situations permit risqué language and others do not, and that some people readily use a diction that others would consider obscene, or at least vulgar. I agree with Edward Sagarin that in our own culture so-called dirty words "are unquestionably the sole vocabulary that many people have at their command to describe [certain] processes and objects."[12] My own conviction is based, among other things, on two years' informal research aboard a U.S. Navy ship. This vessel carried a stout complement of lifetime military men who were so insulated from any taint of gentility that they habitually and unselfconsciously used four-letter words in ordinary communication. In sick bay, talking to the doctor, there was no use of such terms as "urination" or "testicles." It was "Doc, it burns when I piss," or "Doc, I got a pain in my balls." Listening to such speech in that closed environment, one could imagine a continuous tradition of usage going back to the American Navy of the eighteenth century and beyond, perhaps via the British sailor, to medieval times.

Experiences and reflections of this sort, along with a properly and rigorously relativistic stance, make it easier to be skeptical about the conventional view of fabliau diction. Add to the factors supporting relativism the change within cultures regarding what is obscene,[13] and one can begin to imagine a diction—used comically but not obscenely in the deployment of sexual humor—being gradually rendered more and more vulgar by the spread of new codes of conduct with their new codes of speech.

My hypothesis is that some such change was taking place in the early thirteenth century. The situation was, I suggest, remarkably like that in our own culture over the past thirty years, except in reverse. On 3 March 1965, during the Free Speech Movement on the Berkeley campus, a young poet and drifter named John Thompson sat down in Sproul Plaza displaying a hand-lettered sign saying FUCK. He was promptly arrested and a week later, in the ensuing uproar over what was quickly called "the Filthy Speech Movement," both the chancellor and the president of the university had resigned. Our views concerning obscenity have been changing markedly since that time. It is almost as if our new populism and anti-clitism, our wholesale dismantling of courtesy, are finally undoing the courtly doctrine as set down by Guillaume de Lorris in *Le Roman de la rose* in the thirteenth century:

> Aprés garde que tu ne dies
> ces orz moz ne ces ribaudies:
> ja por nomer vilainne chose
> ne doit ta bouche estre desclouse.
> Je ne tien pas a cortois home
> qui orde chose et laide nome.[14]

[Next guard yourself against using any dirty words or expressions. Your mouth should never open to name a vulgar thing. I don't consider a man courtly who mentions dirty and ugly things.]

Reading the actual situation in the thirteenth century is made especially difficult by the nature of the available evidence. It is both sparse and complex. Yet the idea that the rules of usage as set forth in such texts as the *Roman de la rose* are historically significant, that they signal a new turn in standards of speech, does seem to be implemented by the doctrinal tone in which the rules were promulgated. In the *Roman* the rules are among the commandments of the God of Love to the lover; and their justification by reference to the new ideal of the *courtois* becomes common. Thus the romancer Jean Renart says that his telling "a pleasing tale that has in it nothing offensive or ugly"[15] displays his *cortoisie.* Henri d'Andeli opens the charming *Lai d'Aristote* with the promise that the reader will hear no vulgarity in it: "a work that runs to vulgarity should never be heard at court."[16] A matron in one of the few fabliaux that confront the new rules directly, invited by her husband into some sexy dialogue, refuses, says the author, *com cortoise.*[17]

It seems clear enough that the idea of obscenity promulgated by the courtly tradition is a socially based phenomenon, and if the fabliaux were at bottom a courtly genre (as Per Nykrog believes) or tonally dependent on the courtly tradition, there would be little question as to how to read their obscenity. But the external evidence does not point to an audience of a single class, whether aristocratic or bourgeois or popular, but rather to one of all classes. Similarly, within the tales we find a remarkable awareness of all levels of thirteenth-century society, including its accelerating social mobility. The fabliau audience, then, is heterogeneous; the fabliau authors, many of them clerks, consistently favor no social group except clerks, and mostly they use a realistic style and colloquial diction.[18]

On this basis we might conclude that the fabliaux are the only substantial body of evidence that gives us reliable insight into contemporaneous everyday speech. But because it is literature and not transcripts of actual speech, this evidence is inevitably—shall we say—"contaminated," in part because it is surrounded by other genres of literature, having a somewhat different agenda but with which it can easily be confused, and in part by its own frequently literary usage.

Our only resource for solving this problem is literary sensibility, which is sometimes applied to this material and sometimes not. In any case, the results are admittedly subjective. My reading tells me that there is something basically different in tone and attitude between a "typical" fabliau and such a production as the poem "Richeut," or between a fabliau and certain parts of the *Roman de Renart,* just as there are allowances to be made, reading the fabliaux, for the peculiar temperaments of the authors Gautier le Leu and Rutebeuf.

The obscenity of "Richeut," its coupling of sadistic wickedness and bizarre sexual virtuosity, has a pathological flavor that is rare in the fabliaux. Different in tone but similarly alien to fabliau humor are the most obscene episodes of the *Roman de Renart,* which go at it with a self-conscious exhibitionism and an explicitly defiant, satirical effrontery toward the feudal and monastic establishments. Renart's lascivious blasphemy in calling *cons* (cunt) "the most beautiful name in the world"[19] in the course of a "confession" is well beyond the fabliau's casual and playful treatment of religion.

A reasonable distinction must also be made between the preponderantly realistic and everyday style of the fabliaux, and the occasional use that fabliau authors, who often had some literary training, make of formal rhetoric and other resources of the courtly style. The fabliaux do contain a few formal portraits, a few formal descriptions and catalogues, and a few topoi which, as Nykrog has shown, can create an effect of irony or even shock in the setting of fabliau diction or motifs.[20] But I differ with the proposition that this sort of effect is a dominant characteristic of the fabliaux. It seems to me that the attribution of shock or literary artifice too often depends on an *a priori* reading of the situation, as if to say: These authors are knowing and sophisticated, their language or situations are palpably obscene, and so they are consciously being shocking or parodic or satirical.

My point is that sexual humor is not inherently *ein Problem*. Sexual humor does not have to be shocking or satirical. The reason that sexuality is—throughout human culture—the most frequent subject of humor is not because it is so often taboo but because it offers so many opportunities for amusement. It is most often simply . . . funny. It does not *need* to be based on aggression or on relief from repression or on any of the other motives attributed to it in Freudian theory. (It is surprising, in fact, how little a reading of Freud's *Jokes and Their Relation to the Unconscious* helps to account for the humor of the fabliaux.) The anthropologists Finnegan Alford and Richard Alford, in a study of seventy-five societies throughout the world and at many levels of cultural complexity, find that "the more sexually restrictive a society is, the less they employ sexual humor . . . This is in contrast to what we would expect using Freudian theory . . . The opposite seems to be the case; the more sexual behavior is restricted, the less sexuality is available for humor."[21]

The contemplation of sexuality as a source of amusement accords well with what we find to be the place of sexuality in the fabliau ethos itself. Sex, in the fabliaux, is fun; it is set congenially within a hedonistic and materialistic universe alongside food, money, and wit as the things most to be desired and enjoyed. It is set, furthermore, in a context of folk wisdom that comically and ironically recognizes that pleasure is ephemeral, that things can often go wrong. The fabliaux endlessly amuse us with sexuality that somehow goes wrong and then gets righted. The overcoming of difficulties—in opportunity, controllability, privacy, potency, comprehension (*how* do you do it?), initiation, compatibility, rivalry—far outweigh as a source of fabliau humor any specific taboos placed by the culture on the subject itself. I need not mention the manifold added difficulties of married life, the perennial battle of the sexes, with which the subject of sexuality is closely mingled.

To establish historically that the courtly rules of clean speech, which came along with the new courtly rules of feeling and behavior, were intended for a public that was not yet sufficiently sensitive to the obscenity of plain speech—this would ideally require us to examine popular speech before the advent of Courtesy. Unfortunately, there is little extant evidence of popular usage before the fabliaux themselves. There are no French analogues to the tenth-century Old High German phrasebook, a travel glossary for the Latin-speaking visitor to German lands. Here among such useful phrases as "Where do you come from, brother?" and "Where is your wife?" we come across "How many times did you fuck?" and "A dog's ass in your nose!"[22] Without such resources for the early-medieval traveler to France, we have to dig within post-courtly French itself.

There are tantalizing hints in the early romance *Eneas,* in which courtly ladies occasionally let slip military-grade obscenities, as if the new rules were not yet perfectly understood.[23] There are four fabliaux in which obscenity is itself the subject, raised as if it were a newly contested issue and generating such authorial comments as "I want to show by this example that women should not be too proud to say *foutre* when all the same they're doing it."[24] In two of these four tales, all of which are concerned with sexual initiation and seduction by means of animal euphemisms, there are a couple of slips into the bald vernacular that suggest that it was still very close to the surface.[25] There is also, late in the thirteenth century, the celebrated defense of plain speech made by Jean de Meun in his continuation of the *Roman de la rose.*[26] Is Lady Reason's eloquent argument for giving plain, unvarnished names to God's creations simply theory, an argument in philosophical linguistics? Or does it hark back to the popular experience of an earlier generation, perhaps that of Jean's grandfather? Part of the passage has a retrospective flavor. Speaking of the word *coilles* (balls), Reason says:

> Se fames nes noment en France,
> ce n'est fors desacoutumance,
> car li propres nons leur pleüst
> qui acoutumé leur eüst (7101–04)

> [If women don't name them in France, it is nothing but *desacoutumance,*
> for the right names would please those who were used to them.]

Does *desacoutumance* (unaccustomedness) suggest an immemorial taboo or just a period of disuse since the advent of Courtesy? The unvarnished word in question seems more at home in the rest of the passage:

> Chascune qui les va nomant
> les apele ne sai conmant,
> borses, harnais, riens, piches, pines,
> ausint con se fussent espines;
> mes quant les sentent bien joignanz,

els nes tienent pas a poignanz.
Or les noment si conme el seulent. (7111–17)

[Every woman who goes around naming them calls them I don't know
what: purses, gear, things, cruets, even pinecones, as if they were
prickles; but when they feel them right up close they don't find
them prickly. Then they call them what they do usually.]

I have already suggested that our judgment about the relative vulgarity of the fabliaux in their own time will have some consequence for
our idea of French medieval culture. The present hypothesis suggests a
more realistic and thus a richer and more complex picture of the period
than perhaps we are used to. Dualism is so commonplace an idea in our
descriptions of Gothic culture, that we tend to overlook the fact that we
have made some dualisms less equal than others. By drawing question-
able analogies—equating the fabliaux with the realistic and obscene
carvings in otherwise sober churches; or with the playful, perverse, and
obscene decorations in the margins of otherwise sober manuscripts; or
with the impudent and riotous merriment sponsored on selected feast
days by otherwise sober clerics—we have marginalized their values,
pushing them to the edge of the cultural picture as if they were truant,
temporary, and depending for their significance on a contrast with more
orthodox values.

The fabliaux are not, however, as "minor" a literature as they may
appear. Given the fact that they are not establishment literature, and
given all the chances of later suppression, the survival of approximately
160 of these texts suggests the existence of a much larger corpus.
Given, too, the existence of the oral tradition on which almost all of
these tales were borne, we can easily imagine fabliau meanings and
attitudes as having been massively propagated in their time, not to
speak of before and since. Indeed, the twin traditions of hedonism and
materialism, which these stories evoke, can hardly have been of marginal significance in the thirteenth century; nor can they have origi-
nated then. They are old traditions, older then Courtesy and older than
Christianity. Historically, then, it is less likely that the fabliaux rudely
irrupted within the established confines of courtly decorum than that
the courtly system established, within the large area of common usage,
its own exclusive province of polite speech, transforming everything
else, hitherto merely vulgate, into vulgarity.

The dualism I am proposing for our view of medieval culture is one in which hedonistic materialism takes an acknowledged place along-side courtly idealism, and alongside Christian morality as well. But of course I do not mean that we should imagine the population to have been divided irrevocably into separate camps, whether the courtly, the pious, or the unmoral. There were undoubtedly pure souls of various sorts: the saints, the complete courtiers, the irremediable hedonists. But remembering the varieties of relativism described by the anthropologists, we should more realistically imagine a complex culture in which many individuals—perhaps most—belonged simultaneously to a number of subcultures, each having its own ethos, language, and literature. And just as some of the men on my Navy ship could move from the culture and language of the forecastle to the culture and language of the wardroom, without feeling alien in either, so medievals—inheritors of folk tradition, of Christianity, and exposed now to the powerful idealism of Courtesy—at some times felt impelled to honor one of their memberships, at other times others. This is what a mixed fabliau audience of all social classes would suggest: at certain times and places—let's say of an evening, after a good meal and some drinks—many different people would feel free to get together, without tension or guilt, to acknowledge, appreciate, and even mutually celebrate through stories the immemorial pleasures of money, food, wit, and sex.

Taking this relativistic, more even-handed view of medieval obscenity, we are free to ask a last historical question, deeper and perhaps impossible to answer. If the courtly tradition did invent or reinvent obscenity, where did its idea of obscenity come from? The tradition is nothing if not obsessively erotic. Whence, then, comes its linguistic puritanism, its prohibition of plain and simple erotic language as dirty words?

It is tempting to assume that the verbal propriety of courtly love was simply a reappropriation of the old Roman doctrine of decency, available in such writers as Cicero, Quintilian, and Seneca,[27] just as the social and political doctrine of courtesy that emerged in the German imperial courts drew "on the ethical writing of ancient Rome for its articulation."[28] But there is a sense in which courtly love—in working out a new refinement of feeling, a new sensuality, and a new aesthetic of the body—could have invented its own taboos, taboos arising in symbiotic relation to the ideals they defended and the obscenities they proscribed. If there is any such symbiotic relation among ideals, taboos, and obscenity, the Roman/Courtly connection becomes remote indeed. For Roman obscenity is so different from medieval that their taboos and proprieties can hardly be imagined as having had a common base. Roman obscenity was self-conscious, proestablishment, punitive, strongly sanctioned literarily by genre and style, and counterweighted by powerful taboos propagated in authoritative technical manuals.[29] Medieval obscenity, on the other hand, was unselfconscious, popular, genial, ignored by canon law, opposed by Christian moralism (which it mainly ignores) only at a distance, and disowned by a tradition of courtesy that was only just beginning to make its mark on European culture.

THE EMERGENCE OF
PSYCHOLOGICAL ALLEGORY
IN OLD FRENCH ROMANCE*

I

For the student of fiction, the most noteworthy accomplishment of Guillaume de Lorris in the *Roman de la Rose* is his invention of large-scale psychological allegory. C. S. Lewis, who has taught us how to read the poem, suggests that it is an offspring of Old French Romance and the moral allegory of the Prudentius tradition: the *Roman* deals with the erotic content of the romances in a form made newly potent by the moral allegorists of the school of Chartres. Lewis sees an adaptation or borrowing of allegory by romance before Guillaume in Chrétien de Troyes. There, it is suggested, we can see narrative poetry taking over allegory as a tool whenever psychology is in question.[1] The purpose of this paper is to amplify the history of psychological allegory at this point, and thereby to modify Lewis' admittedly general account. Thus, while there are excellent reasons for using Chrétien as the exemplar of courtly romance writing, it can be shown that the tendency toward allegory in the romances is considerably more extensive than his practice would indicate. The romances constitute a virtual encyclopedia of psychological personifications, including illustrations and discussions of most of the "characters" in the *Roman de la Rose*. More important, this tendency does not represent simply a borrowing of the forms and procedures of moral allegory. Indeed, the allegory developing within the romances is not even so much a modification of the preestablished species as an independent invention. Specifically designed for psychological analysis, it points to the unique structural achievement of Guillaume de Lorris.

It is this uniqueness, this difference from the allegory of the Prudentius tradition, that makes the *Roman de la Rose* an ancestor of the novel. Indeed, while the poem had many admirers and "imitators,"[2] it was never fully imitated; no medieval poet reproduces its full, subtle exhibition of human psychology in quite the same literary form. Guessing at the reason for this, one might say that the assumptions behind the old tradition were too strong, and the surface similarity between the two kinds of allegory too great, for the distinctiveness of Guillaume's kind to become clearly apparent. The "imitators" take variously the erotic content, the setting, the actors, the superficial prettiness, but not the basic structure. We are able to see the difference perhaps only as fiction has come to be separable from morally didactic literature, as psychology has come to be distinguishable from ethics. Given this separation (be it good or bad) in modern thinking, if Guillaume deals with psychology, Prudentius deals with morals. In less schismatic terms, Prudentius is a prescriptive psychologist, Guillaume a descriptive one; in morals Prudentius is a cosmographer, Guillaume a biographer.

Lewis describes (pp. 259–260) these two kinds of allegory as the moral or homiletic and the erotic, but he seems to disregard the difference of structure that accompanies the differences of subject and purpose implied by these labels. Long ago Gaston Paris attempted to objectify this difference by briefly listing the features of Guillaume's allegory that set it apart from the old tradition. His main point is that in the *Psychomachia* personifications are the only actors, and their actions represent the constant relationship among them. In the *Roman,* however, the personifications are made the means to something else, to tracing the vicissitudes of a completely individual and human action. Furthermore, Paris asserts, certain of Guillaume's personifications (as *Dangier* and *Bel Acueil*) are completely new, representing transient aspects of being, aspects of personality. In the earlier allegory, only the durable and general qualities had been personified.[3] Ernest Langlois objected to this formula. The action transpiring in the *Roman,* he says, deals with relations just as constant as those in Prudentius; *Dangier* (defined by Paris as "la tendance innée chez la femme à ne pas céder sans résistance à celui qui la prie") is not a new personification at all, but represents a quality just as durable and general as do Chastity, Shame, Pride or any of the other Virtues and Vices of Guillaume's predecessors. It is true, he grants, that Guillaume's terms are less abstract, less metaphysical than those of Prudentius, but the same can be said of the allegories of Raoul de Houdenc and Huon de Méri, whose personifications include Vainglory, Fornication, etc.[4]

These objections illustrate the difficulty of defining the area of Guillaume's originality, but they do not belie the soundness of Paris' feeling for it. The point is that the level of generalization of the individual per-sonifications is hardly as important as how they are used. It is in the pattern of their relationships that their newness resides; here Paris' inti-mation that the personifications are not the only characters in the *Roman* is to the point. The *Roman,* in the part that interests us particu-larly, is largely a representation of a single female psyche, whose ele-ments engage and react to each other according to psychological laws. In the *Psychomachia* we can hardly see any *persona* emerging; we have a shadowy suggestion of the presence of an Everyman or Mankind as the container for this battle-in-the-soul, but he eludes the grasp. A dif-ference in organization can be easily illustrated. *Dangier* is inimical to *Bel Acueil* as the *Libido* of Prudentius is inimical to his *Pudicitia.* But where *Pudicitia* merely conquers *Libido* in one of a series of scarcely related hand-to-hand encounters,[5] the actions of *Dangier* and *Bel Acueil* are part of a whole chain of related circumstances. *Dangier* chastises *Bel Acueil,* then is mollified by *Pitié* and *Franchise.* He becomes lazy and almost gentlemanly, and because of his absence (and the freedom of *Bel Acueil*) *Venus* can make her power felt. Immediately thereafter, *Honte* emerges. Stimulated by outside influences such as *Jalosie,* and in the company of newly-appearing *Paor,* she rouses *Dangier* to his for-mer vigor and watchfulness as *Bel Acueil* is removed from the scene. This sequence (2920–3754), in its fullness the richest, the most delicate and subtle piece of psychologizing in the poem, not only postulates the existence of the Lady, with the psychic events surrounding her first kiss from the Dreamer; with her it constitutes a plot. It is fiction as the *Psychomachia* is only sermon.

This is not to blame moral allegory for what it does not try to do; nor is it, really, to lay the burden of Prudentius' crudeness on the genre as a whole. The middle ages saw many refinements and elaborations of it. To advert to the examples suggested by Langlois, the *Tornoiemenz Antecrit* of Huon de Méri has basically the same structure as the *Psychomachia,* even though it is brought strictly up to date with decorative references to fashionable literature (Chrétien and Raoul de Houdenc), fashionable, secular vices (as *Bobenz, Desdaing, Cointise*), and a lengthy digression on love, including a dream and a *jugement d'amour.*[6]

The two allegories of Raoul de Houdenc, written only a generation before the *Roman de la Rose,* show some of the liveliness and original-ity characteristic of that poet. The structure of the *Voie de Paradis* resembles that of the *Roman;* the narrator is placed among a crowd of personified abstractions. Since Raoul adopts the pilgrimage rather than the pitched battle as a vehicle for his allegory, he has the opportunity for a more delicate, and at the same time more consecutive treatment of his subject. In a passage or two he actually approaches the kind of fictional sequence characteristic of Guillaume—as when the stereotyped progress from Confession to Penitence is interrupted by the loss of the narrator's guide *Perseveranche* and the attack of a band of Vices. In the *Songe d'Enfer,* a kind of allegorized autobiography, there is a sequence beginning at *Vile Taverne*—including a scrape with *Versez* (Brawling) and a visit to *Chastiau-Bordel* with *Yvrece* as guide—which is charmingly satisfactory in its imaginative rendering of the facts of life. But the variety and elaboration of these two poems[7] do not take us very far toward Guillaume's special achievement. For all the colorful particularity which produces in the *Songe d'Enfer* a contemporary moral geography (*Tricherie* is ruler of Poitou),[8] and for all the surface unity which the introduction of a participating narrator creates in both poems, neither of them can be consistently seen through to a local, fictional situation. We have Prudentius' cosmic moral order narrowed down to autobiographical dimensions, but no character emerges from the biography. An "I," a protagonist, is rhetorically present, but the allegory tells us nothing about him as an individual personality. His action is largely dictated by the prescriptive moral sense, from without. The interest, as in moral allegory as late as Spenser's *Faerie Queene,* is to "fashion" the reader "in vertuous and gentle discipline,"[9] and not, as in the *Roman de la Rose,* to analyze the peculiar combination of forces in the individual mind and to display from within the necessary interaction between its experiences and responses. This is to say that in strategy these allegories are more typically medieval than Guillaume's; his is a species which nearly resembles modern psychological fiction.

I I

Guillaume comes upon psychological allegory in Old French romance. His romance heritage supplies him, in the first place, with a great deal of his subject-matter. The *Roman de la Rose,* is, as Lewis has clearly stated (pp. 113–116), essentially the subjective, psychological, emotional matter of conventional romance, separated from the external adventures and set down independently. We can find incidents and sequences in the romances which closely parallel, in largely "realistic" terms, what the *Roman* presents allegorically. In *Galeran de Bretagne,* after the love between Galeran and Fresne has been firmly established,

189

a servant-girl carries the gossip to the Abbess Ermine. The latter, who is both the hero's aunt and the heroine's godmother, is violently opposed to the match, and her reproaches bring about a parting of the lovers. The *Roman de la Rose* continues essentially the same sequence in the arousing of *Jalosie* by *Male Bouche.*[10] A parallel even closer in spirit is that between the frightening of *Bel Acueil* and the emergence of *Dangier* in the *Roman,* and the Lady's initial rejection of the Knight in the *Lai de l'Ombre.*[11] The Lady's speech (422 ff.), which begins with a virtual definition of *bel acueil,* shows just the transition from injured courtesy to the direct snub figured by the allegory. The reverse movement—the mollification of *Dangier* by *Franchise* and *Pitié,* and the reëntrance of *Bel Acueil*—can be clearly seen in *Amadas and Ydoine.* Here Ydoine is moved by the extreme love-sickness of the fainted Amadas; pitying his condition, fearing that he may be dead and she to blame, she shifts from proud and cruel rejection to love.[12]

The reader who examines these parallels will be able to gauge the distance between narrative and allegorical treatments of a given "story," and the greater particularity and precision of the latter whenever psychology is involved. In being able to isolate and personify the active elements in his characters' minds or attitudes, Guillaume can fully dramatize action that in narrative, even at its most dramatic moments, must remain half-hidden. Not bound by surface realism, the allegorist has the license and the leisure to invest these attitudes with a wealth of expressive detail far beyond the means of the narrative poet.

Though Guillaume was the first of the courtly-love poets to perfect a method fully able to satisfy the romantic interest in psychology, he was not the first to seek one. The style of the early French romances shows that many of his predecessors felt that their new subject-matter imposed extraordinary technical demands. By far the most noteworthy response to this demand was the development of the inner monologue—the *Entschluss-* and *Liebesmonolog*[13]—and within this form, for two-thirds of a century before Guillaume, psychological allegory was incubated. For the distinction between psychological and moral allegory,[14] this location is crucial and determinative; for with the exception of its introduction, its doctrinal passages, and certain necessary narrative links, the *Roman* of Guillaume deals with action in the mind. It is in some respects still a series of minutely articulated monologues, lifted from their narrative and dramatic contexts, but retaining all the relevance to a given problem with which a fictional matrix would endow them.

At first glance our incubating material seems unpromising. The love-monologue of the "classical" and *aventure* romance has not often been taken seriously in modern times. It is à la mode by 1160 (in *Eneas*); in Chrétien it is already a stylistic toy, mechanical and frigid, one of the more archaic manifestations of the casuistic of love.[15] When the significant examples have been collected and examined, however, the form takes on an importance far out of proportion to its contribution to any single romance. It does not develop neatly over the chronological period (ca. 1150–ca. 1234) in question; yet we can find variations which seem to indicate possible stages in the development of psychological allegory.

The suggestive link between monologue and allegory is in the fact that from the earliest romances on, there is a widespread tendency for the monologue signalizing mental conflict to break down into two or more voices. These voices represent alternating moods of the ego, or, more significantly, the differing attitudes or positions of different parts of the mind. In the highest stage of technical elaboration, the contending voices have been given names such as *Amor* and *Raison* and they interact dramatically, in accordance with these names, to produce an allegory of the mind's action.[16]

A number of surrounding literary and cultural conditions are relevant to the nature of this development. The psychological matter of the romances represents an elaboration of tendencies inherent in the courtly love tradition itself, and these tendencies are broadly characteristic of what has been called the period of subjectivity, of self-reliance and independent activity, following the crusades.[17] More specifically, the courtly interest in individual psychology finds a suggestive cultural parallel in the contemporary rise of the psychology of mysticism. One need not insist on specific influence in order to see in the solitary self-analysis of the lover a kinship with the passionate introspection of the mystic, searching for God in his own soul.[18] For the mystic school of philosophers and theologians in the twelfth century make of introspection and self-analysis a doctrine, and for it they lay a groundwork of systematic psychology. Their writings are particularly rich in descriptions of the soul. They are highly concerned with the modes of meditation and contemplation and with the mutability and instability of the passions, "ista in corde humano multiformis altercatio."[19] Even in its formal structure, the erotic psychology, like the erotic religion and morality, both reflects and rivals the Christian one.[20] Each has its list of passions. As the psychological treatises divide the basic activities of the

191

soul into the rational and the affective, the basic division in the mind of the lover is that between *Raison* and *Armor.* Each in its own way argues the ultimate sovereignty of Love over Reason.[21] Thus the new world of feeling and sentiment that finds its first expression in the Provençal lyric can be "written up" at length, and in narrative form, in its second and third generations. In the *Liebesmonolog* the romance writers dissect and examine the initial personal utterance, tracing it to its sources and following it to its possible consequences. In this they reflect the newly ready capacity of the age to deal with the inner life and to see the mechanism of the soul in sharp definition.

Introspection begets monologue, but the particular form of the dialogue-in-monologue is exemplary of a further aspect of twelfth-century thinking: its predilection for debate. Plato described thinking as "a silent inner conversation of the soul with itself," and the concept of thought as speech persists until the advent of modern psychology.[22] It is worthwhile to note here that the Stoic and Christian moralists with whom Lewis chooses (pp. 59–66) to illustrate the introspective atmosphere attending the birth of allegory—those whose metaphors of struggle and contest prefigure the full-fledged psychomachy—characteristically turn to inner conversation as a form for their thinking. Seneca and Epictetus adopt it as a means of strengthening and examining the soul.[23] Marcus Aurelius entitles his meditations *To Myself.* Augustine, coining the title *Soliloquia,* writes dialogues between himself and *Ratio.*[24] But in turning this traditional inner conversation into debate, the romance psychologists seem to reflect not only specific psychological theory but also the general and unprecedented prominence of dialectic, "disputationis disciplina," in twelfth-century schools. This is the period of the emergence of the *quaestio* and *disputatio* as general teaching methods, and the evolution of the *summa,* with its carefully marshalled lists of contrary arguments, as a favorite form for theological exposition.[25] In addition, the way in which some dialogues-in-monologue are introduced indicates the inevitable assimilation with a dominant complex of literary forms: *conflictus, altercatio, tenson, débat,* and the perennial battle between the Virtues and the Vices.[26]

The influence of medieval patterns of feeling on the form of the romance monologue is dramatically revealed when we compare it with its Ovidian model.[27] The celebrated monologue of Medea (*Metamorphoses* vii. 9–71) deals with the conflict between passion and reason that was to become a conventional cue for monologue in the romance.

For us the rhetoric of it has three noteworthy features. There are touches of personification and allegory:

. . . aliudque cupido,	(19)

mens aliud suadet:

dixit, et ante oculos rectum pietasque pudorque	(72)
constiterant, et victa dabat iam terga Cupido.	

Ovid makes consistent use of rhetorical self-address:

nam cur iussa patris nimium mihi dura videntur?	(14)

. . . cur, quem modo denique vidi,	(15)
ne pereat, timeo?	

And throughout the monologue he so shifts the person of address (now first, now second) as to create a sense of the lively interplay of moods or emotions. He does no more with it. It should be noted that in the alternation of the *ego* and *tu* voices there is nothing systematic. The monologue opens with the *tu* voice, "frustra, Medea, repugnas," as if to suggest surrender to love. But after an interval of rhetorical question by the *ego* voice, the *tu* voice is urging the rejection of passion. The *ego* then takes Jason's side in a more extended exchange, and maintains this position to the end. The other voice, however, keeps shifting in character, now encouraging (47–50), now censorious (69–71). This is to say that the grammatical division of the monologue between persons is purely a device of rhetoric, and does not suggest dramatically conceived dialogue.

Rhetorical self-address— the simplest stage of the form we are tracing —is of course a common figure in the rhetoric of the romances.[28] What is surprising is that the early "Ovidian" romances do not build on the suggestions of personification and allegory in Ovid, but rather on this, on the notion of alternate voices. The style of *Piramus et Tisbé, Narcisus* and *Eneas* is characterized by extensive and peculiar elaboration of the monologue in two persons. It becomes schematic; there is an immediate impulse to align the *gie* and *tu* voices with consistent and opposing points of view, thus defining them sharply enough to create dialogue-in-monologue. Often, as in the following monologue from *Eneas,* the fact of dialogue is accentuated by the use of alternate lines for each voice. Here Lavinia, after seeing Eneas from the tower window, is confronted by the problem of loving him in the face of her mother's hatred for him. The second voice emerges after fifty lines of monologue:

> Lo Troïen m'estuet amer, (8127)
> mais molt lo me covient celer,
> que la raïne ne lo sache,
> qui m'en destroint et me menace:
> ne velt que vers lui preigne amor.
> Qu'en puis ge, lasse, se ge plor?
> Or l'ain, gehui m'en ert petit.
> —Fole Lavine, qu'as tu dit?
> —Amors me destroint molt por lui.
> —Et tu l'eschive, se lo fui!
> —Nel puis trover an mon corage.
> —Ja n'eres tu ier si salvage.
> —Or m'a Amors tote dontee.
> —Molt malement t'en es gardee.
> —Molt m'an ert po gehui matin,
> or me fet fere male fin;
> ne garrai pas longues issi.
> —Por coi t'arestas tu ici?
> —Por lo Troïen esgarder.
> —Bien t'an peüsses consirrer.
> —Por coi?—Ne fu noiant savoir
> quel venisses ici veor.
> —Maint an i ai ge ja veü,
> unc mes de nul rien ne me fu.[29]

This technique has been criticised for its failure to achieve Ovid's naturalness.[30] It is possible, however, that surface naturalness did not come forward in the poet's mind when dealing with his technical problem. He seems—even after we allow for his inferior skill—to look at mental conflict differently than Ovid did. He tends to see it not as a haphazard shifting of external attitudes but as an inner debate between members of a divisible or divided mind. The poet is not absolutely consistent in this regard. Occasionally—and this is true of a number of the poets we are considering—he allows a more extended argument of the second voice to melt into the first without abrupt transition (8279–99). Here, as the *tu* voice has persuaded the ego to give up the idea of a divided love, it is "natural" that the two then become indistinguishable. In general, however, the clarity with which the voices are separated in character is remarkable.

In the quotation from *Eneas* above we can already see that the second voice has a mildly duenna-like tone[31] in the face of the impulsiveness of the first. Elsewhere it is used to express Lavinia's streak of opportunism (8729 ff.), and her sense of fidelity (8279). In Eneas' monologues it is the voice of common sense (8961 ff.), of antifeminism (8980–88, 8997–9009), and of deceptiveness (9073–88), in opposition to the hero's more romantic and tender inclinations.

A survey of all of the considerable examples of this technique in the romances bears out the pattern we see in *Eneas*. The dialogue-in-monologue appears predominantly in love-scenes or love-crises, and the contending voices are used to express the values and issues central to the doctrines of courtly love. Individual poets vary in their feeling for the proximity of this form to psychological allegory proper. In Gautier D'Arras' *Eracle,* which contains several monologues in two voices, the contending elements are not actually personified, though we can clearly see this tendency in a long monologue of Athanais, for instance, where the second voice addresses the first as *suer, douce amie* (3590, 3657, cf. 3644). Here, the problems are how to communicate her love to Paridès, and how to overcome the temporal and moral dangers of the love affair; the alter ego is close to being a combined personification of prudence, loyalty and honor (3644–3719), and the debate is similar to several which in other romances are actually assigned to *Amor* and *Sen.*[32]

In *Galeran de Bretagne,* among several examples of dialogue-in-monologue, with the voices more-or-less sharply articulated, we find one in which the second voice, though not actually personified, invokes the personification just under the surface. Here Esmeree, daughter of the Duke, debates whether to tell Galeran of her love:

"En la fin m'estuet il ouvrir,"   (4498)
Fait Esmeree en son pourpens,
"A Galeren ce que je pens,
Car la santé est bonne a querre."
"Comment? Veulx tu doncques requerre

Le Breton d'amours tout avant?
Tousjours mes te seroit davant
Mis ytel ledure et tel honte."

Hue de Rotelande similarly verges on psychological allegory while not actually giving the form its fullest possible elaboration. In *Ipomedon* a monologue of La Fiere (956–1098) is presented as essentially a debate between voices espousing *orgoil* and *simplicité* respectively, and the latter wins. This is, with less subtle and refined conceptions of those qualities, an early version of the rivalry between *Dangier* and *Bel Acueil* in the *Roman de la Rose:*

Ostez iceo, ne serreit prus,   (989)
Si jeo m'enbaundenase a tuz,
Trop averoie le quer leger.
Jeo nel deveraie pas prier,
Par droit deveraie estre prie:
Amur, trop vus ai aquointe,
Kant my quers est d'amer si prest
Un hom, dount ne sei, qi il est,
De quele terre ne quele lignage,
C'il est de haut ou bas parage;
Ne sai, coment il ad a non:—
Q'avez vus dit? A grant reison
Doit il par amur estre amez,
Kar si beaus hom ne fust unke nez,
Si curteis hom, mien escient,
Ne nasquit unkes de base gent . . .

At a very similar point in the progress of his love-story, the author of *Guillaume de Palerne* introduces (1587 ff.) the second voice in Melior's monologue as that of *Amor.*

Amor, almost universally present in the minds of lovers, emerges personified in a monologue as early as the *Roman de Troie* (20701–74). Achilles, tormented by the military and amatory dilemma of loving the daughter of the enemy king, is represented as being addressed by *Amor* in a considerable sermon, in which his transgressions of the rules of love's service are brought forcibly to mind. *Athis and Prophilias* contains about seventeen dialogues-in-monologue. In several the author actually names the contending voices, bringing *Amor* into dramatic conflict with another personified attitude of the mind. This degree of specification is also found in *Floire et Blancheflor, Florimont* and *L'Escoufle*.

Amor does not have a uniform character in the romances; it is clear, however, that we are not dealing here with merely a traditional cupid, but rather with a personification of the whole set of desires, impulses and even doctrines that love brings to prominence in the lover's consciousness. He includes the whole range of qualities that Guillaume de Lorris distributes among *Amor, Bel Acueil* and *Venus*. This is to say that the *Athis* poet, for instance, is not nearly so discriminating a psychologist as Guillaume. It is *Amor* who appears in order to urge Prophilias to make love to his friend's wife. The personification emerges from an inner debate, and seconds the advice of the *alter ego:*

Mes trop es fel et orguilleus	(669)
Et vers Amors contralïeus.	

. . . .

Amors vialt fere toz ses buens,	(677)
Plus est nobles que rois ne cuens.	
Amors li dit: "Prophilïas,	
Ne tenir pas cest plet a gas!	
Li deus d'amors t'a si navré	
Que tu ne puez avoir santé,	
Se par li n'est, bien le te di.	
Del tot te met an sa merci,	
A li t'otroie et si t'i rant!"[33]	

The opponent of *Amor* emerges a few lines later:

Savoirs li r'est el cors antrez,	(723)
Qui en met hors les maus pansez.	
De la raige qu'il a eüe	
Toz ses corages li remue.	
Et dit: "Cheitis, que est ce, las?	
Lai toi morir, Prophilias!	
Grant desverie me demeinne.	
Amors, trop par estes vileinne,	
Qui tel chose me rovez feire."	

Savoir is here still so closely identified with the ego that it is doubtful which is speaking. At any rate, when Prophilias (in one of the nearly comic scenes of the romance) debates whether to take advantage of his friend's permission to sleep with Cardionès, the rival personifications reemerge:

> Amors li dit: "Que viaus tu fere? (1185)
> Viaus te tu donc arriere trere?
> Or puez avoir mout bon leisir
> Et mecine de toi garir.
> Que fez, qu'atanz? Sene ta plaie!
> Garis le mal qui si t'esmaie!
> Ja n'aies tu mes de li eise,
> S'or ne fez chose qui te pleise.
> Ja est il nuiz, nus ne te voit:
> Or puez bien fere ton esploit."
> Savoirs le toiche, Amors l'esfroie,
> Qui son corage li desvoie.
> Grant tençon a en son corage:
> L'un de savoir, l'autre de rage.

Savoir, always the weaker, does not even find speech, but *Amor* springs into action:

> Amors le prant, el lit le bote, (1207)
> Puis li a dit: "Or naiez dote!
> Prophilïas, ne t'atardier,
> Car te hastes de comancier!"

Amor has not yet attained the refinement of character he has in the *Roman de la Rose;* here he clearly incorporates some of the sensuality that Guillaume de Lorris personifies in *Venus*.[34] This is again seen where *Amor* is described as displaying the physical attractions of Athis to Gaiete's imagination and burning her as *Venus* makes *Bel Acueil* feel the heat of her torch in the *Roman de la Rose*.[35]

Savoir reappears in Gaiete's monologues with its name changed to *San,* personifying apart from "common sense" and practicality a number of other conservative qualities that appear separately in the *Roman de la Rose* as, for instance, *Honte* and *Dangier:*

An son cuer sant une meslee   (3781)
Qui puet a peinne estre acordee.
Amors et Sans i tienent plet:
Ce qu'Amors viaut, Sans li desfet.

. . . .

Sans la chastie et dit: "Ne fere!   (3801)
De folie te doiz retrere.
Regarde, bele, a ton parage,
Ne fere honte a ton lignage!"[36]

Amor in turn summarizes this attitude by asking: "De coi demeinnes or dongier?" (3781).

In *Floire et Blancheflor* (Version I, 1603–44) Savoir urges Floire to leave Babylon and give up his search for Blancheflor; *Amor* gives him hope of finding her, and reminds him that he cannot live without her. *Pitié* is briefly pitted against *Amor* in *Florimont* (2501–06) when the hero is torn between remaining with his parents and departing with the Pucele de l'Ile Selee. Later in the romance (8948–9036) there is a fuller debate between *Sapience* and *Amor* in the mind of Romadanaple. The lover, Povre Perdu, is already sitting at her bedside as the relative merits of taking a rich or a poor lover are presented to her mind. *Amor,* of course, prevails.

In *L'Escoufle,* the dialogues between *Amor* and its opponents are rendered with an animation that proclaims even further the extent to which allegory has emerged from the romance tissue. Aelis is about to descend from her window by a rope of linens, to elope with Guillaume:

La fenestre qui si haute ere   (3906)
La faisoit douter totes voies,
Et ses sens la remet es voies
De raison, qui mout li keurt seure
E qui li dist: "Fole, demeure.
Vels tu hounir tot ton lignage?
Se tu t'en vas en soignentage,
Tuit ti ami i aront honte."
Mais amors abat et sormonte
Son sens, et boute tot arriere
Raison, et dist: "En quel maniere
Puet cis voiages remanoir?

Lairoit on son ami manoir
Avuec, se ele estoit remese?
Nenil. Dont ne vaut une frese
S'ele ne fait quanqu'ele a empris . . ."

She hears her lover below, and begins to climb out:

Hardemens et amors l'escole   (3946)
K'ele se tiengne bien as dras.
Fait amors: "Bele et ja vendras
La desous a ton douç ami."
Fait sens et raison: "Qu'est ce? aimi!
Aelis, irés vos ent donques?
—Oïl voir.—Or ne fist ce onques
Fille a roi tel descouvenue.
—Por coi? Mes amis m'est venue
Querre, et je ne m'en iroie? . . ."

Much later, after they have long been separated, Aelis is trying to
decide whether the young falconer who is telling his story to the Count
is really Guillaume. Her moments of mounting recognition and hesitation are presented as interpolations in the long recital of Guillaume's
adventures:

Ces paroles li ont percié   (7550)
Le cuer et cangié sa pensée.
Se ses sens ne l'eüst tensée,
El li fust lués salie au col;
Puis se pense: "Se jou l'acol
Et ce n'est il, jou arai honte.
Qui que soit a conté cest conte
A cestui, que ce n'est mie."
Si est desloiaus anemie.
Fait Amors: "C'est il voirement."
Fait ses sens: "Amors, et conment
Savés vous que c'est ses amis?"

. . . .

Ses sens l'en tout le hardement   (7600)
Et hontes, qu'ele crient et doute;
Mais Amours l'oposoit et boute,

200

Et dist: "C'est il, car li ceur seure!
—Non ferai, se Diex me seceure,
Dusqu'il ait tout dit et conté,"
Fait Raisons.

. . . .

Fait Amors: "Or avés vous tort,   (7656)
Aelys, que nel connoissiés.
Vés com li cuens s'est angoissiés
Pour savoir l'ocoison de s'ire."

This, then, is the technical form most highly developed in Old French romance for rendering psychological conflict. I do not wish to minimize here the extent to which a somewhat simpler and more schematic form of allegory also appears. Lewis cites a passage in the *Lancelot,* where Chrétien describes the hero's hesitation before mounting the dwarf's cart as a contest of *Amor* against *Raison.*[37] In the midst of Ydoine's acceptance of Amadas, the poet similarly injects a few lines of allegorical summary of the forces at work in her:

Par le commandement d'Amours
Pitiés et Francise et Paours
Forgent mult tosts un trencant dart:
Communement de la leur part
Li ont lanciet par mi le cuer. (1102–06; cf. 883–889)

A number of poets, including some who also deal in dramatic allegory, put this narrative form into the mouths of their characters,[38] but the procedure is nevertheless the same. Although the two kinds appear together in the romance and between them take up most of the qualities personified in the *Roman de la Rose,*[39] I have segregated them because for our purposes they differ materially. In the first place the narrative form is a less effective mechanism than the dramatic; it gives a less direct view of the workings of the mind.[40] It tends to give up one of the major advantages of personification, that of enabling a passion to speak and act. The passage from *Amadas et Ydoine* above does not replace and improve upon conventional narrative. Rather, it is merely a rhetorical recapitulation of what has been previously said—and said better— in other terms. This form is, then, of intrinsically less technical interest than the allegory we have been thus far studying. Furthermore, it tends to obscure the particular provenience of the latter. For some poets—

Chrétien for instance[41]—it may represent the direct adaptation of moral allegory that critics have seen in the *Roman de la Rose*. The dramatic form, however, shows clearly that the romance writers do not simply find the solution to their problem ready-made in the Prudentius tradition. They have a habit of allegorical narrative and a list of passions ready to hand, and they make use of them. But the dialogue-in-monologue just as often appears without the trimmings of formal personification, and points to a kind of independent discovery of allegory within romance itself.

I I I

It should be clear now that it is the romance matrix that puts the fictional (as opposed to the didactic) stamp on the *Roman de la Rose*. Allegorical psychomachy, as we have seen, can represent either an insight into the basic conflicts of an entire moral world, with issues and developments dictated by the prescriptive moral sense, or it can be devoted to the analysis of an individual psyche, with its course strictly regulated by the conditions in which that psyche happens to be placed and by the combination of traits peculiar to it.[42] This is not to say that these spheres are unrelated, nor to deny that courtly love was susceptible to homiletic treatment. It is part of the vagrancy of courtly love that it rejected conventional moral prescript as few other medieval notions did. But it had its own cosmos, and hardly any of its considerable documents is without some general, didactic element. Many romances, as well as the *Roman de la Rose,* have passages dealing with the standard psychology, physiology and etiquette of love.[43] On the other hand, Guillaume's poem does shift from the doctrinal interest of *Amor*'s lecture to the fictional interest of the love-affair itself. In this he follows the romances. To begin with a local habitation is inevitable in romance psychology. The fact that the characters are often commonplace, and their responses crude or stereotyped, does not matter. The point is that in the psychologizing of the romances we are always in sight of the fictional situation, always aware of the forces surrounding the psychic event. This gives the allegory of the romance, despite its comparative simplicity and crudeness, a pointedness, an initial directness of signification, and a sense of causal relatedness that moral allegory has not. While abolishing almost all the external particulars of romance, Guillaume de Lorris preserves this inner orientation, this scrupulous reference to and organization around individual character. The cat has disappeared, but its grin is distinctly visible.

We can infer with some assurance that the romances gave Guillaume's readers some preparation to understand his method. Important as it is to remember how deep the allegorical mode of thinking went in the medieval mind, I do not think that this alone would make the "particular mechanism" of the *Roman* familiar to thirteenth-century readers.[44] To the extent of the structural difference we have seen, the well-established mode of the moral allegory was not a sufficient guide to the *Roman de la Rose.* To follow the involved and psychically integrated signification of the *Roman* requires a different mental stance, a different orientation, than following the broad moral implications and linear development of, for instance, the *Voie de Paradis.* Medieval readers—like modern readers, I suspect—would find the latter easier, as they would find easier the pretty, erotic and superficially allegorical "imitations" of the *Roman de la Rose,* of the class of *Le Fablel dou Dieu d'Amors*[45] and *De Venus la Déesse d'Amor.*[46] The *Roman de la Rose* was the most subtle and intricate love-poem its audience knew, and in reaching this degree of complexity, in this peculiar orientation, Guillaume tacitly relied, not only on the general medieval grasp of allegory, but more importantly on his audience's particular knowledge of the procedures of romance psychology. When *Dangier* appears on the scene, introducing the first psychological conflict in the *Roman,* his accents are already familiar:

Bel Acueil, por quoi amenez   (2926)
Entor ces rosiers cest vassaut?
Vos faites mal, si Deus me saut,
Qu'il bee a vostre avilement.

Beneath the vivid and elaborated characterization, and the richly figurative, minutely meaningful diction of the entire passage, we can still hear the dissident second voice of romance monologue, locating the action, as it were, not in some general cosmos of lovers, but in the mind of a heroine. The entrance of *Raison* is more clearly fraught with the possibility of ambiguity of significance. In the tradition of moral allegory she has been identified with as lofty a conception as the divine *Nous,* the formal element in the universe.[47] Guillaume's treatment of her preserves some of her antique significance and dignity, enabling her to deliver some general wisdom (2971–98, 3044–72). But the reader remembering the even more prosaic alter ego of Athanais (*Eracle,* 3590 ff.) with its sensible warnings of the difficulty of the specific affair at hand—not to speak of the ever-defeated *Sen* and *Raison* of other romances—will see Guillaume's character first as a psychological force in a single mind. Guillaume, to be sure, gives his reader other signs, not the least of which is the rose itself. He painstakingly makes clear its uniqueness by a progressive narrowing of the attention from the many to the one:

Ou miroer, entre mil choses, (1615)
Choisi rosiers chargiez de roses,

. . . .

Des roses i ot granz monciaus, (1637)
Ausi beles n'avoit soz ciaus;
S'i ot boutons petiz e clos,
E teus qui sont un poi plus gros;

. . . .

Icil bouton mout m'abelurent: (1649)
Onques si bel nul leu ne crurent;

. . . .

Entre ces boutons en eslui (1655)
Un si trés bel qu'envers celui
Nul des autres rien ne prisai,
Puis que je l'oi bien avisé. . .

He expends all this care to prevent the ever-present possibility of confusion—in an age soaked in the procedures of moral allegory—between Ladies' Love in general and the love of a particular Lady. While the poem ultimately stands or falls on the efficacy of its internal organization, it is nonetheless likely that the allegory of the romances prepared the audience for the emergence of a Lady from the complicated web of Guillaume's allegory, a Lady who is initially less a general personification of Womankind than one with all (and more) of the charm and interest of Aelis or Fresne, Melior or La Fiere. It prepared the way, then, for our first full-scale psychological novel.[48]

ERICH AUERBACH, *MIMESIS*

Auerbach, Erich. *Mimesis, The Representation of Reality in Western Litera-ture.* Translated from the German by Willard R. Trask. Princeton: Prince-ton University Press, 1953. Pp. 563

Erich Auerbach's *Mimesis* is one of those rare books that speak to everyone in the literate world. It is itself something of a piece of *belles-lettres;* it is a superb demonstration of practical literary criticism; it makes original historical observations that may profoundly affect our notion of Western, and particularly, of medieval, literature. It can be read with profit and delight by the casual amateur of letters and by the most specialized scholar; but it is *par excellence* the book of a teacher. It is likely to have its deepest influence among that middle group of serious, younger students who are most receptive to literary criticism as an activity, and who will welcome this fresh evidence that philology can be at once important, exciting, and humane. The publication of this admirable translation by Mr. Trask could hardly be better justified.

Mimesis is a series of essays on Western literature, dealing with texts in seven languages, and from Homer to the twentieth century. Its announced theme—the way in which each author represents reality—includes a vast field of interest, which is made manageable through a variety of arbitrary but necessary restrictions. The "representation of reality," with some major exceptions for the sake of point and contrast, is sought in various forms of "realism," and both "reality" and "real-ism" are given special definitions in the course of the book. "Reality" means "objective life," the random, everyday event. It is related to prac-tical purposes and is sensory in quality. Its essential characteristic is change and development. (I am collecting here definitions from scat-tered parts of the book.) It can be described in terms of sociology, pol-itics, and economics. It is the stuff of history. At times Auerbach verges on assigning reality exclusively to the lower classes, or to the sphere of what we now call "social problems." Thus in the discussion of Chré-tien's *Yvain* he passes over the psychologically realistic scenes between Laudine and Lunete to dwell on the sociological realism of the work-room in the Chastel de Pesme Avanture, "in which we even find discussions of such things as working conditions and workmen's compensation" (p. 133). Late in the book (but from as early as the discussion of the Duke of Saint-Simon) his critical sympathy with the subjectivity of modern realism seems to work a change in his definition. "Reality" becomes less objective. There is more and more mention of "the reality which is given to the individual" (p. 489), of "the process of consciousness" (p. 540), as if Auerbach were now giving the psychological, if not the moral, realm more reality in itself. Nevertheless, the definition is consistent enough to provide a usefully limited basis for literary discussion. To be "realistic" in Auerbach's terms, then, a work must embody a sense of history; it must deal with the social forces underlying the facts and conditions presented, rather than with static ethical concepts. It must be able to deal with common people and with everyday life, and to deal with them seriously. It may be problematic or tragic, but not comic. This kind of realism is sharply to be distinguished from the style of most of the literature of Antiquity. For, owing to the doctrine of the separation of styles, antique literature when realistic is also comic, and when serious is at the same time aristocratic, aprioristic, ethical, and rhetorical. Seen through Auerbach's definition, Western literature has two major peaks of realism: Dante, and the school of nineteenth-century French novelists, Stendhal, Balzac, Flaubert, and Zola.

Auerbach does not attempt to "cover" the field. Because he does not read them in the original languages, Ibsen and the Russians are given only passing mention. Because he is a specialist in the Romance literatures, and with some absolute historical justification, the central place is given to French works. And even here, not a few of the subjects have been chosen in response to personal preference, rather than as the best historical or conceptual specimens available. But in most cases— while deploring the omission of a full discussion of Russian realism, which would have given the second half of the book a more convincing climax, and bound it more securely to the first half—one is grateful that the author has been more enthusiastic than tamely dutiful. The essay on Montaigne, for instance, contributes relatively little to the book's "story," but it vibrates with much of the kind of personal sympathy that ultimately holds the book together. Indeed, the explication of Montaigne's style and method, of his elasticity, his experimentalism, his suspicion of *a priori* formulations, is strikingly applicable to Auerbach's own work. Auerbach's essays, with their circling style, turning again and again into the body of his subject, trying each time to bring forth a prize of observation, are very much *essais*. Nevertheless, Auerbach does cover the classic achievements of Western realism. Insofar as his narrative has its dramatics, it is in the emergence of Dante and the French realists from a background of the history of style.

Auerbach brings to his discussion, along with keen sensitivity and wide learning, the whole armory of critical weapons and an admirable tactical sense. He is a master at making just the approach, applying just the term or category that will most handily bring out the essence of his subject. An appreciation of Voltaire calls for particular consideration of tempo. The *Decameron* brings into play an ear for dialect. Montaigne rewards logical analysis. Flaubert and Virginia Woolf require special examination of the relationship between narrator and subject. Stendhal invites extensive biographical observations, and Schiller's *Luise Millerin* observations on genre. The discussion of the Goncourts takes up the relation of the writer to his audience, and involves even a short bibliography. A compendious demonstration of the flexibility and virtuosity of method in Auerbach's hands is the section on Dante, where the material is rich enough to sustain analysis of its dramatics, semantics, syntax, sound, tone, diction, and much more.

Although Auerbach thus concerns himself with almost every possible aspect of the literature in question, his basic approach is a highly sophisticated version of the *explication de texte*. Most often he immediately places before the reader a passage from the work, subjects the passage to a minute stylistic analysis, and thence, in ever-widening circles of reference, and with an impressive capacity to recreate the spirit of the whole, he goes on to the largest questions of literary and cultural history. This is the method of some of the best modern stylistics. It is not only a convenience in dealing with a wide range of literary considerations, but reflects a conviction (which the reader must soon share) that the language of a passage, if analyzed with sufficient insight, can be made to render up important secrets of its author and of its epoch. The method is most finely adapted to the setting of a given style in its historical context. It has a number of concomitant disadvantages. The oscillation of interest between style and history breaks up the historical sequence into pieces, which the reader can put together only with difficulty, despite the abundance of cross-references from essay to essay. Since the passages, often chosen for other than historical reasons, determine what history shall be taken up, in order to connect them chronologically Auerbach sometimes is forced to make shift with synthetic generalizations that too nimbly and unsatisfactorily leap centuries of important development. Thus the rhetorical character of Antoine de La Sale's fifteenth-century prose is identified in the space of two sentences (pp. 242–243) with "formations of the late antique period of decadence," and this is virtually all we are given of the history of formal rhetoric in the Middle Ages.

Another defect of the method is that it must neglect the important middle ground between a style's local texture and its broad sociological significance; it neglects, that is, those stylistic elements, form or structure, which are unique to the individual work of art itself, and which answer most meaningfully to its particular theme. This aspect of style can be elicited only by extended examination of literary works as wholes. Auerbach adopts a very loose definition of literature: he includes collections of essays, memoirs, chronicles, histories, works in which the questions of larger structure and of controlled theme do not always apply. But where he takes up such a work as *Madame Bovary,* one would welcome a more precise, detailed discrimination between the style as created in support of the book's specific theme—"The novel is the representation of an entire human existence which has no issue" (p. 488)—and the style that is more broadly the creature of the *Zeitgeist* and of the author's general literary theories.

But no method is perfect for all uses; and the practical critiques in *Mimesis,* with their superabundance of analytical energy, of fresh and acute literary observations, are the book's most unchallengeable virtue. The whole collection of essays, even where, as in the second half, the historical drama of their sequence begins to lose its force, creates a continuous impression of the sheer fecundity and excitement of the literature itself. For most readers this will be value enough for one book.

But Mimesis is in addition a contribution to literary history. It traces, to my knowledge for the first time, the influence on Western literature of Christian figural realism, of a theory of history and a theory of style. The figural conception of history, hitherto most commonly associated with medieval Biblical exegesis, holds in its simplest form that events in the Old Testament are prophecies or prefigurations of events in the New. More philosophically, it holds that all of history is in a sense simultaneous, that its events have not so much a causal relationship to each other as the relationship of a common participation in God's plan. This view of history would seem at first glance to give small occasion to the rise of a realistically oriented style. Auerbach shows that under special circumstances it fostered a static, crystallized, categorical, exemplary art (p. 116). But uncontaminated figural interpretation—

here Auerbach cites the "Church fathers, especially Tertullian, Jerome, and Augustine" (p. 196)—unlike the allegorical method, preserved nevertheless for each event its own literal meaning. Events are both figure and history. Furthermore each event, encompassed as it is in the grand scheme of divine Providence, is important. Everything is part of the one story whose central feature is the Passion and the Resurrection of Christ. Here are the connecting links with a theory of serious realism, of a style which treats each event, however outwardly insignificant, in its sensory, historical concreteness, and yet manages to invest it with the grandeur and sublimity of the cosmic, Christian story to which it contributes. Auerbach marshals his discussion of this style around the term *sermo humilis.*[1]

Both the figural conception of history and the humble-sublime style are important instruments, and the former is virtually an invention, of St. Paul's mission among the Gentiles. They are defense and propaganda against the dogma and universalist tendencies of Jewish thought, and against the sophisticated abstractionism of Greek thought. Their most powerful opponent on the literary level is the antique doctrine of the separation of styles; their most powerful ally, from which they are in a sense derived, is the story of Christ itself: "The style in which it was presented possessed little if any rhetorical culture in the antique sense; it was *sermo piscatorius* and yet it was extremely moving and much more impressive than the most sublime rhetorico-tragical literary work" (p. 72). The humble style of the Bible is thus functionally related to the story it tells. If antique literature has no place in its scheme for such heroes as Christ and Peter, conversely, in the Judaeo-Christian tradition there can be no categorization of styles according to the social dignity of the subject. "The sublime influence of God here reaches so deeply into the everyday that the two realms of the sublime and the everyday are not only actually unseparated but basically inseparable" (pp. 22–23). The inevitable conflict between the two traditions of style is one of the main themes in Auerbach's discussion of late Antiquity and the Middle Ages. The Christian style, he concludes, emerged victorious.

Since the Christian tradition down to the sixth century and periodically at later times imbibed considerable classical learning, not the least part of which was rhetoric and the doctrine of separation of styles, Auerbach has no little task in explaining just how Christian figural realism could coexist with so powerful an opponent. One reason is that the inner-historical, realistic interpretation of the Bible, and *sermo humilis,* were "popular" devices, and were widely used in the instruction and sermonizing of the missions. The Hellenistic, learned allegory and rhetoric could not come into use on the same scale. Again, the Bible, and the earliest Acts of the Martyrs, true to the original Judaeo-Christian impulse, are realistic. While martyrology and hagiology soon become conventional, the Bible continues to exert itself on Christian writers as a model, preserving the humble style despite the pressure of pagan theory and criticism. The strength of the Biblical Christian material was such, indeed, that it ultimately subjected classical rhetoric to itself. When Christian authors of late Antiquity submitted to the classical literary school discipline, at least two different results were produced. One was the "baroque" style of Jerome, similar to the style of Ammianus Marcellinus, in which a lifeless rhetorical pomp is incongruously mixed with the vivid, gruesome pictorial effects characteristic of the decadent, late-antique style. The other result, actually more classical in its restraint, was a new idiom, impulsive but human, a low rhetoric (*sermo humilis*) unmistakably Christian in spirit despite its use of antique rhetorical forms. The key example of this, both for theory and for practice, is Augustine. In his article "*Sermo Humilis,*" Auerbach exposes the mechanism by which the antique levels of style are admitted into Christian eloquence. Where Cicero grades subjects and styles absolutely—*parua submisse, modica temperate, magna granditer*—Augustine knows only one universal subject, and the levels of style for him become simply differentiations of function. Thus in *De doctrina Christiana* he recommends the low style for teaching, the middle style for praise or blame, and the high style for exciting men to action.[2]

In the sixth-century Gaul of Gregory of Tours, with the virtual disappearance of antique culture and its rhetoric, another *sermo humilis* is generated. The elevated, exemplary realism of original Christianity here finds a strong, practical, native counterpart. It is fed by the coarseness of Merovingian life, by the near presence of the spoken language of the people, and by the peculiar consciousness of the Christian bishop discharging his intensely practical duties. If Gregory's style reflects a deficiency of culture, it also signalizes "a reawakening of the directly sensible" (p. 94).

Gregory had no immediate followers. Auerbach takes up his story next with the *Chanson de Roland* and the *Vie de Saint Alexis.* Figural interpretation has meanwhile undergone a process of simplification, linked both to the decline of antique culture and to the needs of the Church in converting simple, untutored peoples. The early vernacular texts thus express a suffocatingly simple, codified, unambiguous attitude toward experience; it is reflected in their rigid, narrow, paratactic structure. But comparison of the French *Alexis* with a Latin version shows that with this early vernacular poetry a new germ of realism nevertheless appears. Living history has become a series of isolated, juxtaposed pictures. But the represented figures, which in the Latin tradition had completely lost their local identity and become merely conventional signs, here begin to stir in their frames again.

In the mystery cycles—Auerbach analyzes the late–twelfth-century *Mystère d'Adam*—Christian figural realism is well developed. The plays, with their prophets and prophecies and their anachronous handling of time, belong by their very content to the figural-historical tradition. Their familiar setting and diction, and their burgher-like characters, are part and parcel of the essentially realistic style that is, as it were, natural to Christian figuralism. St. Francis, the Franciscan movement, and Dante bring the tradition to a climax.

Auerbach uses the term "creatural" to describe the sense of human suffering and of hopeless transitoriness which pervades the realism of the late Middle Ages. The ethical and metaphysical structure which in Dante, for instance, could hold heaven and earth in a coherent relationship is now breaking down. *Humilitas* and *sublimitas* are beginning to lose their consonance and to clash in grotesque ways. The one often becomes a morbid concern with the flesh, with age, sickness, death, and putrefaction. The other degenerates into popular mysticism, ecstaticism, and superstition. Creatural realism at its most moving— though still perilously close to sentimentality, as Auerbach implies—is illustrated in Antoine de La Sale's *Réconfort de Madame du Fresne.* Here, too, the style has emerged from a strictly Christian frame to serve secular matter.

With Rabelais, the secularization of the tradition is complete; "creatural realism has acquired a new meaning . . . that of the vitalistic-dynamic triumph of the physical body and its functions" (p. 276). Rabelais' seriousness "lies in the joy of discovery—pregnant with all possibilities, ready to try every experiment, whether in the realm of reality or super-reality—which was characteristic of his time . . ." (p. 284). Thence Auerbach traces creatural realism, with decreasing emphasis, to Montaigne and Shakespeare, to seventeenth- and eighteenth-century Germany, and to the nineteenth-century Russian novel.

The second half of the book chronicles the rise of a very different style, of a realism that lacks the traditional theological supports. But

211

although modern realism is hardly therefore self-sustaining, Auerbach does not attempt to describe its conceptual background with anything like the same originality. Thus, while the quality of the literary analysis in the book is consistently high, the first half claims most of our interest in history.

It will take some years, and the attention of specialists in the field, to evaluate Auerbach's contribution justly. The foregoing rough sketch will do, perhaps, to suggest the originality of his thesis and the inherent difficulty of establishing it. He has taken an idea long familiar to theology, and boldly investigated its aesthetic life. The idea—figuralism—is so similar to allegory and symbolism that it is a delicate task to differentiate them even in the abstract, not to speak of the centuries of exegetic and mimetic literature in which they intermingle. Figuralism, furthermore, is the "popular" form among the three, of major use in such media as vernacular sermons. This means that a vast proportion of its literature has disappeared, while, owing to the abundance of sources, and to numerous and vigorous recent researches, allegory and symbolism have been virtually established in the scholarly mind as the preëminent Christian forms of the Middle Ages. And there still lingers among otherwise respectable scholars a strong predisposition to trace back all the important aesthetic characteristics of medieval literature to classical Antiquity.

In dealing with realism and with style at all Auerbach takes on further difficulties. There are half a dozen medieval realisms. It is difficult to distinguish the figural realism directly inspired by the Incarnation from the practical style necessary to holding the attention of an uncivilized audience. Much of the evangelical literature on which Auerbach's history is based must be compounded of both styles. And there are other realisms to be distinguished as well: the late-antique pictorial, the "bourgeois" of Boccaccio, of the fabliaux, and of late drama and sermon, and the "creatural."

Auerbach is enabled to make distinctions among all these by adopting, himself, an Augustinian view of style (cf. p. 199). "Style," in his usage, can often mean ethical import or function, or even intention. Thus by "mixture of styles," he most often means a peculiar combination of style and purpose, rather than of style and style. While this view of style serves a main theme of the book—the search for a "serious" realism—it invites its own problems. To relate literary style to an other-than-literary entity, be it a philosophical concept, a socio-economic situation, or a state of mind, is a difficult business. To demonstrate the

natural and inevitable relationship between style and the other element
is even more difficult. At best the critic brings to the discovery of such
a relationship a set of expectations or deductions, from the style to what
it is expected to express, or vice versa. And it is fatally easy in this
process—Auerbach himself has said as much[3]—to find one's quarry
where it should be rather than where it is. Where in addition a style is
defined not only in terms of its describable traits, but also in such fluid
terms as those of purpose and intention, the error of confusing style and
statement, or of reading-in, is inevitable. Thus Auerbach says of a
Balzac caricature: "What confronts us, then, is the unity of a particular
milieu, felt as a total concept of a demonic-organic nature and presented entirely by suggestive and sensory means." Yet the unity, the
organic totality, of the milieu is largely owing to Balzac's repeated and
overt announcement of it in the passage: "Enfin toute sa personne
explique la pension, comme la pension implique sa personne," and so
on (pp. 470–472). Later on, a passage from *Germinal* is given "classic"
status for its combination of realism and world-historical importance
(pp. 512–515). But most readers, I think, would dismiss the dialogue as
thinly-veiled sermoning by Zola through the characters. "Moi," says the
miner Maheu's wife, "je ne veux du mal à personne, mais il y a des fois
où cette injustice me révolte."

These are, even assuming that I am right, insignificant errors, but
they illustrate the enormous problem in stylistics of maintaining the
rigors of good literary judgment against the pressures of one's formulated expectations. The investigation of figural realism is particularly
beset by this problem. To establish the figuralism of a given text, it is
not enough to identify the typological motives associated with it. The
seriousness or sublimity that goes with the realism, and vice versa,
must be literary, not merely doctrinal or conceptual. It must be demon-
strated in the pressure of the language itself, and not simply in a superimposed, unincorporated idea. For *humilitas* and *sublimitas,* even in
centrally Christian medieval literature, do not necessarily rest easily
together, and either or both may refuse to pass from the category of
concept to that of style. For instance, there is in Saint Bernard a key
passage, quoted by Auerbach, p. 153, on *humilitas-sublimitas* as a theological concept. The idea, dwelt on with all the rapture of the mystic,
has not penetrated the style, which is anything but *humilis.* The reverse
stylistic situation occurs in the Adam-and-Eve scenes of the *Mystère
d'Adam.* Here, says Auerbach, "is a subject of the utmost importance
and the utmost sublimity from the point of view of the author and his

MEDIEVAL LITERATURE, STYLE, AND CULTURE

audience" (p. 151). But the plain though not pointedly popular style of the episode is entirely inadequate to the elevation of its subject. The poet was not equal to his task, nor to Auerbach's estimate of him. Indeed, where elevation is called for, as in Adam's lament, the poet does not rely on the inherent power of his material, nor on the audience's stock response, but on a school-bookish rhetoric, reminiscent of early romance.

If Auerbach overstates his case here and there, if he deals with scanty or difficult materials, and faces some scholarly prejudice, it cannot be denied that his search for the set of attitudes "behind" Dante's realistic style, which was the origin of his whole investigation of figuralism, has been richly rewarded. It seems clearly that it is figuralism in large part— certainly it is not allegory—which makes possible the remarkable if transitory poise, in later thirteenth-century art, between natural and supernatural concerns, which makes it possible for Dante to represent the hereafter as an intensification and fulfillment of human history, rather than as a bloodless, formulated abstraction. Should literary history come to reject figuralism as a continuously important tradition, and to see it rather as a typically mid-medieval revival of apostolic ideas, Auerbach's historical researches will nevertheless have been invaluable in uncovering the aesthetic corollaries of those ideas.

Mimesis has had many reviewers since its first appearance in 1946. I find myself in agreement with those who have found the book, in large, strikingly ambivalent. Auerbach's "reality" is sometimes dynamic, its nature different in different times and places, and sometimes it is more fundamental, "universally valid." His "style" is sometimes the organization of concrete literary traits, and sometimes ethical import, or purpose, or intention. "Literature" is everything from the most highly worked art of Dante and Flaubert to the crude, disconnected, raw material of a Gregory of Tours. Its nature is determined at times by milieu, by the state of history; but at other times it is the product of a shaping will, of an intention, even of an intention to escape history. Few of these conceptions are really incompatible, yet one feels that in Auerbach's hands their contradictions have rather been embraced than resolved. The book contains a wealth of historical data, and repeated recommendations of historicism, yet it is itself only semi-history. At its center is something intuitive and creative, aesthetic, even moral, though for himself Auerbach treats "ethical" literature tangentially and even slightingly. This is the book's encompassing ambivalence. One should perhaps not seek the reason for it within the book, as some have done.[4] It lies not in the author's rather painstaking avoidance of definitions and of theoretical discussion, nor in any defect of theoretical capacity, but rather in his actual condition as author. The book, we find, was written in exile, "during the war and at Istanbul. . . ." One can fill in the rest. To have produced such a book under these unpromising circumstances is to have been both beset by history and fortified by something personal, internal, unhistorical, but equally real. The book reflects this great dialectic of its time and place. Instead of a serene, theoretical unity, it has rather a humane inconclusiveness. It has its contradictions, but also a precious immediacy. Its literary criticism is the better for a range of insight into history and into private human existence that can give us comments as far apart in their relation to literature, and yet as resonant, as these:

> [on Stendhal] For Europe there began that process of temporal concentration, both of historical events themselves and of everyone's knowledge of them which has since made tremendous progress and which not only permits us to prophesy a unification of human life throughout the world but has in a certain sense already achieved it. Such a development abrogates or renders powerless the entire social structure of orders and categories previously held valid; the tempo of the changes demands a perpetual and extremely difficult effort toward inner adaptation and produces intense concomitant crises. He who would account to himself for his real life and his place in human society is obliged to do so upon a far wider practical foundation and in a far larger context than before, and to be continually conscious that the social base upon which he lives is not constant for a moment but is perpetually changing through convulsions of the most various kinds [p. 459].

> [on Madame de Chastel] It is hard to decide what is most praiseworthy in this speech, its self-effacement or its self-control, its goodness or its clarity. That a woman under such a trial does not abandon herself to grief but sees the situation clearly as it really is; that she understands there can be no question of surrendering the fortress and hence that the boy is lost in any case if the Prince is in earnest; that she manages by her intervention to restore her husband's inner poise, by her example to give him the courage to make a decision, and even, by her reference to the fame he will gain, to offer him some consolation and most certainly to

give him back the pride and self-respect which will make it easier for him to play the part assigned to him—all this has a simple beauty and grandeur which can vie with any classical text [pp. 245–246].

NOTES

THE CANTERBURY TALES

1. Miller's Prologue, l. 3177; see B. H. Bronson,"Chaucer's Art in Relation to his Audience," in *Five Studies in Literature,* Univ. of Calif. Publ. English, VIII, no. I (1940); Ruth Crosby, "Chaucer and the Custom of Oral Delivery," *Speculum,* XIII (1938) 413–32.

2. See Margaret Schlauch, "Chaucer's Colloquial English: Its Structural Traits," *PMLA,* LXVII (1952) 1103–16; Dorothy Everett, "Chaucer's 'Good Ear,'" in her *Essays on Medieval Literature,* Oxford 1955, pp. 139–48.

3. ll. 1425–56; see Germaine Dempster, "Chaucer at Work on the Complaint in the Franklin's Tale," *Modern Language Notes,* LII (1937) 16–23.

4. E.g. *The Physician's Tale,* ll. 240–4; *The Summoner's Tale,* from l. 2001 to 2088; the "hasardrye" section of *The Pardoner's Tale,* ll. 590–650, similarly lacks energy.

5. *The Miller's Tale,* ll. 3337–8.

6. See Arthur Hoffman, "Chaucer's Prologue to Pilgrimage: The Two Voices," *ELH,* XXI (1954) 1–16; Ralph Baldwin, "The Unity of the Canterbury Tales," *Anglistica,* V (Copenhagen 1955), pp. 19–32.

7. See, e.g., J. L. Lowes, *Geoffrey Chaucer and the Development of his Genius,* Boston 1934, pp. 243–4; H. S. Bennett, *Chaucer and the Fifteenth Century,* Oxford 1947, pp. 88–95.

8. E.g. *The Squire's Tale,* ll. 401–8.

9. Ideas propagated by J. M. Manly, "Chaucer and the Rhetoricians," *Proceedings of the British Academy,* XII (1926) 95–113.

10. This, with some of the ensuing remarks, is the thesis of the present writer's *Chaucer and the French Tradition,* Berkeley and Cambridge 1957; on the style of the Old French fabliaux, see Per Nykrog, *Les Fabliaux,* Copenhagen 1957, esp. Chap. IX.

11. John Speirs, *Chaucer the Maker,* London 1951, pp. 171–4.

CHAUCER'S RELIGION AND THE CHAUCER RELIGION

1. Derek Brewer, "Images of Chaucer 1386–1900," in *Chaucer and Chaucerians,* ed. D. S. Brewer (London, 1966), pp. 258–60.

2. Brewer, "Images," p. 269.

3. Thomas R. Lounsbury, *Studies in Chaucer,* 3 vols. (New York, 1892), vol. II, p. 508.

4. George Lyman Kittredge, *Chaucer and His Poetry* (Cambridge, Mass., 1915).

5. Florence Ridley, "The State of Chaucer Studies," *Studies in the Age of Chaucer,* I (1979), p. 14.

6. Donald Howard, *The Idea of the Canterbury Tales* (Berkeley, 1976).

7. V. A. Kolve, *Chaucer and the Imagery of Narrative: The First Five Canterbury Tales* (Stanford, 1984), p. 369.

8. Alfred David, *The Strumpet Muse: Art and Morals in Chaucer's Poetry* (Bloomington, 1976).

9. Howard, *Idea of the Canterbury Tales,* p. 381.

10. Lee Patterson, "The 'Parson's Tale' and the Quitting of the 'Canterbury Tales,'" *Traditio,* 34 (1978), pp. 376–9.

11. Lounsbury, *Studies,* vol. I, p. 206.

12. I am preparing a more detailed study of the use of the term "meditation" to denote genre in Middle English. My preliminary impression is that among Middle English genres there is a reasonably clear distinction between works chiefly devoted to the inculcation of formal Christian doctrine and its practical application in daily life, and the meditation, which is more affective in character, approaching the nature of prayer. But in many works the two motives were combined. See, e.g., Peter Revell, *Fifteenth Century English Prayers and Meditations: A Descriptive List of Manuscripts in the British Library* (New York, 1975), pp. vii–viii; P. S. Jolliffe, *A Check-List of Middle English Prose Writings of Spiritual Guidance* (Toronto, 1974), pp. 29–30; John C. Hirsh, "Prayer and Meditation in Late Medieval England," *Medium Aevum,* 48 (1979), pp. 55–66; C. A. Martin, "Middle English Manuals of Religious Instruction," in *So Meny People Longages and Tonges* (*Essays presented to Angus McIntosh*), ed. Michael Benskin and M. L. Samuels (Edinburgh, 1981), p. 291.

13. E. Talbot Donaldson, *Speaking of Chaucer* (London, 1970), p. 172.

14. Kolve, *Chaucer and the Imagery of Narrative,* p. 370.

15. Howard, *Idea of the Canterbury Tales,* p. 385.

16. Kittredge's famous remark, that "Chaucer always knew what he was about" (*Poetry of Chaucer,* p. 15), was defensible in 1915, amid readers relatively untutored in medieval convention. In terms of the biographies of most poets, however, it seems absurd.

17. An idea suggested by Professor Wendy Clein in discussion of the present essay.

CHAUCER IN AN AGE OF CRITICISM

1. Wolfgang Clemen. *Chaucer's Early Poetry.* Translated by C. A. M. Sym. New York: Barnes and Noble, 1964.

Robert O. Payne. *The Key of Remembrance: A Study of Chaucer's Poetics.* New Haven and London: Yale University Press [for the University of Cincinnati], 1963.

Bernard F. Huppé and D. W. Robertson, Jr. *Fruyt and Chaf: Studies in Chaucer's Allegories.* Princeton: Princeton University Press, 1963.

POETRY AND CRISIS IN THE AGE OF CHAUCER

Relevance, Poetic Style, and Cultural Crisis

1. See, for instance, the two volumes of *Daedalus, Proceedings of the American Academy of Arts and Sciences* 98, no. 3 (1969): *The Future of the Humanities;* and 99, no. 2 (1970): *Theory in Humanistic Studies;* also J. Mitchell Morse, "The Case for Irrelevance," *College English* 30 (1968): 201–211, and the issue of *College English* 30, no. 8 (1969).

2. Roy Harvey Pearce, *Historicism Once More: Problems & Occasions for the American Scholar* (Princeton: Princeton Univ. Press, 1969), p. vii.

3. See René Wellek and Austin Warren, *Theory of Literature* (New York: Harcourt, Brace, 1949), which well represents the New Criticism in its institutional form, as summarized in this paragraph. Chapter 12 deals partly with the ontological status of literature.

4. A more extended critique of the New Criticism in these terms is made by Pearce, "Historicism Once More," *Kenyon Review* 20 (1958): 558–566, reprinted in his collection of the same name, pp. 8–17; cf. also Robert Weimann, "Past Significance and Present Meaning in Literary History," *New Literary History* 1 (1969): esp. 93–98; and John Gerber, "Literature—Our Untamable Discipline," *College English* 28 (1967): 351–358.

5. The ahistorical bent of the first three seems to me self-evident. But since the "exegetical" approach to medieval studies sometimes comes with an air of superior historicity   as approaching medieval literature as the medievals saw it rather than with modern (and thus with anachronistic) assumptions   I should explain that the approach seems to me ahistorical in two related ways. Its "medievalism" has almost no nuances; that is, it tends to posit a uniform set of ideas, and by implication a homogenous culture, over a thousand years of history in which historians of art, music, philosophy, etc., see a great diversity; secondly, its assumption that the bulk of medieval literature is Christian and didactic in a specific way leads to a method that is essentially the same as that of the other ahistorical approaches: a search for recurrent patterns, which (whether rooted in prehistory, biology, the collective unconscious, or in Christian revelation) are regarded a priori as permanently valid, and are thus of little historical interest.

6. See Leo Marx, "American Studies—A Defense of an Unscientific Method," *New Literary History* 1 (1969): 75–90, and the references in his note 2.

219

7. My favorite students of style are both medievalists and both profoundly interested in cultural history: Erich Auerbach, as in *Mimesis: The Representation of Reality in Western Literature* [1946], trans. Willard R. Trask (Princeton: Princeton Univ. Press, 1953); and Leo Spitzer, as in *Linguistics and Literary History: Essays in Stylistics* (Princeton: Princeton Univ. Press, 1948). A bibliography of Auerbach's works appears in his *Literary Language and Its Public in Late Latin Antiquity and in the Middle Ages,* trans. Ralph Manheim, Bollingen Series 74 (New York: Pantheon, 1965), pp. 395–405. There is as yet no complete bibliography of the very prolific Spitzer; a selected bibliography is appended to the obituary article by René Wellek on Spitzer as critic and theorist in *Comparative Literature* 12 (1960): 310–330, with supplement in volume 13 (1961): 378–379. For modern English stylistics in general, see Richard W. Bailey and Dolores M. Burton, S.N.D., *English Stylistics: A Bibliography* (Cambridge, Mass.: M.I.T. Press, 1968) with periodic supplements in the journal *Style.* On linguistics and literature, see the article by Samuel Levin and Seymour Chatman in *Current Trends in Linguistics,* ed. W. Bright et al. ('S-Gravenhage: Mouton [announced for 1971]); Seymour Chatman, ed., *Literary Style: A Symposium* (London: Oxford Univ. Press, 1971), esp. the article by Richard Ohmann, "Speech, Action, and Style"; and D. C. Freeman, ed., *Linguistics and Literary Style* (New York: Holt, Rinehart, and Winston, 1970).

8. The matter is of course a complicated one, and our notions and definitions of period style are continually being refined. See the issue of *New Literary History* 1, no. 2 (Winter, 1970), entitled "A Symposium on Periods." The liveliness of this new journal is symptomatic of the current interest of our subject.

9. See Wellek and Warren, *Theory of Literature,* pp. 117–123; E. H. Gombrich, *In Search of Cultural History* (Oxford: Clarendon, 1969) offers a broad critique of *Geistesgeschichte.*

10. See Spitzer, *Linguistics and Literary History,* chaps. 1–4.

11. Johan Huizinga's term "autumn" or "waning" is the mildest epithet I have found to describe the general setting of the period. *The Age of Adversity* is the title of a recent study by Robert E. Lerner (Ithaca: Cornell Univ. Press, 1968). Norman E. Cantor remarks of the fourteenth and fifteenth centuries: "In France, England, Germany, and Flanders it is the death agonies of medieval civilization which predominate. . . ." (*Medieval History* [New York: Macmillan, 1963], p. 577). In a textbook more restrained in its approach, Jeffrey Burton Russell nevertheless comments, vis-à-vis economic conditions, "The period from 1349 to 1470 was a Golden Age only for bacteria" (*Medieval Civilization* [New York: John Wiley, 1968], p. 559). F. R. H. DuBoulay, in the first chapter of his *An Age of Ambition: English Society in the Late Middle Ages* (London: Nelson, 1970) announces an attack on the "Myth of Decline," but there is little in his study to change the prevailing view of the last half of

the fourteenth century. In his chapter entitled "The Apparatus of Religion," moreover, he admits that "it was on all hands an age of special anxiety. Every literary and artistic form tells us so. The pestilence and sudden death which actually brought social betterment to the survivors, the social mobility and conflict that resulted, the need for thousands of families to adjust themselves in one way or another under the lowering clouds of sudden mortality, brought with them also a sense of insecurity and terror" (p. 145).

12. Brief resumés on the economic state of Europe will be found in Jacques Heers, *L'Occident aux XIVe et XVe siècles: aspects économiques et sociaux,* 2d ed. (Paris: Presses Universitaires, 1966), pp. 104–107, and in Ruggiero Romano and Alberto Tenenti, *Die Grundlegung der modernen Welt: Spätmittelalter, Renaissance, Reformation* (Frankfurt am Main: Fischer, 1967), pp. 9–47 ("Die 'Krise' des 14 Jahrhunderts"); on England see May McKisack, *The Fourteenth Century: 1307–1399,* vol. 5 in *The Oxford History of England* (Oxford: Clarendon, 1959), pp. 328–348.

13. See R. B. Dobson, ed., *The Peasants' Revolt of 1381* (London: Macmillan, 1970), p. 375. This is an excellent collection of original documents in modern English translation; a good general account of the revolt is C. Oman, *The Great Revolt of 1381* [orig. pub. 1906], new ed by E. B. Fryde (Oxford: Clarendon, 1969).

14. Dobson, *Peasants' Revolt,* p. 311.

15. May McKisack, *The Fourteenth Century,* p. 423; cf. p. 384: "The first and least sensational of these attacks resulted in the substitution, in 1371, of lay for clerical ministers of state; the second, in 1376, in the impeachment of the king's chamberlain and a number of lesser officials; the third, in 1381, in the murder of the chancellor and treasurer and the indiscriminate massacre of certain officers of the law and minor civil servants."

16. Gervase Mathew, *The Court of Richard II* (London: John Murray, 1968), p. 114; cf. A. R. Myers, *England in the Late Middle Ages* (Harmondsworth: Penguin, 1952), pp. xiii–xiv. On politics in the reign of Richard II, see Anthony Steel, *Richard II* (Cambridge: Cambridge Univ. Press, 1941), and R. H. Jones, *The Royal Policy of Richard II: Absolutism in the Later Middle Ages* (New York: Barnes and Noble, 1968).

17. Dobson, *Peasants' Revolt,* p. 374.

18. Gordon Leff, *Heresy in the Later Middle Ages: The Relation of Heterodoxy to Dissent c. 1250–c. 1450,* 2 vols. (Manchester: Manchester Univ. Press), I, 14.

19. On Wyclif and Lollardy, see Leff, *Heresy in the Late Middle Ages,* II, 494–558.

20. Leff, *Heresy in the Late Middle Ages,* I, 31. The early-fifteenth-century Margery Kempe is more notably histrionic, or hysterical, than any fourteenth-century English mystic; W. A. Pantin, *The English Church in the Fourteenth*

Century (Cambridge: Cambridge Univ. Press, 1955), considers her, however, "a product of fourteenth-century conditions" (p. 256), and "a creditable specimen of the devout lay person in the later Middle Ages" (p. 261).

21. Joan Evans, *English Art: 1307–1461* (Oxford: Clarendon, 1949), p. 74. "It is a remarkable fact that it has been possible to give a continuous history of the early Perpendicular style without reference to the national disasters which occurred in its years of growth. Yet these were so great that it seems miraculous that they did not leave a greater scar upon the art of England." On the art of Richard II's reign, see *ibid.,* pp. 82–86, 100–105; also Margaret Rickert, *Painting in Britain: The Middle Ages* (London: Penguin, 1954), pp. 165–189; Mathew, *Court of Richard II,* chaps. 5 and 10 (the latter chapter contains interesting and original remarks on some remnants of didactic "provincial" art related to the themes of *Piers Plowman*); Lawrence Stone, *Sculpture in Britain: The Middle Ages* (Harmondsworth: Penguin, 1955), pp. 177–195.

22. Émile Mâle, *L'Art réligieux du XIIe au XVIIIe siècle* (Paris: Colin [1945], repr. 1961), p. 91, my translation.

23. Émile Mâle, *L'Art réligieux de la fin du moyen âge en France: étude sur l'iconographie du moyen âge et sur ses sources d'inspiration,* 5th ed. (Paris: Colin, 1949), pp. 85–86, my translation.

24. Mâle, *L'Art réligieux de la fin du moyen âge,* pp. 122–132, 146–150, 157–221.

25. Johan Huizinga, *The Waning of the Middle Ages: A Study of the Forms of Life, Thought and Art in France and the Netherlands in the XIVth and XVth Centuries* [1919: Engl. trans. 1924] (London: Arnold, 1937), p. 240.

26. Huizinga, *Waning of the Middle Ages,* pp. 126, 189. On the period generally, Huizinga is still our principal authority. On the literature see also Italo Siciliano, *François Villon et les thèmes poétiques du moyen âge* (Paris: Colin, 1934), esp. pp. 115–199; on the imagery of Death, see Mâle, *L'Art réligieux de la fin du moyen âge,* pp. 347–389. It may be worth noting that the Dance of Death is a well-documented motif in English art of the fifteenth century, and that the earlier, related theme of the Three Living and Three Dead appears plentifully in the surviving English mural paintings of the fourteenth century. See the two articles by Ethel Carleton Williams, "The Dance of Death in Painting and Sculpture in the Middle Ages," *Journal of the British Archaeological Association,* 3d ser., I (1937): 237–239, and "Mural Paintings of the Three Living and the Three Dead in England," *ibid.,* 7 (1942): 31–40.

27. Martin M. Crow and Clair C. Olson, *Chaucer Life-Records* (Oxford: Clarendon, 1966).

28. John S. P. Tatlock, *The Development and Chronology of Chaucer's Works,* Chaucer Society Pubs., 2d ser., 37 (London, 1907) is still the most authoritative single treatment of the chronology.

29. George Lyman Kittredge, *Chaucer and His Poetry* (Cambridge, Mass.: Harvard Univ. Press, 1915), p. 45.

30. E. Talbot Donaldson, "Chaucer the Pilgrim," *PMLA* 49 (1954): 935.

31. See, respectively, Crow and Olson, *Life-Records,* pp. 269, 364–369; 269–270; 343–347. Two of the articles of a recently discovered ordinance of Parliament in 1385 are of particular interest as regards Chaucer's giving up of his customs posts. As a result of an inquest, Parliament recommended to the King:

> Item les profitz de sa graunt custume et petit custume serrount grandement encruz sil luy plest que les custumez et aultrez officers appendantz aycellez soiont ordeynez des bons et loyalx gentz par avys de son conseill et ses officers et nient par priere ne desir singuler, et remuablez selonc lour deserte; et qilz soient demouranuntz sur lour office sanz leutenantz ou attournez . . . .
>
> Item le subside dez laynes a luy grauntez et pelles lanutez poet graundement estre encruz sil luy plest suffrer que lez custumers, controllours et poysers porront estre ordenez des bonez et loyalx gentz par avys soun conseillers et ses officers et nient par singuler desir ne requeste, et remuablez selonck lour deserts, et demourauntz sur leur office en propre persone.

Since Chaucer was controller of both the wool custom and subsidy and the petty custom at London at the time, he cannot but have fallen under suspicion of neglect of his posts at the very least, no matter what his deserts. See J. J. N. Palmer, "The Impeachment of Michael de la Pole in 1386," *Bulletin of the Institute of Historical Research* 42 (1969): 96–101; *idem,* "The Parliament of 1385 and the Constitutional Crisis of 1386," *Speculum* 46 (1971): esp. 483. The ordinance is printed in the former of these, pp. 100–101.

32. In *Chaucer and the French Tradition: A Study in Style and Meaning* (Berkeley: Univ. of California Press, 1957).

33. George Kane, *Piers Plowman: The Evidence for Authorship* (London: Univ. of London, Athlone Press, 1965).

The *Pearl* Poet

1. For the works of the *Pearl* poet I use the following editions: *Purity,* ed. Robert J. Menner, Yale Studies in English 61 (New Haven: Yale Univ. Press, 1920); *Pearl,* ed. E. V. Gordon (Oxford: Clarendon, 1953); *Sir Gawain and the Green Knight,* ed. J. R. R. Tolkien and E. V. Gordon, 2d ed. rev. Norman Davis (Oxford: Clarendon, 1967); *Patience,* ed. J. J. Anderson (Manchester, Manchester Univ. Press, 1969).

2. See respectively *Purity,* vv. 285–292, 303–308, 363–406, 947–972, 1215–1260, 1767–1792; *Patience,* vv. 137–232, 273–280.

3. Menner, ed. *Purity,* p. 67, remarks that "even here his condemnation of

wicked priests is quite different from the violent denunciations of the author of *Piers Plowman,* since he is careful to contrast impartially the behavior and reward of righteous priests . . . with the sin of those who are vile and hypocritical."

4. See Carleton Brown, "The Author of the Pearl Considered in the Light of His Theological Opinions," *PMLA* 19 (1904): 115–153; René Wellek, "The *Pearl:* An Interpretation of the Middle English Poem," [orig. pub. 1933] in Robert J. Blanch, ed., *Sir Gawain and Pearl: Critical Essays* (Bloomington: Indiana Univ. Press, 1966), pp. 11–12, 24–33; Gordon, ed., *Pearl,* pp. xxiii–xxvii.

5. Cf. A. C. Spearing, "Symbolic and Dramatic Development in *Pearl,*" *Modern Philology* 60 (1962): 11 [repr. Blanch, ed., *Sir Gawain and Pearl,* pp. 117–118.]

6. A study of the various meanings of the term "courtesy" as used by the poet will be found in D. S. Brewer, "Courtesy and the Gawain-Poet," in John Lawlor, ed., *Patterns of Love and Courtesy: Essays in Memory of C. S. Lewis* (London: Arnold, 1966), pp. 54–85 [repr. in Helaine Newstead, ed., *Chaucer and his Contemporaries* (Greenwich, Conn.: Fawcett, 1968), pp. 310–343].

7. Wendell Stacy Johnson, "The Imagery and Diction of *The Pearl:* Toward an Interpretation," *ELH* 20 (1953): 165 [repr. in Edward Vasta, ed., *Middle English Survey: Critical Essays* (Notre Dame, Ind.: Univ. of Notre Dame Press, 1965), p. 98]. Johnson's analysis has been challenged by P. M. Kean, *The Pearl: An Interpretation* (London: Routledge, 1967), pp. 83–84: " . . . the imagery of treasure, of the garden, of the plant in all its parts and aspects, of spices, wheat, and harvest, forms an inextricably linked whole; not brought together by the poet but joined by long traditional use. It is not, therefore, possible to interpret the poem as developing its themes through juxtaposition of contrasted groups of images; for example, by opposing the artificiality and nonorganic quality of treasure and jewels to the natural imagery of the plant." However, Johnson's thesis is I think strongly supported by such passages as vv. 269–272:

> "For þat þou lesteȝ watȝ bot a rose
> Þat flowred and fayled as kynde hyt gef.
> Now þurz kynde of þe kyste þat hyt con close
> To a perle of prys hit is put in pref."

Though elsewhere allusion is made to the immortal rose (v. 906), the opposition in the present passage is clear.

8. So A. C. Cawley, ed. and trans., *Pearl, Sir Gawain and the Green Knight,* Everyman's Library 346 (London: Dent, 1962), p. xvi; Dorothy Everett, in *Essays on Middle English Literature,* ed. Patricia Kean (Oxford: Clarendon, 1955), remarks (p. 88): "The same stanza form, and the linking, are

found elsewhere in Middle English, and in some lyrics in the Vernon MS. for instance, but nowhere else is there anything like this complex scheme, nor is the stanza handled with such mastery."

9. Donald R. Howard, "Structure and Symmetry in Sir Gawain," *Speculum* 39 (1964): 425; see also pp. 430–431; Dale B. J. Randall, "A Note on Structure in *Sir Gawain and the Green Knight,*" *MLN* 71 (1956): 319.

10. This interpretation follows particularly upon Larry D. Benson's study of variation in the diction, syntax, structure, and meaning of *Sir Gawain;* see his *Art and Tradition in Sir Gawain and the Green Knight* (New Brunswick, N.J.: Rutgers Univ. Press, 1965), esp. pp. 126–166, 247–248.

11. Johnson, "Imagery," pp. 166–167; cf. p. 172; and C. A. Luttrell, "*Pearl:* Symbolism in a Garden Setting," in Blanch, ed., *Sir Gawain and Pearl,* pp. 82–84.

12. See the excellent treatment by Spearing, "Symbolic and Dramatic Development," pp. 1–12 [repr. Blanch, ed., *Sir Gawain and Pearl,* pp. 98–119], to which I am much indebted in this discussion.

13. Marie Borroff, in *Sir Gawain and the Green Knight: A Stylistic and Metrical Study* (New Haven: Yale Univ. Press, 1962), pp. 121–129, points out certain highly interesting characteristics of the narrating "eye," some of which clearly intensify the descriptive richness of the poem: "The narrator tends to see a given object or agent in relation to other objects or agents within a limited space. The resultant effect is one of fullness or crowding. . ." (p. 123); "Descriptive details . . . are frequently circumstantial, expressing temporary conditions or relationships. . . . The result, as with the narrator's treatment of space, is to people or crowd the scene" (p. 124). "He tends also to adopt the point of view of the character central in a given narrative passage as that character responds to the circumstances of the action. The result is vividness, but it is vividness of a special kind. When it is visual, it depends as much on the exact appropriateness of what is seen, by whom, and from where, as on the color, texture, or other intrinsic sensory or aesthetic qualities of the object" (p. 128).

14. So, notably, Francis Berry, "Sir Gawayne and the Grene Knight," in *The Age of Chaucer,* ed. Boris Ford (London: Pelican, 1954), pp. 156–158.

15. The effect of the verse-form has been so described by J. B. Bessinger, Jr., on the cover of the Caedmon recording [TC2024] of his reading of the poem with Marie Borroff. A general tension in the poem between "formal" and "primitive" elements is noted by Berry, "Sir Gawayne," pp. 151–153; it is finely described in greater detail by William Goldhurst, "The Green and the Gold: The Major Theme of *Gawain and the Green Knight.*" *College English* 20 (1958–59): 61–65.

16. P. B. Taylor, "'Blysse and blunder,' Nature and Ritual in *Sir Gawain and the Green Knight,*" *English Studies* 50 (1969): 165–175, begins at the same point but offers quite a different interpretation: "the focus of the story is

on the extension and consequences of [Gawain's] blunder, which is misuse of heroic, or courtly, ritual" (p. 166).

17. Harvey Cox, *The Feast of Fools: A Theological Essay on Festival and Fantasy* (Cambridge, Mass.: Harvard Univ. Press, 1969), pp. 22–23.

18. Borroff, *Sir Gawain,* p. 121: "The narrator tends to see actions, whether major or minor, as reciprocal, giving explicit attention to the reciprocating or responding agent even when the response is of no importance to the story line or could be omitted as obvious. The germ of such a tendency may be discerned in the traditional style of alliterative poetry, which provides for the expression of qualities of promptness and readiness in response to commands and requests. . . . But the tendency is sufficiently consistent and systematic in *Gawain* to distinguish that poem from the works of other poets."

19. See Morton W. Bloomfield, "Sir Gawain and the Green Knight: An Appraisal," *PMLA* 76 (1961): 16, 19; Donald R. Howard, *The Three Temptations: Medieval Man in Search of the World* (Princeton: Princeton Univ. Press, 1966), pp. 243–244, 284–285. Bloomfield and Howard principally call attention to the "game" that is the poem, that is, to the game being played by the poet with his audience. J. A. Burrow, *A Reading of Sir Gawain and the Green Knight* (London: Routledge, 1965), pp. 21–23, notes the seriousness, the "vein of legal earnest," with which the Green Knight's Christmas game is taken up. Robert G. Cook, "The Play Element in Sir Gawain and the Green Knight," *Tulane Studies in English* 13 (1963): 5–31, collects the numerous references to and examples of "play" in the poem itself, with some reference to the ideas of Johan Huizinga's *Homo Ludens* (see note 22 below). Huizinga's ideas have been taken up and applied illuminatingly to medieval drama by V. A. Kolve, *The Play Called Corpus Christi* (Stanford: Stanford Univ. Press, 1966). On "game" in Chaucer, see Richard A. Lanham, "Game, Play, and High Seriousness in Chaucer's Poetry," *English Studies* 48 (1967): 1–24. Huizinga's book founded a whole "anthropology of play." One of its principal documents is Roger Caillois, *Les Jeux et les hommes* (Paris: Gallimard, 1958); see also the issue of *Yale French Studies,* no. 41 (1968), entitled "Game, Play, Literature," and the references in Lanham's article cited above.

20. The precise nature of the game has not been determined. All the elements in the description, vv. 66–70, would be accounted for by a sort of handicapping game (similar to that called "newe faire" in *Piers Plowman,* B V 327 ff.) in which, after New Year's gifts had been exchanged, the giver of the gift judged the less valuable had to make up the difference in kisses.

21. Henry L. Savage, "The Significance of the Hunting Scenes in Sir Gawain and the Green Knight," *JEGP* 27 (1928): 1–15 [repr. in his *The Gawain Poet: Studies in his Personality and Background* (Chapel Hill: Univ. of North Carolina Press, 1956) chap. 2].

22. Johan Huizinga, *Homo Ludens: A Study of the Play-Element in Culture* [1938], Engl. trans. (Boston: Beacon, 1955), p. 45.

23. See vv. 1–5. That it is Aeneas and not Antenor and that Aeneas is meant to be regarded as *trewest on erthe,* despite the *tricherie* attributed to him by medieval tradition, is ably argued, in the context of the whole poem, by Alfred David, "Gawain and Aeneas," *English Studies* 49 (1968): 402–409; cf. also Phillip W. Damon, "Dante's Ulysses and the Mythic Tradition," in William Matthews, ed., *Medieval Secular Literature* (Berkeley: Univ. of California Press, 1965), p. 41.

Piers Plowman

1. See, for instance, the three recent collections of *Piers Plowman* criticism: Robert J. Blanch, ed., *Style and Symbolism in Piers Plowman: A Modern Critical Anthology* (Knoxville: Univ. of Tennessee Press, 1969); S. S. Hussey, ed., *Piers Plowman: Critical Approaches* (London: Methuen, 1969); Edward Vasta, ed., *Interpretations of Piers Plowman* (Notre Dame, Ind.: Univ. of Notre Dame Press, 1968). In my references to the three texts of the poem I shall for convenience use the single edition of Walter W. Skeat, *The Vision of William Concerning Piers the Plowman,* 2 vols. (London: Oxford Univ. Press, 1886; repr. 1954), with some additional punctuation; however, references to the A-text have been checked for meaningful variants against the more authoritative edition of George Kane, *Piers Plowman: the A Version* (London: Univ. of London, the Athlone Press, 1960). My references to events in the poem are to the B-text unless otherwise specified.

2. George Kane, "The Vision of Piers Plowman," in his *Middle English Literature: A Critical Study of the Romances, the Religious Lyrics, Piers Plowman* (London: Methuen, 1951), p. 185; A. C. Spearing, "The Art of Preaching and *Piers Plowman,*" in his *Criticism and Medieval Poetry* (New York: Barnes and Noble, 1964), p. 92; Morton Bloomfield, *Piers Plowman as a Fourteenth-century Apocalypse* (New Brunswick, N.J.: Rutgers Univ. Press, 1963), p. 20; John Lawlor, "The Imaginative Unity of Piers Plowman," *Review of English Studies,* n.s., 8 (1957): 126; Elizabeth Salter and Derek Pearsall, eds., *Piers Plowman* (Evanston: Northwestern Univ. Press, 1967), pp. 42, 47.

3. On literary theory see Edmond Faral, ed., *Les Arts poétiques du XIIe* et du XIIIe siècle (Paris: Champion, 1924); on aesthetic theory see Edgar de Bruyne, *Etudes d'esthétique médiévale,* 3 vols. (Bruges: De Tempel, 1946). There is a convenient summary of these subjects in Robert M. Jordan, *Chaucer and the Shape of Creation: The Aesthetic Possibilities of Inorganic Structure* (Cambridge, Mass.: Harvard Univ. Press, 1967), chap. 2. Arthur K. Moore, "Medieval English Literature and the Question of Unity," *Modern Philology* 65 (1968): 285–300, discusses the theoretical and practical difficulties of applying modern conceptions of "unity" to medieval literature; a few pages (289, 294–296) take up *Piers Plowman.*

4. Robert Worth Frank, Jr., *Piers Plowman and the Scheme of Salvation:*

An Interpretation of Dowel, Dobet and Dobest (New Haven: Yale Univ. Press, 1957), p. 34.

5. The principal older theories are summarized by S. S. Hussey, "Langland, Hilton, and the Three Lives," *RES,* n.s., 7 (1956), pp. 132–150 (repr. Vasta, *Interpretations,* pp. 232–258).

6. See Hussey, "Langland," p. 148 and note; Salter and Pearsall, *Piers,* pp. 29–30.

7. Kane, "Vision," pp. 240–241.

8. Bloomfield, *Piers as Apocalypse,* p. 116.

9. This is the implication of Lawlor, "Imaginative Unity," passim, and Spearing, "Art of Preaching," pp. 92–94.

10. *Piers as Apocalypse,* pp. 20–21.

11. Rosemary Woolf, "Some Non-Medieval Qualities of *Piers Plowman,*" *Essays in Criticism* 12 (1962): 120.

12. Salter and Pearsall, *Piers,* pp. 8, 42–43.

13. "Vision," p. 244.

14. "Imaginative Unity," pp. 125–126. Lawlor is one of the ablest and most sympathetic readers of the poem. In accepting the poem's incoherencies as part of its artistic plan, he wisely does not insist on its complete artfulness: "We may well, if we choose, identify the poet behind the Dreamer, manoeuvering the reader through his guide until vision is inescapable. But we should be very sure that we allow for the activity of the poem itself, bringing to the poet, in the act of telling, new relations and significances. Our criticism will be beside the mark if we do not see that the poem succeeds in communicating the mind, not behind, but *in* the poem—a poem which is always, in a sense, unfinished." *(Ibid.)* Lawlor's ideas appear in expanded form in his book *Piers Plowman: An Essay in Criticism* (London: Arnold, 1962); see esp. chap. 7.

15. All three texts contain the pairing: AB Prologus 20, 24; C Prologus 22, 25; it is echoed in B XIX 331 (C XXII 337): "Now is Pieres to the plow and Pruyde it aspyde." Kane's edition of the A-text (Prol. 20) offers the reading "to plouz," making "plow" a verb instead of a noun. In either sense, the word comes, of course, with powerful symbolic value in itself, but this does not alter the contrast in concreteness of the paired terms. Another obvious example of the equivalence, in the poet's mind, of terms on different levels of abstraction, comes in the ride to Westminster (Passus II, vv. 161 ff.), where the classes of civil and ecclesiastical officers are mingled freely but not uniformly with moral abstractions. Meed rides on a sheriff; Falsehood on a juryman; Deceit on a flatterer; Simony on the group of summoners and provisors; bishops on deans and other episcopal officers, etc. For further discussion of the mixture of allegory and literalism in Langland, see Salter and Pearsall, *Piers,* pp. 5, 12, 24; Bloomfield, *Piers as Apocalypse,* pp. 41–42; Lawlor, *Piers,* pp. 252 ff; and Priscilla Jenkins, "Conscience: the Frustration of Allegory," in Hussey, ed., *Piers,* pp. 125–142, where the "interplay between the modes" is provocatively

read as "the structural basis of the poem" (p. 125); " . . . allegory is a mode of thought which Langland is investigating and defining through the juxtaposition of allegorical and literal" (p. 142).

16. Raoul de Houdenc, *Le Songe d'Enfer,* in Aug. Scheler, ed., *Trouvères Belges,* Nouvelle Série (Louvain: Lefever, 1879), 2: 176–200.

17. The ensuing two paragraphs repeat observations on Langland's space offered in my "Locus of Action in Medieval Narrative," *Romance Philology* 17 (1963): 115–22, with discussion of space in earlier allegory.

18. Guillaume de Deguileville, *Le Pèlerinage de Vie Humaine,* ed. J. J. Stürzinger (London: Roxburghe Club, 1893), vv. 6503 ff.

19. Spearing, "Art of Preaching," p. 95; cf. Woolf, "Some Non-Medieval Qualities," pp. 114–116.

20. *Piers as Apocalypse,* p. 32; cf. Spearing, "Art of Preaching," p. 87: "one has the impression that the poet is engaged in a contest against an unpredictable opponent."

21. J. F. Goodridge, trans., *Piers the Ploughman* (Harmondsworth: Penguin, 1959), p. 57.

22. See particularly, Spearing, "Art of Preaching," *passim.*

23. See Elizabeth Salter, *Piers Plowman: An Introduction* (Cambridge, Mass.: Harvard Univ. Press, 1962), pp. 24–34; Spearing, "Art of Preaching," pp. 84–89; Salter and Pearsall, *Piers,* pp. 32–35, 48–51, 54. Donald Wesling, "Eschatology and the Language of Satire in 'Piers Plowman,'" *Criticism* 10 (1968): 287, explains Langland's digressiveness as "unavoidable in the narrative technique of satire."

24. See Lawlor, "Imaginative Unity," pp. 118–119, 124–126; Lawlor, *Piers,* pp. 232–233, 306–316; Salter, *Piers: An Introduction,* pp. 90, 95; Salter and Pearsall, *Piers,* pp. 32, 42–43, 47, 49, 51; Woolf, "Some Non-Medieval Qualities," pp. 120–122; Kane, "Vision," pp. 189–192, 243–245, 247.

25. There is still much to be learned about Langland's poetic style. Perhaps the best brief characterization of the quality of his "making" is Nevill Coghill's "God's Wenches and the Light That Spoke," *English and Medieval Studies Presented to J. R. R. Tolkien,* ed. N. Davis and C. L. Wrenn (London: Allen and Unwin, 1962), pp. 200–218 [rcpr. Newstead, *Chaucer and His Contemporaries,* pp. 236–254]. See also Kane, "Vision," *passim;* Elizabeth Suddaby, "The Poem *Piers Plowman,*" *JEGP* 54 (1955): 91–103; Salter, *Piers: An Introduction,* pp. 19–24, 31–44; R. E. Kaske, "The Use of Simple Figures of Speech in *Piers Plowman* B: A Study in the Figurative Expression of Ideas and Opinions," *Studies in Philology* 48 (1951): 571–600; Lawlor, *Piers,* esp. pp. 187–280; B. F. Huppé, *"Petrus id est Christus:* Word Play in Piers Plowman, the B-Text," *ELH* 17 (1950): 163–190; E. Talbot Donaldson, *Piers Plowman: The C-Text and Its Poet* (New Haven: Yale Univ. Press, 1949; repr. 1966), chap. 3.

26. The tradition of the *sermo humilis* is substantially the discovery of

Erich Auerbach; see his *Mimesis,* esp. chaps. 7, 8, and 10; and "Sermo
Humilis," in his *Literary Language and Its Public in Late Latin Antiquity and
in the Middle Ages,* Bollingen Series 74 (New York: Pantheon, 1965), pp.
27–66. Auerbach, however, does not mention *Piers Plowman* in this connection. The applicability of Auerbach's category to Langland's plain style has
been recently noted by J. A. W. Bennett, "Chaucer's Contemporary," in
Hussey, ed., *Piers,* p. 316. However, I do not agree that it is equally applicable to "the rich medley of the *Canterbury Tales.*"

27. "Iurdan" is a pun on "jordan," chamber pot, and "Jordan," the name of
a contemporary friar; on Langland's general propensity for puns, see Huppé,
"Word Play."

28. Lawlor, *Piers,* pp. 262–263; Woolf, "Some Non-Medieval Qualities,"
p. 118.

29. Conveniently listed by Huppé, "Word Play," esp. pp. 179 ff. Langland's
thematic repetitions, like most repetitions, at least give the reader a sense of
security and familiarity on the level of ideas. Whether they give the poem
structural coherence is another matter, which cannot at any rate be proved by
the mere listing of them. Some of Langland's repetitions, as for instance his
frequent attacks on the friars, and his defenses of the poor, seem to work
against coherence; they begin to take on an obsessive quality that threatens
interruption of the argument rather than support of it.

30. *Piers as Apocalypse,* pp. 35–36.

31. *Piers: The C-Text,* pp. 78–79. Donaldson continues: "Knowing A and
B, brilliance mingled with mediocrity is just what we should expect from C."

32. I have not taken up the even more complex question of a *four*-fold or
four-level structure of meaning in *Piers Plowman,* in which what I have variously called the allegorical or spiritual significance is further divided into
three separate levels of meaning. See D. W. Robertson, Jr., and Bernard F.
Huppé, *Piers Plowman and Scriptural Tradition* (Princeton: Princeton Univ.
Press, 1951), esp. pp. 2–3, 14, 236–240. According to the present reading of
the poem, a four-level edifice is even more likely to have collapsed together
in Langland's imagination than a two-level one.

33. I embrace together here the remark by Kane, "Vision," p. 236, that the
author has "an unusually powerful visual imagination," and that by Woolf,
"Some Non-Medieval Qualities," p. 115, that the poem "lacks the visual quality . . . characteristic of Medieval literature."

34. See in particular, in addition to the works already cited, T. P. Dunning,
C.M., *Piers Plowman: An Interpretation of the A Text* (London: Longmans,
Green, 1937; excerpts in Vasta, ed., *Interpretations,* pp. 87–114) and his "The
Structure of the B-Text of *Piers Plowman,*" *RES,* n.s., 6 (1956): 225–237
(repr. in Vasta, ed., *Interpretations,* pp. 259–277, and in Blanch, ed., *Style and
Symbolism,* pp. 87–100); and Sister Mary Clemente Davlin, O.P., "Kynde
Knowyng as a Major Theme in *Piers Plowman* B," *RES,* n.s., 22 (1971): 1–19.

35. Robertson and Huppé, *Piers,* p. 236.

36. See Salter, *Piers,* pp. 71–72; Salter and Pearsall, *Piers,* pp. 22–23. That segment of medieval "surrealism" which borders on the grotesque is taken up by Jurgis Baltrušaitis, *Réveils et prodigues: le gothique fantastique* (Paris: Colin, 1960).

37. Millard Meiss, *Painting in Florence and Siena after the Black Death* (Princeton: Princeton Univ. Press, 1951), pp. 25, 93.

Chaucer

1. See chap. I above, pp. 31–32 and footnote 32. For the text of Chaucer, I use *The Works of Geoffrey Chaucer,* ed. F. N. Robinson, 2d ed. (Boston: Houghton Mifflin, 1957).

2. This idea is discussed in some detail in my *"The Canterbury Tales:* Style of the Man and Style of the Work," in D. S. Brewer, ed., *Chaucer and Chaucerians: Critical Studies in Middle English Literature* (London: Nelson, 1966), pp. 88–114, [reprinted above, pp. 1–25].

3. This is the import of recent "exegetical" criticism; see, for instance, D. W. Robertson, Jr., *A Preface to Chaucer: Studies in Medieval Perspectives* (Princeton: Princeton Univ. Press, 1962), pp. 317–331, 380–382.

4. Ernest Langlois, ed., *Le Roman de la Rose par Guillaume de Lorris et Jean de Meun,* Société des Anciens Textes Française, 5 vols. (Paris: Champion, 1914–1924), vv. 11969–974:

> "Mais a vous n'ose je mentir;
> Mis se je peüsse sentir
> Que vous ne l'aperceüssiez,
> La mençonge ou poing ëussiez:
> Certainement je vous boulasse,
> Ja pour pechié ne la laissasse. . . ."

The Middle English translation (Robinson, ed., *Chaucer,* p. 633), vv. 7287–7292:

> "But unto you dar I not lye:
> But myght I felen or aspie
> That ye perceyved it no thyng,
> Ye shulde have a stark lesyng
> Right in youre honde thus, to bigynne;
> I nolde it lette for no synne."

5. See Erich Auerbach, "Camilla, or, the Rebirth of the Sublime," in his *Literary Language and Its Public,* trans. Ralph Manheim, Bollingen Series 74 (New York: Pantheon, 1965), pp. 183–233. Auerbach discusses the reasons

for the decline of the sublime style and describes the steps leading to Dante's full revival of it in the *Divine Comedy.*

6. Robert Kilburn Root, ed., *The Book of Troilus and Criseyde* by Geoffrey Chaucer (Princeton: Princeton Univ. Press, 1926 [repr. 1945]), p. xlv. Cf. Daniel C. Boughner. "Elements of Epic Grandeur in the 'Troilus,'" *ELH* 6 (1939): 200–210; and Paul M. Clogan, "Chaucer's Use of the 'Thebaid,'" *English Miscellany* 18 (1967): 9–31. The best study of the *Teseida's* influence on Chaucer's epic style is R. A. Pratt, "Chaucer's Use of the *Teseida,*" *PMLA* 62 (1947): 598–621. Pratt suggests (p. 612) that the example of the *Teseida* "may have had more to do with Chaucer's decision to rework the story of *Il Filostrato* in a heightened manner than the example of Dante's *Commedia.* . . ."

7. Giovanni Boccaccio, *Teseida delle nozze d'Emilia,* ed. Aurelio Roncaglia (Bari: Laterza, 1941), XII, 84; cf. Boccaccio's *chiose* to XII, 84 and 85, p. 465. Boccaccio is referring to *De Vulgari eloquentia* II, ii, 8: "Quare hec tria, salus videlicet, venus et virtus, apparent esse illa magnalia que sint maxime pertractanda, hoc est ea que maxime sunt ad ista, ut armorum probitas, amoris accensio et directio voluntatis" (ed. A. Marigo, 3d ed. [Firenze: Le Monnier, 1957]).

8. See Robert S. Haller, *"The Knight's Tale* and the Epic Tradition," *Chaucer Review* 1 (1966): 67–84; dealing mainly with the ethical and political import of epic, Professor Haller argues persuasively that "it is in his treatment of love that Chaucer is most epic, for what Chaucer has done is to make love take the place of the usual political center of the epic . . ."; love is "the means whereby the cosmic and political implications of the epic are conveyed" (p. 68).

9. See Derek Pearsall, "The Squire as Story-Teller," *UTQ* 34 (1965): 82–92; Robert S. Haller, "Chaucer's *Squire's Tale* and the Uses of Rhetoric," *Modern Philology* 62 (1965): 285–295.

10. Brian Wilkie, "What is Sentimentality?," *College English* 28 (1967): 564–575, is an excellent statement of the problem.

11. Medieval romance contains from the first an "Ovidian" strain of pathos having to do with unhappy heroines, but it is rarely so overstated as to approach sentimentality. Mr. Richard Lock has pointed out to me a rare instance (and the earliest I know) of the introduction of a child for pathetic effect in romance: *The Continuations of the Old French Perceval of Chrétien de Troyes,* vol. I, *The First Continuation,* ed. William Roach (Philadelphia: Univ. of Pennsylvania Press, 1949), vv. 10857–10948, 11035–11079.

12. On Mâle, see above, pp. 22–23 in this volume. The very popular *Meditations on the Life of Christ,* written probably first in Latin by a Franciscan living in Tuscany in the second half of the thirteenth century, still exists in over two hundred manuscripts in various languages. See *Meditations on the Life of Christ,* ed. and trans. Isa Ragusa and Rosalie B. Green (Princeton: Princeton Univ. Press, 1961), a modern English translation based mainly on an

Italian version. The *Meditations* were translated into English in the fifteenth century by Nicholas Love; see Elizabeth Zeeman, "Nicholas Love—A Fifteenth-Century Translator," *RES,* n.s., 6 (1955): 113–127. In the same approximate period as the pseudo-Bonaventura, or slightly earlier, is the *Legenda Aurea* (ca. 1255) of Jacobus de Voragine, with quite a few saints' legends containing pathetic incidents.

13. Treatment of mothers and children in a pathetic vein is rare in English literature between Chaucer and the eighteenth century. Addison's *Spectator* paper no. 44 (April 20, 1711) signals the change of taste: "A disconsolate Mother, with a Child in her Hand, has frequently drawn Compassion from the Audience, and has therefore gained a Place in several Tragedies. A Modern Writer, that observed how this had took in other Plays, being resolved to double the Distress, and melt his Audience twice as much as those before him had done, brought a Princess upon the Stage with a little Boy in one Hand and a Girl in the other. . . ." (ed. G. Gregory Smith, vol. 1, Everyman's Library, no. 164 [London: Dent, 1945], p. 133.)

14. See William S. Wilson, "Exegetical Grammar in the *House of Fame,*" *English Language Notes* 1 (1964): 246.

15. Johan Huizinga, *Waning of the Middle Ages* [1919; Eng. trans. 1924] (London: Arnold, 1937), pp. 126–128.

16. The thirteenth has been called "the century of the discovery of childhood." See Philippe Ariès, *Centuries of Childhood: A Social History of Family Life,* trans. Robert Baldick (New York: Knopf, 1962), esp. pp. 33–49, "The Discovery of Childhood"; E. Delaruelle, "L'Idée de croisade chez Saint Louis," *Bulletin de Littérature Ecclésiastique* 61 (1960): 252. I have been unable to obtain the 36-page work cited by both: Pierre Colombier, *L'Enfant au Moyen Age* (Villefranche-sur-Rhône: Jacquemaire, 1951).

17. D. S. Brewer, "Children in Chaucer," *Review of English Literature* 5 (1964): 55–56.

18. Quoted in Erich Auerbach, *Mimesis: The Representation of Reality in Western Literature* [1946], trans. Willard R. Trask (Princeton: Princeton Univ. Press, 1953), p. 239.

19. Theodore Spencer, "The Story of Ugolino in Dante and Chaucer," *Speculum* 9 (1934): 295–301.

20. See, for flaccid narration, 105 ff.; 155–157, 174, 217; and for vague plot, 139 ff., 260 ff.

21. The "soft" view of the tale, accepting its pathos fully, is the traditional view, dominant until recent times; for an excellent presentation of the "hard" view, see Alan T. Gaylord, "The Unconquered Tale of the Prioress," *Papers of the Michigan Academy of Science, Arts, and Letters* 47 (1962): 613–636.

22. This argument is elaborated in my *Chaucer and the French Tradition: A Study in Style and Meaning* (Berkeley: Univ. of California Press, 1957), pp. 190–197.

23. Alfred David, "The Man of Law vs. Chaucer: A Case in Poetics," *PMLA* 82 (1967): 223.

24. See, e.g., vv. 267–273, 295–315, 358–371, 421–427, 470–504, 631–637, 652–658, etc.

25. Frederick A. Pottle, *The Idiom of Poetry* (Ithaca: Cornell Univ. Press, 1941), p. 32: "Poetry in the bulk, poetry by and large, infallibly expresses the sensibility of the age which produced it. If it did not, it would not be poetry at all. And hence I say that poetry, in the collective sense, cannot go wrong."

THE WIFE OF BATH AND GAUTIER'S *LA VEUVE*

1. See the present writer's *Chaucer and the French Tradition [CFT]* (Berkeley, 1957), p. 5; William W. Heist, "Folklore Study and Chaucer's Fabliau-like Tales," *Papers of the Michigan Acad. of Science, Art, and Letters,* 36 (1950), 251–258; and, e.g., J. V. Cunningham, "The Literary Form of the Prologue to the *Canterbury Tales,"* MP, 49 (1952), 172–181.

2. Cf. Robert P. Miller, *"The Wife of Bath's Tale* and Medieval Exempla," *ELH,* 32 (1965), 442–456.

3. Ed., respectively, by F. N. Robinson, *The Works of Geoffrey Chaucer,* 2d ed. (Boston, 1957) *[WBP];* and by Charles H. Livingston, *Le Jongleur Gautier Le Leu* (Cambridge, Mass. 1951) *[LaV.].* Livingston (p. 99) dates *La Veuve* "après 1248" and concludes that Gautier's career extended well into the second half of the century.

4. See Dorothy Everett, "Chaucer's 'Good Ear,'" in her *Essays on Middle English Literature* (Oxford, 1955), pp. 139–148; *CFT,* pp. 101–107, 110, 120–123, 134–137, 172; Donald R. Howard, "Chaucer the Man," *PMLA,* 80 (1965), 337–343, and the references therein.

5. The principal authority is Robert A. Pratt. See, e.g., his "The Development of the Wife of Bath" in MacEdward Leach, ed., *Studies in Medieval Literature in Honor of Albert C. Baugh* (Philadelphia, 1961), pp. 45–79, and his forthcoming edition of "Jankyn's Book."

6. Ed. E. Langlois, *Le Roman de la Rose par Guillaume de Lorris et Jean de Meun,* 5 vols., SATF (Paris, 1914–1924), vv. 12740–14546; most of the resemblances are noted in Robinson's *Chaucer.* Cf. also *CFT,* pp. 79–88, 94–96, 205–206. According to Félix Lecoy, ed., *Le Roman de la Rose,* I, CFMA (Paris, 1965), p. viii, Jean's part of the poem was composed between 1269 and 1278.

7. See Livingston, op. cit., pp. 160–163; *CFT,* pp. 81–82.

8. *CFT,* pp. 83, 205–208.

9. *LaV.* 311–312 ("When it comes to the threshing, I don't want my grain without seeds"); compare, for quality of imagery, *WBP* 477–9:

The flour is goon, ther is namoore to telle;
The bren, as I best kan, now moste I selle. . . .

10. *LaV.* 527–8, 535–7; the closest other parallel to this speech that I know
is in Eustache Deschamps' *Miroir de Mariage,* ed. Gaston Raynaud, *OEuvres
Complètes,* IX, SATF (Paris, 1894), vv. 3705–7:

Elle souspire:
"Et que me voulez vous, beau sire?
Me voulez vous ceans tuer?"

But here there has been no fist fight at all.

THE FABLIAUX, COURTLY CULTURE, AND THE (RE)INVENTION OF VULGARITY

1. Charles Muscatine, *The Old French Fabliaux* (New Haven, 1986), esp.
chap. 5.
2. See e.g. Per Nykrog, *Les Fabliaux: Étude d'histoire littéraire et de styl-
istique médiévale* (Copenhagen, 1957), 216; Jürgen Beyer, *Schwank und
Moral: Untersuchungen zum altfranzösischen Fabliau und verwandten For-
men* (Heidelberg, 1969), 100–111; Sarah Melhado White, "Sexual Language
and Human Conflict in Old French Fabliaux," *Comparative Studies in Society
and History* 24 (1982), 191: "The impact of sexual and scatological words
depends not on an absence of inhibition, but on a dynamic interaction of taboo
and defiance."
3. Wolf-Dieter Stempel, "Mittelalterliche Obszönität als literarästhetis-
ches Problem," in H. R. Jauss, ed., *Die nicht mehr schönen Künste* (Munich,
1968), 187–205.
4. As in Nykrog's theory; see his *Les Fabliaux,* 18 and passim. Cf. Pierre
Bec, *Burlesque et obscénité chez les troubadours* (Paris, 1984), 13. Bec makes
a clear distinction between the obscenity of the fabliaux and that of the
Provençal "contre-texte," which does depend on its opposite for comic and
parodic effect.
5. Weston LaBarre, "Obscenity: An Anthropological Appraisal," *Law and
Contemporary Problems* 20 (1955), 541–542.
6. John J. Honigmann, "A Cultural Theory of Obscenity," in Manfred F.
DeMartino, ed., *Sexual Behavior and Personality Characteristics* (New York,
1963), 40–41, citing H. Powdermaker, *Life in Lesu* (New York, 1933), 286.
7. LaBarre, "Obscenity," 538.
8. I have this from the anthropologist D. Michael Warren. He points out

that in these languages, which have no words comparable to our four-letter ones, obscenity involves complex and imaginative uses of language, particularly language denying the humanity of the person addressed.

9. Honigmann, "Cultural Theory," 43n, citing Reo Fortune, *Sorcerers of Dobu* (London, 1932), 245.

10. Harry Feldman, "*Kapekape:* Contexts of Malediction in Tonga," *Maledicta* 5 (1981), 148.

11. Ibid., 143-150.

12. Edward Sagarin, *The Anatomy of Dirty Words* (New York, 1969), 47.

13. See, e.g. Herbert Halpert, "Folklore and Obscenity: Definitions and Problems," *Journal of American Folklore* 75 (1962), 191.

14. *Le Roman de la rose,* ed. Félix Lecoy, 3 vols. (Paris, 1965-1970), lines 2097-2102.

15. Jean Renart, *Le Lai de l'ombre,* ed. John Orr (Edinburgh, 1948), lines 8-13.

16. T. B. W. Reid, ed., *Twelve Fabliaux* (Manchester, 1958), lines 38-59, 45-46.

17. "La Dame qui aveine demandoit pour Morel," in A. de Montaiglon and G. Raynaud, eds., *Recueil général et complet des fabliaux des XIIIe et XIVe siècles,* 6 vols. (Paris, 1872-1890), I.321.

18. On the social background, see Muscatine, *Old French Fabliaux,* chap. 2; on style and diction, 30-33, 55-72.

19. *Le Roman de Renart,* ed. Mario Roques, 6 vols. (Paris, 1948-1963) [branche 14, "La Confession de Renart," lines 14559-69], 5.48. On these aspects of "Richeut" and *Renart,* see Muscatine, *Old French Fabliaux,* 161-163.

20. Nykrog, *Fabliaux,* 72-97; Per Nykrog, "Courtliness and the Townspeople: The Fabliaux as a Courtly Burlesque," in Thomas D. Cooke and Benjamin L. Honeycutt, eds., *The Humor of the Fabliaux* (Columbia, Missouri, 1974), 59-73.

21. See Finnegan Alford and Richard Alford, "A Holo-Cultural Study of Humor," *Ethos* [Journal of the Society for Psychological Anthropology] 9 (1981), 155.

22. See Theodor Wilhelm Braune, *Althochdeutsches Lesebauch,* 15th ed., rev. Ernst A. Ebbinghaus (Tübingen, 1969), 9-10:

"Guane cumet ger, brothro? (unde uenis, frater?)"
"E guas mer in gene francia. (in francia fui.)"
"Guaez ge dar daden? (quid fecisti ibi?)"
"Guar is tin quenna? (ubi est tua femina?)"
"Guanna sarden ger? (quot uices fotisti?)"
"Vndes ars in tine naso. (canis culum in tuo naso)."

The list also includes "Narra *er* sarda gerra (stultus uoluntarie fottit)" and "Guathere, latz mer serte."

23. See *Eneas,* ed. J. J. Salverda de Grave, 2 vols. (Paris, 1925–1929), lines 8567ff (with a pun on *con/connin* in line 8595), 9155–65.

24. Their traditional titles are "La Damoisele qui ne pooit oïr parler de foutre" (2 versions), "La Pucele qui abevra le polain," and "L'Esquiriel." The first three are edited under the first title as versions of the same story in *Nouveau recueil complet des fabliaux [NRCF],* ed. Willem Noomen and Nico van den Boogard, 10 vols. (Assen, 1983–), vol. 4; "L'Esquiriel" appears in vol. 5.

The quotation is from "La Damoisele," (*NRCF,* 4.77– 78):

Par cest essanple monstrer uueil
Que femes n'aient point d'orgueil
De foutre paller hautement
Quant il foutent tot igalment (223–226)

25. In "La Damoisele," v. 147 (*NRCF,* 4.73), the young lady, who is all along supposed to be using euphemisms, refers to her breasts as "two sheep's balls" (*coilles de mouton*); when she finds the clerk's testicles and asks what they are, he uses the common euphemism "two marshals" (*dui mareschal* [v. 193, *NRCF,* 4.77]); cf. "L'Esquiriel," v. 130 (*NRCF,* 6.47), where the expected euphemism is replaced by *con.*

26. Ed. Lecoy, lines 5670–94; 6898–7198.

27. See Jan Ziolkowski, "Obscenity in the Latin Grammatical and Rhetorical Tradition," in this volume.

28. C. Stephen Jaeger, *The Origins of Courtliness: Civilizing Trends and the Formation of Courtly Ideals 939–1210* (Philadelphia, 1985), 238.

29. On all these traits, see Amy Richlin, *The Garden of Priapus: Sexuality and Aggression in Roman Humor* (New Haven, 1983).

THE EMERGENCE OF PSYCHOLOGICAL ALLEGORY IN OLD FRENCH ROMANCE

*In keeping with the character of the present volume, some of the extensive documentation in the notes has been omitted, as indicated by [. . .]; the full documentation may be found in *PMLA* 68 (1953), 1160–1182.

1. *The Allegory of Love* (Oxford, 1936), pp. 111, 30–32 ("Chrétien can hardly turn to the inner world without, at the same time, turning to allegory"), 112–116 (". . . allegory had been born and perfected for the very purpose to which Chrétien put it." "In Chrétien Guillaume de Lorris found, on the one hand, fantastic adventure, on the other, a realistic account of imaginative passion. . . . It was the second that interested him. He conceived the idea that this,

stripped of its Arthurian supports, might stand on its own feet and make the subject of a poem. As such a poem would concern itself exclusively with what the lovers felt, it would, of course, be allegorical."). Cf. Karl Voretzsch, *Einführung in das Studium der altfranzösischen Lieteratur,* 3d ed. (Halle, 1925), p. 420: "In allen diesen dichtungen dienen allegorie und personifikation geistlichen oder wenigstens moralischen zwecken. Aber auch die weltliche dichtung entwickelt solche stilformen, so wenn in den höfischen romanen und chansons 'Amor' personifiziert wird, wenn der dichter vernunft und liebe in seinem herzen streiten lässt. . . . Hiermit wird die allegorie aus der religiösen in die weltliche sphäre, speziell in die liebesdichtung übergeführt, was für den Rosenroman bedeutungsvoll wird"; Edmond Faral, "*Le Roman de la Rose* et la Pensée Française au XIIIe Siècle," *Revue des Deux Mondes,* XXXV (Sept. 1926), 433: "Il [Guillaume de Lorris] anime des entités psychologiques: l'exemple lui en avait été donné par Martianus Capella, par Raoul de Houdenc, par Huon de Méry."

2. See E. Langlois, ed. *Le Roman de la Rose* (Paris, 1914–24), I, 3–8; Lewis, *Allegory of Love,* pp. 176–259.

3. *La Littérature Française au Moyen Age* (Paris, 1888), par. 111.

4. *Origines et Sources du Roman de la Rose* (Paris, 1891), pp. 66–67.

5. *Psychomachia,* ed. & trans. H. J. Thomson, Loeb Classical Library (London & Cambridge, Mass., 1949), vv. 40–108.

6. Georg Wimmer, ed. *Ausgaben und Abhandlungen aus dem Gebiete der romanischen Philologie,* LXXVI (Marburg, 1888). Here, as elsewhere, I cite names of personifications in the *cas-régime* unless no such form occurs in the text.

7. Aug. Scheler ed., in *Trouvères Belges,* nouvelle série (Louvain, 1879); see *Paradis* 461–607, *Enfer* 216–321.

8. Lines 75–79. See also the references to what appear to be actual persons: 167, 189–201, 223.

9. See the *Faerie Queene,* ed. J. C. Smith (Oxford, 1909), II, 485 (letter to Sir Walter Ralegh).

10. Jean Renart [?], *Galeran de Bretagne,* ed. Lucien Foulet, CFMA (Paris, 1925), vv. 2914–3016; cf. *Roman de la Rose* 3511–52. There are, of course, differences of character, situation and emphasis. Since Galeran is supposedly much above Fresne in station, this looms largest in the Abbess' mind, and it is *his bel acueil* which she tries to banish by her reproaches. The Lady of the *Roman* is much less tough than Fresne; while the latter stands up well to the Abbess (*Galeran* 3788–3995), the former allows *Honte* and *Peor* to reawaken *Dangier,* and *Jalosie* to imprison *Bel Acueil* (*Roman* 3561–3754).

11. The two may be profitably compared section by section, viz.: Jean Renart, *Le Lai de l'Ombre* [MS.E], ed. John Orr (Edinburgh, 1948), vv. 342–49, *Roman de la Rose* 2879–85; *Lai* 350–67, 399–421, *Roman* 2886–2906; *Lai* 422–37, *Roman* 2907–19; *Lai* 438–47, *Roman* 2920–50.

12. *Roman de la Rose* 3221–3356; cf. *Amadas et Ydoine*, ed. John Reinhard (Paris, 1926), vv. 1006–1140. The *Amadas* poet uses a few lines of allegory here; [see below, p. 201].

13. See Alfons Hilka, *Die direkte Rede als stilistisches Kunstmittel in den Romanen des Kristian von Troyes* (Halle, 1903), pp. 71–92; Gunnar Biller, *Etude sur le Style des premiers Romans français en Vers (1150–75)*, Göteborgs Högskolas Arsskrift, XXII (Göteborg, 1916), pp. 160–165.

14. Perhaps better defined, according to the locus of the action, as "psychic" and cosmic."

15. Cf. Hilka, *Direkte Rede*, pp. 80–84.

16. Significant examples of some stage of this technique may be found in 14 romances. I list them in roughly chronological order: *Piramus et Tisbé, Narcisus, Eneas, Le Roman de Troie, Athis et Prophilias, Floire et Blancheflor, Eracle, Cligès, Ipomedon, Florimont, Guillaume de Palerne, L'Escoufle, Yder, Galeran de Bretagne.* [. . .]

17. G. W. F. Hegel, *Vorlesungen über die Philosophie der Weltgeschichte*, ed. Georg Lasson, Vol. IV: *Die germanische Welt* (Leipzig, 1920), p. 850; cf. Eduard Wechssler, *Das Kultur-problem des Minnesangs* (Halle, 1909), esp. Ch. vii, "Der Individualismus seit dem Ersten Kreuzzug." A broader picture of the cultural situation is provided by Friedrich Heer, *Aufgang Europas, eine Studie zu den Zusammenhängen zwischen politischer Religiosität, Frömmigkeitsstil und dem Werden Europas im 12. Jahrhundert*, 2 vols. (Vienna & Zürich, 1949). [. . .] I am indebted to Professors Ludwig Edelstein and Morton W. Bloomfield for valuable advice in the preparation of this section of the essay.

18. Wechssler, *Kulturproblem*, passim; Heer, *Aufgang Europas*, see above, n. 17. Against the notion of direct influence of Christian mysticism on the courtly love of the Troubadours, see Etienne Gilson, *La Theologie Mystique de Saint Bernard, Etudes de Philosophie médiévale* (Paris, 1947), XX, 193–215; A. J. Denomy, C.S.B., "An Inquiry into the Origins of Courtly Love," *Med. Stud.*, VI (1944), 188–193. But both authors recognize certain similarities between the two. Cf. Denomy, "Fin' Amors: the Pure Love of the Troubadours," *Med. Stud.*, VII (1944), 147. In the present essay the term "courtly love" is used more loosely, to embrace the variations of concept and principle found in the romances.

19. Richard of St. Victor, *De Statu Interioris Hominis*, I, cap. xix (In Migne, *Patrologia Latina*, CXCVI, col. 1130A). See Bernhard Geyer, ed. *Friedrich Ueberwegs Grundriss der Geschichte der Philosophie*, Vol. II, *Die patristische und scholastische Philosophie*, 11th ed. (Berlin, 1928), pp. 252–272; Pierre Michaud-Quantin, "La Classification des Puissances de l'Ame au XIIe Siècle," *Revue du Moyen Age Latin*, V (1949), 15–34.

20. On the love-religion see Lewis, *Allegory of Love*, pp. 18–22, 29. Cf. the opinion of Helmut Hatzfeld in *Sym.*, II (1948), 286: "the attitude [of the early

troubadours is better explained] by a parodistic-cultural challenge on the part of the worldlings of Cistercian Mysticism. . . .”; and see Myrrha Lot-Borodine, “Sur les Origines et les Fins du *Service d'Amour*,” in *Mélanges . . . Alfred Jeanroy* (Paris, 1928), pp. 223–235.

21. Cf. Isaac of Stella, *De Anima*, in Migne, *PL*, CXCIV, col. 1878C, D; Richard of St. Victor, *Benjamin Minor*, cap. iii (in Migne, *PL*, CXCVI, col. 3); Bernard of Clairvaux, *Sermo LXXIX in Cantica*, 1 (in *Opera Omnia*, ed. J. Mabillon [Paris, 1839], I, col. 3153 B). [. . .]

22. Plato, *Theaetetus* 189E, *Sophist* 263E, quoted by Georg Misch, *A History of Autobiography in Antiquity*, 3rd ed. trans. G. Misch & E. W. Dickes (London, 1950), II, 445, q.v.

23. Misch, *Autobiography*, II, 448–450.

24. See his *Retractationes*, I, cap. iv, 1 (in Benedictine ed. [Paris, 1836], I, vol. 29A, B): “ . . . me interrogans, mihique respondens, tanquam duo essemus, ratio et ego, cum solus essem”; *Soliloquiorum Libri Duo*, II, cap. vii (in ed. cit., I, col. 626C).

25. See G. Paré et al., *La Renaissance du XIIᵉ Siècle: Les Ecoles et l'Enseignement, Publications de l'Institut d'Etudes Médiévales d'Ottawa*, III (Paris & Ottawa, 1933), 125–129, 281–289; Geyer, ed. *Geschichte der Philosophie*, II, 272–281. Cf. Wechssler, *Kulturproblem*, pp. 400–401; Helmut Hatzfeld, “Literarisches Hochmittelalter in Frankreich,” *Tijdschrift voor Taal en Letteren*, XXV (1937), 90–92.

26. [. . .]

27. Edmond Faral, *Recherches sur les Sources latines des Contes et Romans courtois du moyen Age* (Paris, 1913), pp. 150–154, cites the resemblances.

28. See Biller, *Le Style des premiers Romans*, pp. 164–165; Hue de Rotelande, *Prothesilaus*, ed. Franz Kluckow, *Gesellschaft für romanische Literatur*, XLV (Göttingen, 1924), vv. 2777–78; *Galeran* 2622–42; *Cligès* 475 ff.; *Guillaume de Palerne* 864–890, 1200–05; Raoul de Houdenc, *Meraugis von Portlesguez*, ed. Mathias Friedwagner (Halle, 1897), vv. 1240–43, 4357–87.

29. Cf. *Eneas* 8348–52, 8434–87, 8679–8742, 8961–9088, 9867–82; *Narcisus* 267–294, 353–390, 539–548, 597–613; *Piramus et Tisbé* 221–280.

30. See Faral, *Recherches*, p. 154.

31. See also *Eneas* 8348–52, 8434–37.

32. See below, pp. 198–99.

33. The poet does not here appear to be making any material distinction between *Amor*, speaking in vv. 679 ff., and *li deus d'amors* referred to in v. 681 (cf. 691).

34. See Lewis, *Allegory of Love*, p. 121.

35. *Athis et Prophilias* 3933–76. Cf. *Roman de la Rose* 3424–26, 3440–76.

36. Cf. 3977–78, where the quality which restrains Gaiete from imaginar-

ily embracing her lover is called *Honte,* and 4505–10, where Athis' hesitation to reveal his love for Gaiete to Prophilias is attributed to *Honte* and *Peor.*

37. *Lancelot,* ed. Wendelin Foerster (Halle, 1899), vv. 369–381:

> Mes reisons qui d'amors se part
> Li dit que de monter se gart,
> Si le chastie et si l'ansaingne
> Que rien ne face ne n'anpraingne,
> Don il et honte ne reproche.
> N'est pas el cuer, mes an la boche
> Reisons qui ce dire li ose;
> Mes amors est el cuer anclose,
> Qui li comandë et semont
> Que tost sor la charrete mont.
> Amors le viaut, et il i saut;
> Que de la honte ne li chaut
> Puis qu'amors le comande et viaut.

Lewis, *Allegory of Love,* pp. 30–31, cites a number of other examples from Chrétien.

38. [. . .]

39. Of the major personifications in the *Roman,* I have been unable to find either *Bel Acueil,* or Venus as a personification of the sexual appetite, or *Jalosie* in Guillaume's sense, actually named in the romances. The first two, as we have seen above, are crudely subsumed within Amor. Lewis, *Allegory of Love,* p. 122, n. 2, notes an example of *bel acueil* from the Provençal Guilhem de Peitieu. *Jalosie* (see above p. 189) is well illustrated, if not named, in *Galeran.* For the rest, I have found *Amor, Avarice, Biaus Semblanz, Biauté, Chasteé, Cortoisie, Covoitise, Dangier, Envie, Franchise, Gentilesse, Haïne, Honte, Jonece, Largece, Male Bouche, Peor, Pitié, Povreté,* and *Raison* (including *Sen, Sapience, Savoir*). [. . .] *Floire* 1603 ff., *Lancelot* 369 ff., *Florimont* 8949 ff., *Escoufle* 3908 ff., 7600 ff., *Ombre* 599. In a number of passages considerable groups of qualities or personifications are discussed; see *Eracle* 3264 ff., 3720 ff., *Ille* 3579–3602, *Partonopeus* 6225–64, *Meraugis* (601 ff.), 998 ff. For personification in early Old French generally see Richard Herzhoff, *Personificationen lebloser Dinge in der altfranzösischen Literatur des 10. bis 12. Jahrhunderts, Teil II: Personificationen von Abstrakten* (diss. Berlin, 1904); Hyacinthe Binet, *Le Style de la Lyrique courtoise en France au XII* et XIII*ᵉ Siècles* (Paris, 1891) pp. 48–49, 52–54.

40. Cf. the distinction between internal analysis and interior monologue made by L. E. Bowling, "What is the Stream of Consciousness Technique?" *PMLA,* LXV (1950), 345.

41. Chrétien, despite his other virtues, does not appear to have seen the strong kinship between dialogue-in-monologue and psychological allegory as instruments of analysis. Both, in his work, tend to degenerate into preciosity (see above, n. 26, and Lewis, *Allegory of Love,* p. 31) without coming together. On the other hand, the daring passage in *Yvain* 1757–75 where Yvain is imaginarily summoned up to the bar of Laudine's reason and speaks in his own defence, is structurally similar to dialogue-in-monologue, and, it could be argued, constitutes a colloquy between "reison" and "droit" (*Yvain* 1755, 1774). [. . .]

42. The same alternatives, raised to the proportions of "the two major branches of poetry," the didactic and the mimetic, are discussed by Elder Olson, "William Empson, Contemporary Criticism, and Poetic Diction," in *Critics and Criticism, Ancient and Modern,* ed. R. S. Crane (Chicago, 1952), pp. 65–68 ("Reprinted from *Modern Philology,* May 1950"). On p. 66 Olson is concerned with the incompleteness of the reading of certain moral allegories as romances, prescription as plot. My concern here is just the reverse. If in the *Faerie Queene* we have moral allegory superficially resembling romance, we have in the latter part of Guillaume's *Roman* primarily romance, mimesis, using machinery resembling that of moral allegory.

43. See, for doctrine in lecture form, *Roman de la Rose* 2077–2580; *Eneas* 7902–31, 7957–8000; *Athis* 3430–92; *Florimont* 2534–70, 2597–2622, 2751–2889; *Amadas* 1227–61. Many other passages, in their endlessness and irrelevance of detail, have a primarily doctrinal interest despite the pretense of narrative; see, e.g., *Eneas* 8083–8126.

44. Cf. Lewis, *Allegory of Love,* p. 116. There is no doubt that Guillaume follows the older tradition in such features as the set introduction and elaborate portraiture of some personifications. Of the latter there is practically nothing in the romances. But this is not much a question of "mechanism."

45. I. C. LeComte ed., in *MP,* VIII (1910–11), 63–86.

46. W. Foerster ed. (Bonn, 1880). One may also doubt whether an attentiveness bred solely on the hermeneutic tradition, with its multiple levels of meaning, or on certain versions of the notion of Man as microcosm, would yield a full, satisfactory reading of the poem. Both would tend to see it only in cosmic, "universal," and therefore moral and doctrinal terms. For an example of a recent exegetical reading on the tropological or moral level, see D. W. Robertson, Jr., "The Doctrine of Charity in Medieval Literary Gardens: A Topical Approach through Symbolism and Allegory," *Speculum,* XXVI (1951), 40–43. On "cosmocentric microcosmism," see Rudolf Allers, "Microcosmus," *Traditio,* II (1944), 322, 348–351.

47. See the discussion of Bernardus Silvestris' *De Mundi Universitate* and Alanus' *Anticlaudianus* in Lewis, *Allegory of Love,* pp. 90–91, 100–103. I need not mention the large role of *Ratio* in medieval psychology and epistemology.

48. The recent study of the completed poem by Alan M. F. Gunn, *The Mirror of Love, A Reinterpretation of "The Romance of the Rose"* (Lubbock, Texas, 1952) does not directly take up the question of the provenience of the form, but such references as there are to allegory, e.g. as "the dominant poetic method of the thirteenth century" and as "the literary method of the age" (pp. 502–503), indicate that Gunn is not concerned with the structural distinction I have discussed here. [. . .]

ERICH AUERBACH, *MIMESIS*

1. The ensuing account of Auerbach's views contains some material omitted in *Mimesis,* but included in two articles to which he refers the reader: *"Figura,"* AR, XXII (1938), 436–489; *"Sermo Humilis,"* RF, LXIV (1952), 304–306. A continuation of the latter appears in "Lateinische Prosa des 9. und 10. Jahrhunderts," ibid., LXVI (1954), 1–64.

2. E. R. Curtius, "Die Lehre von den drei Stilen in Altertum und Mittelalter," *RF,* LXIV (1952), 57–70, argues "that the antique rule of style-division is neither so uniform nor so absolute as might appear according to Auerbach." The latter replies, I think satisfactorily, in "Epilegomena zu *Mimesis,*" ibid., LXV (1953), 5–10.

3. *Introduction aux études de philologie romane* (Frankfurt, 1949), pp. 36–37.

4. See, for instance, the perceptive review by R. Wellek, *Kenyon Review,* XVI (1954), 299–307.

INDEX

Index

Borroff, Marie, 105, 225n. 13, 225n. 14, 226n. 18
Bosch, Hieronymus, 137
Boucher d'Abbeville, 164
Boughner, Daniel C., 232n. 6
Bourgeoise d'Orléans, 165
Bowling, L. E., 241n. 40
Braies au Cordelier, 165
Braune, Theodor Wilhelm, 236n. 22
Brewer, Derek S., 26–27, 44, 156, 217n. 1, 217n. 2, 224n. 6, 233n. 17
Bright, W., 220n. 7
Bronson, B. H., 217n. 1
Brooks, Cleanth, 71
Brown, Carleton, 90, 224n. 4
Brunain, la vache au prêtre, 165
Burrow, J. A., 226n. 19
Burton, Dolores, S. N. D., 220n. 7

Caillois, Roger, 226n. 19
Canon Yeoman's Prologue, 8, 18
Canterbury Tales, 1–25, 28, 35–37, 40, 61, 86, 113, 139–140, 149, 162, 171–72. *See also individual titles*
Cantor, Norman E., 220n. 11
Cawley, A. C., 224n. 8
Chanson des Saisnes, 164
Chatman, Seymour, 220n. 7
Chaucer, Geoffrey, 81–86, 87, 138–63; allegory, 46, 140; career, 82–85, 223n. 31; catalogues in, 7–8, 23, 52–53; characterization, 24, 45; criticism, 26–31, 38–40, 42–47, 54–55; descriptions, 10–11; dramatic verse, 14, 16; heroic style, 144–50, 232n. 6; idealism, 17, 143–44; imagery, 3–5, 9–10, 17, 20–24, 172–73; inconsistency, 2–3; insouciance, 1–3, 20; irony, 17, 18, 20, 22, 24–25, 46, 85–86, 139–40, 162;

Italian influence, 144–46; language, 3–6, 20–23; metaphors, 3–6; "mixed style," 18, 20–25; narrative technique, 13–14, 83; narrator, 2, 20, 83, 140, 171; on scholarship, 48–55; oral tradition, 2, 171–75; pathos, 18–20, 32–34, 140, 145, 151–62, 233n. 21; plan for *Canterbury Tales,* 35; portraits in, 8–10, 85; realism, 17–18, 24, 27, 140–43; reception of, 26–27; religion, 27–41, 140; rhetoric, 14–16, 23, 33–34, 44–45, 53; romance, 150–51; *sentence* and doctrine, 6; similes, 3–6; sound and rhythm, 11–13; style, 1–25. *See also individual works*
Chevalier à la corbeille, 165
chivalry, fourteenth-century, 77
Chrétien de Troyes, 144, 186, 188, 191, 201, 202, 232n. 11, 241n. 37, 242n. 41. *See also individual works*
Church, fourteenth-century, 77–79
Cicero, 184, 210
Clein, Wendy, 218n. 17
Clemen, Wolfgang, 42–44, 45–46, 218n. 1
Clerk's Tale, 17, 19, 33, 152, 156, 160, 161
Cligès, 239n. 16, 240n. 28
Clogan, Paul M., 232n. 6
Coghill, Nevill, 229n. 25
coilles (term), 182–83
Colombier, Pierre, 233n. 16
con (term), 167, 180, 237n. 25
Consolation of Philosophy, 85
Cook, Robert G., 226, n. 19
Cox, Harvey 226n. 17
Crosby, Ruth, 217, n. 1
Crotte, 165
Crow, Martin M., 222n. 27, 223n. 31